John Ruskin

The Crown of Wild Olive and Lectures on Art

John Ruskin

The Crown of Wild Olive and Lectures on Art

ISBN/EAN: 9783337269210

Printed in Europe, USA, Canada, Australia, Japan

Cover: Foto ©Thomas Meinert / pixelio.de

More available books at **www.hansebooks.com**

THE
CROWN OF WILD OLIVE

—AND—

LECTURES ON ART.

By JOHN RUSKIN, M.A., LL.D.

And indeed it should have been of gold, had not Jupiter been so poor.
—ARISTOPHANES (*Plutus*).

A. L. BURT COMPANY, Publishers
52-58 Duane Street, New York

CONTENTS.

THE CROWN OF WILD OLIVE.

LECTURE I.
	PAGE
WORK	1

LECTURE II.
TRAFFIC	42

LECTURE III.
WAR	76

LECTURES ON ART.

LECTURE I.
INAUGURAL	123

LECTURE II.
THE RELATION OF ART TO RELIGION	156

LECTURE III.
THE RELATION OF ART TO MORALS	188

LECTURE IV.
THE RELATION OF ART TO USE	217

LECTURE V.
LINE	246

LECTURE VI.
LIGHT	270

LECTURE VII.
COLOR	301

PREFACE.

TWENTY years ago, there was no lovelier piece of lowland scenery in South England, nor any more pathetic in the world, by its expression of sweet human character and life, than that immediately bordering on the sources of the Wandle, and including the lower moors of Addington, and the villages of Beddington and Carshalton, with all their pools and streams. No clearer or diviner waters ever sung with constant lips of the hand which "giveth rain from heaven;" no pastures ever lightened in springtime with more passionate blossoming; no sweeter homes ever hallowed the heart of the passer-by with their pride of peaceful gladness—fain-hidden—yet full confessed. The place remains, or, until a few months ago, remained, nearly unchanged in its larger features; but, with deliberate mind I say, that I have never seen anything so ghastly in its inner tragic meaning—not in Pisan Maremma—not by Campagna tomb—not by the sand-isles of the Torcellan shore—as the slow stealing of aspects of reckless, indolent, animal neglect, over the delicate sweetness of that English scene: nor is any blasphemy or impiety—any frantic saying or godless thought more appalling to me, using the best power of judgment I have to discern its sense and scope, than the insolent defilings of those springs by the human herds that drink of them. Just where the welling of stainless water, trembling and pure, like a body of light, enters the pool of Carshalton, cutting itself a radiant channel down to the gravel, through warp of feathery weeds, all waving, which it traverses with its deep threads of clearness, like the chalcedony in moss-agate, starred here and there with white grenouillette; just in the very rush and murmur of the first spreading currents, the human wretches of the place cast their street and house foulness; heaps of dust and slime, and broken shreds of old metal, and rags of putrid clothes; they having neither energy to cart it away, nor decency enough to dig it into the ground, thus shed into the stream, to diffuse what venom of it will float and melt, far away, in all places where God meant those waters to bring joy and health. And, in a little pool, behind some houses further in the village, where another spring rises, the shattered stones of the well, and of the little fretted channel which was long ago built and traced for it by gentler hands, lie scattered, each from each, under a ragged bank of mortar, and scoria; and bricklayers' refuse, on one side, which the clear water nevertheless chastises to purity; but it cannot conquer the dead earth beyond; and there, circled and coiled under festering scum, the stagnant edge of the pool effaces itself into a slope of black slime, the accumulation of indolent years. Half a dozen men, with one day's work, could cleanse those pools, and trim the flowers about their banks, and make every breath of summer air above them rich with cool balm; and every glittering wave medicinal, as if it ran, troubled of angels, from the porch of Bethesda. But that day's work is never given, nor will be; nor will any joy be possible to heart of man, forevermore, about those wells of English waters.

When I last left them, I walked up slowly through the back streets of Croydon, from the old church to the hospital; and, just on the left, before coming up to the crossing of the High Street, there was a new public-house built. And the front of it was built in so wise manner, that a recess of two feet was left below its front windows, between them and the street-pavement— a recess too narrow for any possible use (for even if it had been occupied by a seat, as in old time it might have been, everybody walking along the street would have fallen over the legs of the reposing wayfarers). But, by way of making this two feet depth of freehold land more expressive of the dignity of an establishment for the sale of spirituous liquors, it was fenced from the pavement by an imposing iron railing, having four or five spear-heads to the yard of it, and six feet high; containing as much iron and iron-work, indeed, as could well be put into the space; and by this stately arrangement, the little piece of dead ground within, between wall and street, became a protective receptacle of refuse; cigar-ends, and oyster-shells, and the like, such as an open-handed English street-populace habitually scatters from its presence, and was thus left, unsweepable by any ordinary methods. Now the iron bars which, uselessly (or in great degree worse than uselessly), inclosed this bit of ground, and made it pestilent, represented a quantity of work which would have cleansed the Carshalton pools three times over—of work, partly cramped and deadly, in the mine; partly fierce* and exhaustive, at the furnace; partly foolish and sedentary, of ill-taught students

---

* "A fearful occurrence took place a few days since, near Wolverhampton. Thomas Snape, aged nineteen, was on duty as the 'keeper' of a blast-furnace at Deepfield, assisted by John Gardner, aged eighteen, and Joseph Swift, aged thirty-seven. The furnace contained four tons of molten iron, and an equal amount of cinders, and ought to have been run out at 7:30 P. M. But Snape and his mates, engaged in talking and drinking, neglected their duty, and, in the meantime, the iron rose in the furnace until it reached a pipe wherein water was contained. Just as the men had stripped, and were proceeding to tap the furnace, the water in the pipe, converted into steam, burst down its front and let loose on them the molten metal, which instantaneously consumed Gardner. Snape, terribly burnt, and mad with pain, leaped into the canal and then ran home and fell dead on the threshold. Swift survived to reach the hospital, where he died too."

making bad designs: work from the beginning to the last fruits of it, and in all the branches of it, venomous, deathful, and miserable. Now, how did it come to pass that this work was done instead of the other; that the strength and life of the English operative were spent in defiling ground, instead of redeeming it; and in producing an entirely (in that place) valueless piece of metal, which can neither be eaten nor breathed, instead of medicinal fresh air, and pure water?

There is but one reason for it, and at present a conclusive one—that the capitalist can charge percentage on the work in the one case, and cannot in the other. If, having certain funds for supporting labor at my disposal, I pay men merely to keep my ground in order, my money is, in that function, spent once for all; but if I pay them to dig iron out of my ground, and work it, and sell it, I can charge rent for the ground, and percentage both on the manufacture and the sale, and make my capital profitable in these three by-ways. The greater part of the profitable investment of capital, in the present day, is in operations of this kind, in which the public is persuaded to buy something of no use to it, on production, or sale, of which, the capitalist may charge percentage; the said public remaining all the while under the persuasion that the percentages thus obtained are real national gains, whereas, they are merely filchings out of partially light pockets, to swell heavy ones.

Thus, the Croydon publican buys the iron railing, to make himself more conspicuous to drunkards. The public-house-keeper on the other side of the way presently buys another railing, to out-rail him with. Both are, as to their *relative* attractivness to customers of taste, just where they were before; but they have lost the price of the railings; which they must either themselves finally lose, or make their aforesaid customers of taste pay, by raising the price of their beer, or adulterating it. Either the publicans, or their customers, are thus poorer by precisely what the capitalist has gained; and the value of the work itself, meantime, has been lost to the nation; the iron bars in that form and place being wholly useless. It is this mode of taxation of the poor by the rich which is referred to in the text (page 29), in comparing the modern acquisitive power of capital with that of the lance and sword; the only difference being that the levy of blackmail in old times was by force, and is now by cozening. The old rider and reiver frankly quartered himself on the publican for the night; the modern one merely makes his lance into an iron spike, and persuades his host to buy it. One comes as an open robber, the other as a cheating peddler; but the result, to the injured person's pocket, is absolutely the same.

Of course many useful industries mingle with, and disguise the useless ones; and in the habits of energy aroused by the struggle, there is a certain direct good. It is far better to spend four thousand pounds in making a good gun, and then to blow it to pieces, than to pass life in idleness. Only do not 'et it be called "political economy." There is also a confused notion in the minds of many persons, that the gathering of the property of the poor into the hands of the rich does no ultimate harm; since, in whosesoever hands it may be, it must be spent at last, and thus, they think, return to the poor again. This fallacy has been again and again exposed; but grant the plea true, and the same apology may, of course, be made for black mail, or any other form of robbery. It might be (though practically it never is) as advantageous for the nation that the robber should have the spending of the money he extorts, as that the person robbed should have spent it. But this is no excuse for the theft. If I were to put a turnpike on the road where it passes my own gate, and endeavor to exact a shilling from every passenger, the public would soon do away with my gate, without listening to any plea on my part that "it was as advantageous to them, in the end, that I should spend their shillings, as that they themselves should." But if, instead of out-facing them with a turnpike

I can only persuade them to come in and buy stones, or old iron, or any other useless thing, out of my ground, I may rob them to the same extent and be, moreover, thanked as a public benefactor, and promoter of commercial prosperity. And this main question for the poor of England—for the poor of all countries—is wholly omitted in every common treatise on the subject of wealth. Even by the laborers themselves, the operation of capital is regarded only in its effect on their immediate interests; never in the far more terrific power of its appointment of the kind and the object of labor. It matters little, ultimately, how much a laborer is paid for making anything; but it matters fearfully what the thing is, which he is compelled to make. If his labor is so ordered as to produce food, and fresh air, and fresh water, no matter that his wages are low—the food and fresh air and water will be at last there; and he will at last get them. But if he is paid to destroy food and fresh air, or to produce iron bars instead of them—the food and air will finally *not* be there, and he will *not* get them, to his great and final inconvenience. So that, conclusively, in political as in household economy, the great question is, not so much what money you have in your pocket, as what you will buy with it, and do with it.

I have been long accustomed, as all men engaged

in work of investigation must be, to hear my statements laughed at for years, before they are examined or believed; and I am generally content to wait the public's time. But it has not been without displeased surprise that I have found myself totally unable, as yet, by any repetition, or illustration, to force this plain thought into my readers' heads—that the wealth of nations, as of men, consists in substance, not in ciphers; and that the real good of all work, and of all commerce, depends on the final worth of the thing you make, or get by it. This is a practical enough statement, one would think: but the English public has been so possessed by its modern school of economists with the notion that Business is always good, whether it be busy in mischief or in benefit; and that buying and selling are always salutary, whatever the intrinsic worth of what you buy or sell— that it seems impossible to gain so much as a patient hearing for any inquiry respecting the substantial result of our eager modern labors. I have never felt more checked by the sense of this impossibility than in arranging the heads of the following three lectures, which, though delivered at considerable intervals of time, and in different places, were not prepared without reference to each other. Their connection would, however, have been made far more distinct, if I had not been prevented, by what I feel to be another great difficulty in addressing English audiences, from enforcing, with any decision, the common, and to me the most important, part of their subjects. I chiefly desired (as I have just said) to question my hearers—operatives, merchants, and soldiers, as to the ultimate meaning of the *business* they had in hand; and to know from them what they expected or intended their manufacture to come to, their selling to come to, and their killing to come to. That appeared the first point needing determination before I could speak to them with any real utility or effect. "You craftsmen—salesmen—swordsmen—do but tell me clearly what you want, then, if I can say anything to help you, I will; and if not, I will account to you as I best may for my inability." But in order to put this question into any terms, one had first of all to face the difficulty just spoken of—to me for the present insuperable—the difficulty of knowing whether to address one's audience as believing, or not believing, in any other world than this. For if you address any average modern English company as believing in an Eternal life, and endeavor to draw any conclusions, from this assumed belief, as to their present business, they will forthwith tell you that what you say is very beautiful, but it is not practical. If, on the contrary, you frankly address them as unbelievers in Eternal life, and try to draw any consequences from that unbelief—they immediately hold you for an accursed person, and shake off the dust from their feet at you. And the more I thought over what I had got to say, the less I found I could say it, without some reference to this intangible or intractable part of the subject. It made all the difference, in asserting any principle of war, whether one assumed that a discharge of artillery would merely knead down a certain quantity of red clay into a level line, as in a brick field; or whether, out of every separately Christian-named portion of the ruinous heap, there went out, into the smoke and deadfallen air of battle, some astonished condition of soul, unwillingly released. It made all the difference, in speaking of the possible range of commerce, whether one assumed that all bargains related only to visible property—or whether property, for the present invisible, but nevertheless real, was elsewhere purchasable on other terms. It made all the difference in addressing a body of men subject to considerable hardship, and having to find some way out of it—whether one could confidently say to them, "My friends—you have only to die, and all will be right;" or whether one had any secret misgiving that such advice was more blessed to him that gave, than to him that took it. And therefore the deliberate reader will find throughout these lectures, a hesitation in driving points home, and a pausing short of conclusions which he will feel I would fain have come to; hesitation which arises wholly from this uncertainty of my hearers' temper. For I do not now speak, nor have I ever spoken, since the time of first forward youth, in any proselyting temper, as desiring to persuade any one of what, in such matters, I thought myself; but, whomsoever I venture to address, I take for the time his creed as I find it, and endeavor to push it into such vital fruit as it seems capable of. Thus, it is a creed with a great part of the existing English people, that they are in possession of a book which tells them, straight from the lips of God all they ought to do, and need to know. I have read that book, with as much care as most of them, for some forty years; and am thankful that, on those who trust it, I can press its pleadings. My endeavor has been uniformly to make them trust it more deeply than they do; trust it, not in their own favorite verses only, but in the sum of all; trust it not as a fetich or talisman, which they are to be saved by daily repetitions of; but as a Captain's order, to be heard and obeyed at their peril. I was always encouraged by supposing my hearers to hold such belief. To these, if to any, I once had hope of addressing, with acceptance, words which insisted on the guilt of pride, and the futility of avarice; from these, if from any, I once expected ratification of a political economy, which asserted that the life was more than the meat, and the body than raiment; and these, it once seemed to me, I might ask, without accusation of fanaticism, not merely in doctrine of the lips, but in the bestowal of their heart's treasure, to separate themselves from the crowd of whom it is written, "After all these things do the Gentiles seek."

It cannot, however, be assumed, with any semblance of reason, that a general audience is now wholly, or even in majority composed of these religious persons. A large portion must always consist of men who admit no such creed; or who, at least, are inaccessible to appeals founded on it. And as, with the so-called Christian, I desired to plead for honest declaration and fulfillment of his belief in life—with the so-called Infidel, I desired to plead for an honest declaration and fulfillment of his belief in death. The dilemma is inevitable. Men must either hereafter live, or hereafter die; fate may be bravely met, and conduct wisely ordered, on either expectation; but never in hesitation between ungrasped hope, and unconfronted fear. We usually believe in immortality, so far as to avoid preparation for death; and in mortality, so far as to avoid preparation for anything after death. Whereas, a wise man will at least hold himself prepared for one or other of two events, of which one or other is inevitable; and will have all things in order, for his sleep, or in readiness, for his awakening.

Nor have we any right to call it an ignoble judgment, if he determine to put them in order, as for sleep. A brave belief in life is indeed an enviable state of mind, but, as far as I can discern, an unusual one. I know few Christians so convinced of the splendor of the rooms in their Father's house, as to be happier when their friends are called to those mansions, than they would have been if the Queen had sent for them to live at court: nor has the Church's most ardent "desire to depart, and be with Christ," ever cured it of the singular habit of putting on mourning for every person summoned to such departure. On the contrary, a brave belief in death has been assuredly held by many not ignoble persons, and it is a sign of the last depravity in the Church itself, when it assumes that such a belief is inconsistent with either purity of character, or energy of hand. The shortness of life is not, to any rational person, a conclusive reason for wasting the space of it which may be granted him; nor does the anticipation of death to-morrow suggest, to any one but a drunkard, the expediency of drunkenness to-day. To teach that there is no device in the grave, may indeed make the deviceless person more contented in his dullness; but it will make the deviser only more earnest in devising; nor is human conduct likely, in every case, to be purer under the conviction that all its evil may in a moment be pardoned, and all its wrong-doing in a moment redeemed; and that the sigh of repentance, which purges the guilt of the past, will waft the soul into a felicity which forgets its pain—than it may be under the sterner, and to many not unwise minds, more probable, apprehension, that "what a man soweth that shall he also reap"—or others reap—when he, the living seed of pestilence, walketh no more in darkness, but lies down therein.

But to men whose feebleness of sight, or bitterness of soul, or the offense given by the conduct of those who claim higher hope, may have rendered this painful creed the only possible one, there is an appeal to be made, more secure in its ground than any which can be addressed to happier persons. I would fain, if I might offenselessly, have spoken to them as if none others heard; and have said thus: Hear me, you dying men, who will soon be deaf forever. For these others, at your right hand and your left, who look forward to a state of infinite existence, in which all their errors will be overruled, and all their faults forgiven; for these, who, stained and blackened in the battle smoke of mortality, have but to dip themselves for an instant in the font of death, and to rise renewed of plumage, as a dove that is covered with silver, and her feathers like gold; for these, indeed, it may be permissible to waste their numbered moments, through faith in a future of innumerable hours; to these, in their weakness, it may be conceded that they should tamper with sin which can only bring forth fruit of righteousness, and profit by the iniquity which, one day, will be remembered no more. In them, it may be no sign of hardness of heart to neglect the poor, over whom they know their Master is watching; and to leave those to perish temporarily who cannot perish eternally. But, for you, there is no such hope, and therefore no such excuse. This fate, which you ordain for the wretched, you believe to be all their inheritance; you may crush them, before the moth, and they will never rise to rebuke you—their breath, which fails for lack of food, once expiring, will never be recalled to whisper against you a word of accusing—they and you, as you think, shall lie down together in the dust, and the worms cover you—and for them there shall be no consolation, and on you no vengeance—only the question murmured above your grave: "Who shall repay him what he hath done?" Is it therefore easier for you in your heart to inflict the sorrow for which there is no remedy? Will you take, wantonly, this little all of his life from your poor brother, and make his brief hours long to him with pain? Will you be readier to the injustice which can never be redressed; and niggardly of mercy which you *can* bestow but once, and which, refusing, you refuse forever? I think better of you, even of the most selfish, than that you would do this, well understood. And for yourselves, it seems to me, the question becomes not less grave, in these curt limits. If your life were but a fever fit—the madness of a night, whose follies were all to be forgotten in the dawn, it might matter little how you fretted away the sickly hours—what toys you snatched at, or let fall— what visions you followed wistfully with the deceived eyes of sleepless frenzy. Is the earth only an hospital? Play, if you care to play, on the floor of the hospital dens. Knit its straw into what crowns please you; gather the dust of it for treasure, and die rich in that, clutching at the black motes in the air with your dying hands—and yet, it may be well with you. But if this life be no dream, and the world no hospital; if all the peace and power and joy you can ever win, must be won now; and all fruit of victory gathered here, or never—will you still, throughout the puny totality of your life, weary yourselves in the fire of vanity? If there is no rest which remaineth for you, is there none you might presently take? was this grass of the earth made green for your shroud only, not for your bed? and can you never lie down *upon* it, but only *under* it? The heathen, to whose creed you have returned, thought not so. They knew that life brought its contest, but they expected from it also the crown of all contest. No proud one! no jeweled circlet flaming through Heaven above the height of the unmerited throne, only some few leaves of wild olive, cool to the tired brow, through a few years of peace. It should have been of gold, they thought; but Jupiter was poor; this was the best the god could give them. Seeking a greater than this, they had known it a mockery. Not in war, not in wealth, not in tyranny, was there any happiness to be found for them—only in kindly peace, fruitful and free. The wreath was to be of *wild* olive, mark you— the tree that grows carelessly, tufting the rocks with no vivid bloom, no verdure of branch; only with soft snow of blossom, and scarcely fulfilled fruit, mixed with gray leaf and thorn-set stem; no fastening of diadem for you but with such sharp embroidery! But this, such as it is, you may win while yet you live; type of gray honor and sweet rest. Free-heartedness, and graciousness, and undisturbed trust and requited love, and the sight of the peace of others, and the ministry to their pain—these, and the blue sky above you, and the sweet waters and flowers of the earth beneath; and mysteries and presences, innumerable, of living things—these may yet be here your riches; untormenting and divine: serviceable for the life that now is; nor, it may be, without promise of that which is to come.

THE CROWN OF WILD OLIVE.

THREE LECTURES.

1. WORK.
2. TRAFFIC.
3. WAR.

LECTURE I.

WORK.

(Delivered before the Working Men's Institute, at Camberwell.)

My Friends—I have not come among you to-night to endeavor to give you an entertaining lecture; but to tell you a few plain facts, and ask you some plain, but necessary questions. I have seen and known too much of the struggle for life among our laboring population, to feel at ease, even under any circumstances, in inviting them to dwell on the trivialities of my own studies; but, much more, as I meet to-night, for the first time, the members of a working Institute established in the district in which I have passed the greater part of my life, I am desirous that we should at once understand each other, on graver matters. I would fain tell you, with what feelings, and with what hope, I regard this Institution, as one of many such, now happily established throughout England, as well as in other countries—Institutions which are preparing the way for a great change in all the circumstances of industrial life; but of which the success must wholly depend upon our clearly understanding the circumstances and necessary *limits* of this change. No teacher can truly promote the cause of education until he knows the conditions of the life for which that education is to prepare his pupil. And the fact that he is called upon to address you, nominally, as a "Working Class," must compel him, if he is in any wise earnest or thoughtful, to inquire in the outset, on what you yourselves suppose this class distinction has been founded in the past, and must be founded in the future. The manner of the amusement, and the matter of the teaching, which any of us can offer you, must depend wholly on our first understanding from you, whether you think the distinction heretofore drawn between workingmen and others, is truly or falsely founded. Do you accept it as it stands? do you wish it to be modified? or do you think the object of education is to efface it, and make us forget it forever?

Let me make myself more distinctly understood. We call this—you and I—a "Working Men's" Institute, and our college in London, a "Working Men's" College. Now, how do you consider that these several institutes differ, or ought to differ, from "idle men's" institutes and "idle men's" colleges? Or by what other word than "idle" shall I distinguish those whom the happiest and wisest of workingmen do not object to call the "Upper Classes?" Are there really upper classes—are there lower? How much should they always be elevated, how much always depressed? And, gentlemen and ladies—I pray those of you who are here to forgive me the offense there may be in what I am going to say. It is not *I* who wish to say it. Bitter voices say it; voices of battle and of famine through all the world, which must be heard some day, whoever keeps silence. Neither is it to *you* specially that I say it. I am sure that most now present know their duties of kindness, and fulfill them, better perhaps than I do mine. But I speak to you as representing your whole class, which errs, I know, chiefly by thoughtlessness, but not therefore the less terribly. Willful error is limited by the will, but what limit is there to that of which we are unconscious?

Bear with me, therefore, while I turn to these workmen, and ask them, also as representing a great multitude, what they think the "upper classes" are, and ought to be, in relation to them. Answer, you workmen who are here, as you would among yourselves, frankly; and tell me how you would have me call those classes. Am I to call them—would *you* think me right in calling them—the idle classes? I think you would feel somewhat uneasy, and as if I were not treating my subject honestly, or speaking from my heart, if I went on under the supposition that all rich people were idle. You would be both unjust and unwise if you would allow me to say that—not less unjust than the rich people who say that all the poor are idle, and will never work if they can help it, or more than they can help.

For indeed the fact is, that there are idle poor and idle rich; and there are busy poor and busy rich. Many a beggar is as lazy as if he had ten thousand a year; and many a man of large fortune is busier than his errand-boy, and never would think of stopping in the street to play marbles. So that, in a large view, the distinction between workers and idlers, as between knaves and honest men, runs through the very heart and innermost economies of men of all ranks and in all positions. There is a working class—strong and happy—among both rich and poor; there is an idle class—weak, wicked and miserable—among both rich and poor. And the worst of the misunderstandings arising between the two orders come of the unlucky fact that the wise of one class habitually contemplate the foolish of the other. If the busy rich people watched and rebuked the idle rich people, all would be right; and if the busy poor people watched and rebuked the idle poor people, all would be right. But each class has a tendency to look for the faults of the other. A hard-working man of property is particularly offended by an idle beggar; but an orderly, but poor, workman is naturally intolerant of the licentious luxury of the rich. And what is severe judgment in the minds of the just men of either class, becomes fierce enmity in the unjust—but among the unjust *only*. None but the dissolute among the poor look upon the rich as their natural enemies, or desire to pillage their houses and divide their property. None but the dissolute among the rich speak in opprobrious terms of the vices and follies of the poor.

There is, then, no class distinction between idle and industrious people; and I am going to-night to speak only of the industrious. The idle people we will put out of our thoughts at once—they are mere nuisances —what ought to be done with *them*, we'll talk of at another time. But there are class distinctions among the industrious themselves—tremendous distinctions, which rise and fall to every degree in the infinite thermometer of human pain and of human power—distinctions of high and low, of lost and won, to the whole reach of man's soul and body.

These separations we will study, and the laws of them, among energetic men only, who, whether they work or whether they play, put their strength into the work, and their strength into the game; being in the full sense of the word "industrious," one way or another—with a purpose, or without. And these distinctions are mainly four:

1. Between those who work, and those who play.

II. Between those who produce the means of life, and those who consume them.

III. Between those who work with the head, and those who work with the hand.

IV. Between those who work wisely, and who work foolishly.

For easier memory, let us say we are going to oppose, in our examination:

    I. Work to play;

    II. Production to consumption;

    III. Head to hand; and,

    IV. Sense to nonsense.

I. First, then, of the distinction between the classes who work and the classes who play. Of course we must agree upon a definition of these terms—work and play—before going further. Now, roughly, not with vain subtlety of definition, but for plain use of the words, "play" is an exertion of body or mind, made to please ourselves, and with no determined end; and work is a thing done because it ought to be done, and with a determined end. You play, as you call it, at cricket, for instance. This is as hard work as anything else; but it amuses you, and it has no result but the amusement. If it were done as an ordered form of exercise, for health's sake, it would become work directly. So, in like manner, whatever we do to please ourselves, and only for the sake of the pleasure, not for an ultimate object, is "play," the "pleasing thing," not the useful thing. Play may be useful in a secondary sense (nothing is indeed more useful or necessary); but the use of it depends on its being spontaneous.

Let us, then, inquire together what sort of games the playing class in England spend their lives in playing at.

The first of all English games is making money. That is an all-absorbing game; and we knock each other down oftener in playing at that than at football, or any other roughest sport; and it is absolutely without purpose; no one who engages heartily in that game ever knows why. Ask a great money-maker what he wants to do with his money—he never knows. He doesn't make it to do anything with it. He gets it only that he *may* get it. "What will you make of what you have got?" you ask. "Well, I'll get more," he says. Just as, at cricket, you get more runs. There's no use in the runs, but to get more of them than other people is the game. And there's no use in the money, but to have more of it than other people is the game. So all that great foul city of London there—rattling, growling, smoking, stinking—a ghastly heap of fermenting brick-work, pouring out poison at every pore—you fancy it is a city of work? Not a street of it! It is a great city of play; very nasty play, and very hard play, but still play. It is only Lord's cricket ground without the turf—a huge billiard-table without the cloth, and with pockets as deep as the bottomless pit; but mainly a billiard-table, after all.

Well, the first great English game is this playing at counters. It differs from the rest in that it appears always to be producing money, while every other game is expensive. But it does not always produce money. There's a great difference between "winning" money and "making" it; a great difference between getting it out of another man's pocket into ours, or filling both. Collecting money is by no means the same thing as making it; the tax-gatherer's house is not the Mint; and much of the apparent gain (so-called), in commerce, is only a form of taxation on carriage or exchange.

Our next great English game, however, hunting and shooting, is costly altogether; and how much we are fined for it annually in land, horses, gamekeepers, and game laws, and all else that accompanies that beautiful and special English game, I will not endeavor to count now: but note only that, except for exercise, this is not merely a useless game, but a deadly one, to all connected with it. For through horse-racing, you get every form of what the higher classes everywhere call "Play," in distinction from all other plays; that is—gambling; by no means a beneficial or recreative game: and, through game-preserving, you get also some curious laying out of ground; that beautiful arrangement of dwelling-house for man and beast, by which we have grouse and blackcock—so many brace to the acre, and men and women—so many brace to the garret. I often wonder what the angelic builders and surveyors—the angelic builders who build the "many mansions" up above there; and the angelic surveyors, who measured that four-square city with their measuring reeds—I wonder what they think, or are supposed to think, of the laying out of ground by this nation, which has set itself, as it seems, literally to accomplish, word for word, or rather fact for word, in the persons of those poor whom its Master left to represent him, what that Master said of himself—that foxes and birds had homes, but He none.

Then, next to the gentlemen's game of hunting, we must put the ladies' game of dressing. It is not the cheapest of games. I saw a brooch at a jeweler's in Bond Street a fortnight ago, not an inch wide, and without any singular jewel in it, yet worth £3,000. And I wish I could tell you what this "play" costs, altogether, in England, France, and Russia annually. But it is a pretty game, and on certain terms, I like it; nay, I don't see it played quite as much as I would fain have it. You ladies like to lead the fashion—by all means lead it—lead it thoroughly, lead it far enough. Dress yourselves nicely, and dress everybody else nicely. Lead the *fashions for the poor* first; make *them* look well, and you yourselves will look, in ways of which you have no conception, all the better. The fashions you have set for some time among your peasantry are not pretty ones; their doublets are too irregularly slashed, and the wind blows too frankly through them.

Then there are other games, wild enough, as I could show you if I had time.

There's playing at literature, and playing at art—very different, both, from working at literature, or working at art, but I've no time to speak of these. I pass to the greatest of all—the play of plays, the great gentlemen's game, which ladies like them best to play at—the game of War. It is entrancingly pleasant to the imagination; the facts of it, not always so pleasant. We dress for it, however, more finely than for any other sport; and go out to it, not merely in scarlet, as to hunt, but in scarlet and gold, and all manner of fine colors: of course we could fight better in gray, and without feathers; but all nations have agreed that it is good to be well dressed at this play. Then the bats and balls are very costly; our English and French bats, with the balls and wickets, even those which we don't make use of, costing, I suppose, now about fifteen millions of money annually to each nation; all of which you know is paid for by hard laborer's work in the furrow and furnace. A costly game!—not to speak of its consequences; I will say at present nothing of these. The mere immediate cost of all these plays is what I want you to consider; they all cost deadly work somewhere, as many of us know too well. The jewel-cutter, whose sight fails over the diamonds; the weaver, whose arms fails over the web; the iron-forger, whose breath fails before the furnace—*they* know what work is—they, who have all the work and none of the play, except a kind they have named for themselves down in the black north country, where "play" means being laid up by sickness. It is a pretty example for philologists, of varying dialect, this change in the sense of the word "play," as used in the black country of Birmingham, and the red-and-black country of Baden Baden. Yes, gentlemen, and gentlewomen, of England, who think "one moment unamused a misery, not made for feeble man," this is what you have brought the word "play" to mean, in the heart of merry England! You may have your fluting and piping; but there are sad children sitting in the market-place, who indeed cannot say to you, "We have piped unto you, and ye have not danced:" but eternally shall say to you, "We have mourned unto you, and ye have not lamented."

This, then, is the first distinction between the "upper and lower" classes. And this is one which is by no means necessary; which indeed must, in process of good time, be by all honest men's consent abolished. Men will be taught that an existence of play, sustained by the blood of other creatures, is a good existence for gnats and sucking fish; but not for men: that neither days, nor lives, can be made holy by doing nothing in them: that the best prayer at the beginning of a day is that we may not lose its moments; and the best grace before meat, the consciousness that we have justly earned our dinner. And when we have this much of plain Christianity preached to us again, and enough respect what we regard as inspiration, as not to think that "Son, go work to-day in my vineyard," means "Fool, go play to-day in my vineyard," we shall all be workers, in one way or another; and this much at least of the distinction between "upper" and "lower" forgotten.

II. I pass then to our second distinction; between the rich and poor, between Dives and Lazarus—distinction which exists more sternly, I suppose, in this day, than ever in the world, Pagan or Christian, till now. I will put it sharply before you, to begin with, merely by reading two paragraphs which I cut from two papers that lay on my breakfast-table on the same morning, the 25th of November, 1864. The piece about the rich Russian at Paris is commonplace enough, and stupid besides (for fifteen francs—12$s.$ 6$d.$—is nothing for a rich man to give for a couple of peaches, out of season). Still, the two paragraphs printed on the same day are worth putting side by side.

"Such a man is now here. He is a Russian, and

with your permission, we will call him Count Teufelskine. In dress he is sublime; art is considered in that toilet, the harmony of color respected, the *chiaroscuro* evident in well-selected contrast. In manners he is dignified—nay, perhaps apathetic; nothing disturbs the placid serenity of that calm exterior. One day our friend breakfasted *chez* Bignon. When the bill came he read, 'Two peaches, 15f.' He paid. 'Peaches scarce, I presume?' was his sole remark. 'No, sir,' replied the waiter, 'but Teufelskines are.'" *Telegraph*, November 25, 1864.

"Yesterday morning, at eight o'clock, a woman, passing a dung heap in the stone-yard near the recently-erected almshouses in Shadwell Gap, High street, Shadwell, called the attention of a Thames police-constable to a man in a sitting position on the dung heap, and said she was afraid he was dead. Her fears proved to be true. The wretched creature appeared to have been dead several hours. He had perished of cold and wet, and the rain had been beating down on him all night. The deceased was a bone-picker. He was in the lowest stage of poverty, poorly clad, and half-starved. The police had frequently driven him away from the stone-yard, between sunset and sunrise, and told him to go home. He selected a most desolate spot for his wretched death. A penny and some bones were found in his pockets. The deceased was between fifty and sixty years of age. Inspector Roberts, of the K division, has given directions for inquiries to be made at the lodging-houses respecting the deceased, to ascertain his identity, if possible."—*Morning Post*, November 25, 1864.

You have the separation thus in brief compass; and I want you to take notice of the " a penny and some bones were found in his pockets," and to compare it with this third statement, from the *Telegraph* of January 16th of this year:

" Again, the dietary scale for adult and juvenile paupers was drawn up by the most conspicuous political economists in England. It is low in quantity, but it is sufficient to support nature; yet within ten years of the passing of the Poor Law Act, we heard of the paupers in the Andover Union gnawing the scraps of putrid flesh and sucking the marrow from the bones of horses which they were employed to crush."

You see my reason for thinking that our Lazarus of Christianity has some advantage over the Jewish one. Jewish Lazarus expected, or at least prayed, to be fed with crumbs from the rich man's table; but *our* Lazarus is fed with crumbs from the dog's table.

Now this distinction between rich and poor rests on two bases. Within its proper limits, on a basis which is lawful and everlastingly necessary; beyond them, on a basis unlawful, and everlastingly corrupting the frame-work of society. The lawful basis of wealth is, that a man who works should be paid the fair value of his work; and that if he does not choose to spend it to-day, he should have free leave to keep it, and spend it to-morrow. Thus, an industrious man working daily, and laying by daily, attains at last the possession of an accumulated sum of wealth, to which he has absolute right. The idle person who will not work, and the wasteful person who lays nothing by, at the end of the same time will be doubly poor—poor in possession, and dissolute in moral habit; and he will then naturally covet the money which the other has saved. And if he is then allowed to attack the other, and rob him of his well-earned wealth, there is no more any motive for saving, or any reward for good conduct; and all society is thereupon dissolved, or exists only in systems of rapine. Therefore the first necessity of social life is the clearness of national conscience in enforcing the law—that he should keep who has JUSTLY EARNED.

That law, I say, is the proper basis of distinction between rich and poor. But there is also a false basis of distinction; namely, the power held over those who earn wealth by those who levy or exact it. There will be always a number of men who would fain set themselves to the accumulation of wealth as the sole object of their lives. Necessarily, that class of men is an uneducated class, inferior in intellect, and more or less cowardly. It is physically impossible for a well-educated, intellectual, or brave man to make money the chief object of his thoughts; as physically impossible as it is for him to make his dinner the principal object of them. All healthy people like their dinners, but their dinner is not the main object of their lives. So all healthily minded people like making money—ought to like it, and to enjoy the sensation of winning it; but the main object of their life is not money; it is something better than money. A good soldier, for instance, mainly wishes to do his fighting well. He is glad of his pay—very properly so, and justly grumbles when you keep him ten years without it—still, his main notion of life is to win battles, not to be paid for winning them. So of clergymen. They like pew-rents, and baptismal fees, of course; but yet, if they are brave and well educated, the pew-rent is not the sole object of their lives, and the baptismal fee is not the sole purpose of the baptism; the clergyman's object is essentially to baptize and preach, not to be paid for preaching. So of doctors. They like fees no doubt—ought to like them; yet if they are brave and well educated, the entire object of their lives is not fees. They, on the whole, desire to cure the sick; and—if they are good doctors, and the choice were fairly put to them—would rather cure their patient, and lose their fee, than kill him, and get it. And so with all other brave and rightly trained men; their work is first, their fee second—very important always, but still *second.* But in every nation, as I said, there are a vast class who are ill-educated, cowardly, and more or less stupid. And with these people, just as certainly the fee is first, and the work second, as with brave people the work is first and the fee second. And this is no small distinction. It is the whole distinction in a man; distinction between life and death *in* him, between heaven and hell *for* him. You cannot serve two masters—you *must* serve one or other. If your work is first with you, and your fee second, work is your master, and the lord of work, who is God. But if your fee is first with you, and your work second, fee is your master, and the lord of fee, who is the Devil; and not only the Devil, but the lowest of devils—the "least erected fiend that fell." So there you have it in brief terms; Work first—you are God's servants; Fee first—you are the Fiend's. And it makes a difference, now and ever, believe me, whether you serve Him who has on His vesture and thigh written, "King of Kings," and whose service is perfect freedom; or him on whose vesture and thigh the name is written, "Slave of Slaves," and whose service is perfect slavery.

However, in every nation there are, and must always be a certain number of these Fiend's servants, who have it principally for the object of their lives to make money. They are always, as I said, more or less stupid, and cannot conceive of anything else so nice as money. Stupidity is always the basis of the Judas bargain. We do great injustice to Iscariot, in thinking him wicked above all common wickedness. He was only a common money-lover, and, like all money-lovers, didn't understand Christ—couldn't make out the worth of Him, or meaning of Him. He didn't want Him to be killed. He was horror-struck when he found that Christ would be killed; threw his money away instantly, and hanged himself. How many of our present money-seekers, think you, would have the grace to hang themselves, whoever was killed? But Judas was a common, selfish, muddle-headed, pilfering fellow; his hand always in the bag of the poor, not caring for them. He didn't understand Christ—yet believed in Him, much more than most of us do; had seen Him do miracles, thought He was quite strong enough to shift for Himself, and he, Judas, might as well make his own little by-perquisites out of the affair. Christ would come out of it well enough, and he have his thirty pieces. Now, that is the money-seeker's idea, all over the world. He doesn't hate Christ, but can't understand Him—doesn't care for Him—sees no good in that benevolent business; makes his own little job out of it at all events, come what will. And thus, out of every mass of men, you have a certain number of bag-men—your "fee-first" men, whose main object is to make money. And they do make it—make it in all sorts of unfair ways, chiefly by the weight and force of money itself or what is called the power of capital; that is to say, the power which money, once obtained, has over the labor of the poor, so that the capitalist can take all its produce to himself, except the laborer's food. That is the modern Judas' way of "carrying the bag," and "bearing what is put therein."

Nay, but (it is asked) how is that an unfair advantage? Has not the man who has worked for the money a right to use it as he best can? No; in this respect, money is now exactly what mountain promontories over public roads were in old times. The barons fought for them fairly—the strongest and cunningest got them; then fortified them, and made every one who passed below pay toll. Well, capital now is exactly what crags were then. Men fight fairly (we will, at least, grant so much, though it is more than we ought) for their money; but, once having got it, the fortified millionaire can make everybody who passes below pay toll to his million, and build another tower of his money castle. And I can tell you, the poor vagrants by the roadside suffer now quite as much from the bag-baron, as ever they did from the crag-baron. Bags and crags have just the same result on rags. I have not time, however, to-night to show you in how many ways the power of capital is unjust; but this one great principle I have to assert —you will find it quite indisputably true—that whenever money is the principal object of life with either man or nation, it is both got ill, and spent ill; and does harm both in the getting and spending; but when it is not the principal object, it and all other things will be well got, and well spent. And here is the test, with every man, of whether money is the principal object with him, or not. If in mid-life he could pause and say, "Now I have enough to live upon, I'll live upon it; and having well earned it, I will also well spend it, and go out of the world poor, as I came into it," then money is not principal with him; but if, having enough to live upon in the manner befitting his character and rank, he still wants to make more, and to *die* rich, then money is the principal object with him, and it becomes a curse to himself, and generally to those who spend it after him. For you know it *must* be spent some day; the only question is whether the man who makes it shall spend it, or some one else. And generally it is better for the maker to spend it, for he will know best its value and use. This is the true law of life. And if a man does not choose thus to spend his money, he must either hoard it or lend it, and the worst thing he can generally do is to lend it; for borrowers are nearly always ill-spenders, and it is with lent money that all evil is mainly done, and all unjust war protracted.

For observe what the real fact is, respecting loans to foreign military governments, and how strange it is. If your little boy came to you to ask for money to spend in squibs and crackers, you would think twice before you gave it to him, and you would have some idea that it was wasted, when you saw it fly off in fireworks, even though he did no mischief with it. But the Russian children, and Austrian children, come to you, borrowing money, not to spend in innocent squibs, but in cartridges and bayonets to attack you in India with, and to keep down all noble life in Italy with, and to murder Polish women and children with; and *that* you will give at once, because they pay you interest for it. Now, in order to pay you that interest, they must tax every working peasant in their dominions: and on that work you live. You therefore at once rob the Austrian peasant, assassinate or banish the Polish peasant, and you live on the produce of the theft, and the bribe for the assassination! That is the broad fact—that is the practical meaning of your foreign loans, and of most large interest of money; and then you quarrel with Bishop Colenso, forsooth, as if *he* denied the Bible, and you believed it! though, wretches as you are, every deliberate act of your lives is a new defiance of its primary orders; and as if, for most of the rich men of England at this moment, it were not indeed to be desired, as the best thing at least for *them*, that the Bible should *not* be true, since against them these words are written in it: "The rust of your gold and silver shall be a witness against you, and shall eat your flesh, as it were fire."

III. I pass now to our third condition of separation, between the men who work with the hand, and those who work with the head.

And here we have at last an inevitable distinction. There *must* be work done by the arms, or none of us could live. There *must* be work done by the brains, or the life we get would not be worth having. And the same men cannot do both. There is rough work to be done, and rough men must do it; there is gentle work to be done, and gentlemen must do it; and it is physically impossible that one class should do, or divide, the work of the other. And it is of no use to try to conceal this sorrowful fact by fine words, and to talk to the workman about the honorableness of manual labor, and the dignity of humanity. That is a grand old proverb of Sancho Panza's, " Fine words butter no parsnips;" and I can tell you that, all over England just now, you workmen are buying a great deal too much butter at that dairy. Rough work, honorable or not, takes the life out of us; and the man who has been heaving clay out of a ditch all day, or driving an express train against the north wind all night, or holding a collier's helm in a gale on a lee-shore, or whirling white-hot iron at a furnace mouth, that man is not the same at the end of his day, or night, as one who has been sitting in a quiet room, with everything comfortable about him, reading books, or classing butterflies, or painting pictures. If it is any comfort to you to be told that the rough work is the more honorable of the two, I should be sorry to take that much of consolation from you; and in some sense I need not. The rough work is at all events real, honest, and generally, though not always, useful; while the fine work is, a great deal of it, foolish and false as well as fine, and therefore dishonorable: but when both kinds are equally well and worthily done, the head's is the noble work, and the hand's the ignoble; and of all hand work whatsoever, necessary for the maintenance of life, those old words, "In the sweat of thy face thou shalt eat bread," indicate that the inherent nature of it is one of calamity; and that the ground, cursed for our sake, casts also some shadow of degradation into our contest with its thorn and its thistle; so that all nations have held their days honorable, or "holy," and constituted them "holydays" or "holidays," by making them days of rest; and the promise, which, among all our distant hopes, seems to cast the chief brightness over death, is that blessing of the dead who die in the Lord, that "they rest from their labors, and their works do follow them."

And thus the perpetual question and contest must arise, who is to do this rough work? and how is the worker of it to be comforted, redeemed, and rewarded? and what kind of play should he have, and what rest, in this world, sometimes, as well as in the next? Well, my good working friends, these questions will take a little time to answer yet. They must be answered: all good men are occupied with them, and all honest thinkers. There's grand head-work doing about them; but much must be discovered, and much attempted in vain, before anything decisive can be told you. Only note these few particulars, which are already sure.

As to the distribution of the hard work. None of us, or very few of us, do either hard or soft work because we think we ought; but because we have chanced to fall into the way of it, and cannot help ourselves. Now, nobody does anything well that they cannot help doing: work is only done well when it is done with a will; and no man has a thoroughly sound will unless he knows he is doing what he should, and is in his place. And, depend upon it, all work must be done at last, not in a disorderly, scrambling, doggish way, but in an ordered, soldierly, human way—a lawful way. Men are enlisted for the labor that kills— the labor of war: they are counted, trained, fed, dressed, and praised for that. Let them be enlisted also for the labor that feeds: let them be counted, trained, fed, dressed, praised for that. Teach the plow exercise as carefully as you do the sword exercise, and let the officers of troops of life be held as much gentlemen as the officers of troops of death; and all is done: but neither this, nor any other right thing, can be accomplished—you can't even see your way to it—unless, first of all, both servant and master are resolved that come what will of it, they will do each other justice. People are perpetually squabbling about what will be best to do, or easiest to do, or advisablest to do, or profitablest to do; but they never, so far as I hear them talk, ever ask what it is *just* to do. And it is the law of heaven that you shall not be able to judge what is wise or easy, unless you are first resolved to judge what is just, and to do it. That is the one thing constantly reiterated by our Master—the order of all others that is given oftenest—"Do justice and judgment." That's your Bible order; that's the "Service of God," not praying nor psalm-singing. You are told, indeed, to sing psalms when you are merry, and to pray when you need anything; and, by the perversion of the Evil Spirit, we get to think that praying and psalm-singing are "service." If a child finds itself in want of anything, it runs in and asks its father for it—does it call that, doing its father a service? If it begs for a toy or a piece of cake—does it call that serving its father? That, with God, is prayer, and He likes to hear it: He likes you to ask Him for cake when you want it; but He doesn't call that "serving Him." Begging is not serving: God likes mere beggars as little as you do—He likes honest servants, not beggars. So when a child loves its father very much, and is very happy, it may sing little songs about him; but it doesn't call that serving its father; neither is singing songs about God, serving God. It is enjoying ourselves, if it's anything; most probably it is nothing; but if it's anything, it is serving ourselves, not God. And yet we are impudent enough to call our beggings and chantings "Divine Service:" we say "Divine service will be 'performed'" (that's our word—the form of it gone through) "at eleven o'clock." Alas!—unless we perform Divine service in every willing act of our life, we never perform it at all. The one Divine work—the one ordered sacrifice—is to do justice; and it is the last we are ever inclined to do. Anything rather than that! As much charity as you choose, but no justice. "Nay," you will say, "charity is greater than justice." Yes, it is greater; it is the summit of justice—it is the temple of which justice is the foundation. But you can't have the top without the bottom; you cannot build upon charity. You must build upon justice, for this main reason, that you have not, at first, charity to build with. It is the last reward of good work. Do justice to your brother (you can do that, whether you love him or not), and you will come to love him. But do injustice to him, because you don't love him; and you will come to hate him. It is all very fine to think you can build upon charity to begin with; but you will find all you have got to begin with, begins at home, and is essentially love of yourself. You well-to-do people, for instance, who are here to-night, will go to "Divine service" next

Sunday, all nice and tidy, and your little children will have their tight little Sunday boots on, and lovely little Sunday feathers in their hats; and you'll think, complacently and piously, how lovely they look! So they do; and you love them heartily, and you like sticking feathers in their hats. That's all right: that *is* charity; but it is charity beginning at home. Then you will come to the poor little crossing-sweeper, got up also—it, in its Sunday dress—the dirtiest rags it has—that it may beg the better: we shall give it a penny, and think how good we are. That's charity going abroad. But what does Justice say, walking and watching near us? Christian Justice has been strangely mute, and seemingly blind; and, if not blind, decrepit, this many a day: she keeps her accounts still, however—quite steadily—doing them at nights, carefully, with her bandage off, and through acutest spectacles (the only modern scientific invention she cares about). You must put your ear down ever so close to her lips to hear her speak; and then you will start at what she first whispers, for it will certainly be, "Why shouldn't that little crossing-sweeper have a feather on its head, as well as your own child?" Then you may ask Justice, in an amazed manner, "How she can possibly be so foolish as to think children could sweep crossings with feathers on their heads?" Then you stoop again, and Justice says—still in her dull, stupid way—"Then, why don't you, every other Sunday, leave your child to sweep the crossing, and take the little sweeper to church in a hat and feather?" Mercy on us (you think), what will she say next? And you answer, of course, that "you don't, because everybody ought to remain content in the position in which Providence has placed them." Ah, my friends, that's the gist of the whole question. *Did* Providence put them in that position, or did *you?* You knock a man into a ditch, and then you tell him to remain content in the "position in which Providence has placed him." That's modern Christianity. You say—"*We* did not knock him into the ditch." How do you know what you have done, or are doing? That's just what we have all got to know, and what we shall never know, until the question with us every morning, is, not how to do the gainful thing, but how to do the just thing; nor until we are at least so far on the way to being Christian, as to have understood that maxim of the poor half-way Mohammedan, "One hour in the execution of justice is worth seventy years of prayer."

Supposing, then, we have it determined with appropriate justice, *who* is to do the hand-work, the next questions must be how the hand-workers are to be paid, and how they are to be refreshed, and what play they are to have. Now, the possible quantity of play depends on the possible quantity of pay; and the quantity of pay is not a matter for consideration to hand-workers only, but to all workers. Generally, good, useful work, whether of the hand or head, is either ill-paid, or not paid at all. I don't say it should be so, but it always is so. People, as a rule, only pay for being amused or being cheated, not for being served. Five thousand a year to your talker, and a shilling a day to your fighter, digger, and thinker is the rule. None of the best head-work in art, literature, or science, is ever paid for. How much do you think Homer got for his Iliad? or Dante for his Paradise? only bitter bread and salt, and going up and down other people's stairs. In science, the man who discovered the telescope, and first saw heaven, was paid with a dungeon; the man who invented the microscope, and first saw earth, died of starvation, driven from his home: it is indeed very clear that God means all thoroughly good work and talk to be done for nothing. Baruch, the scribe, did not get a penny a line for writing Jeremiah's second roll for him, I fancy; and St. Stephen did not get bishop's pay for that long sermon of his to the Pharisees; nothing but stones. For indeed that is the world-father's proper payment. So surely as any of the world's children work for the world's good, honestly, with head and heart; and come to it, saying, "Give us a little bread, just to keep the life in us," the world-father answers them, "No, my children, not bread; a stone, if you like, or as many as you need, to keep you quiet." But the hand-workers are not so ill off as all this comes to. The worst that can happen to *you* is to break stones; not be broken by them. And for you there will come a time for better payment; some day, assuredly, more pence will be paid to Peter the Fisherman and fewer to Peter the Pope; we shall pay people not quite so much for talking in Parliament and doing nothing, as for holding their tongues out of it and doing something; we shall pay our plowman a little more and our lawyer a little less, and so on: but, at least, we may even now take care that whatever work is done shall be fully paid for; and the man who does it paid for it, not somebody else; and that it shall be done in an orderly, soldierly, well-guided, wholesome way, under good captains and lieutenants of labor; and that it shall have its appointed times of rest, and enough of them; and that in those times the play shall be wholesome play, not in theatrical gardens, with tin flowers and gas sunshine, and girls dancing because of their misery; but in true gardens, with real flowers and real sunshine, and children dancing because of their gladness; so that truly the streets shall be full (the "streets," mind you, not the gutters) of children, playing in the midst thereof. We may take care that workingmen shall have at least as good books to read as anybody else, when they've time to read them; and as comfortable firesides to sit at as anybody else, when they've time to sit at them. This, I think, can be managed for you, my working friends, in the good time .

IV. I must go on, however, to our last head, concerning ourselves all, as workers. What is wise work, and what is foolish work? What the difference between sense and nonsense, in daily occupation?

Well, wise work is, briefly, work *with* God. Foolish work is work *against* God. And work done with God, which He will help, may be briefly described as "Putting in Order"—that is, enforcing God's law of order, spiritual and material, over men and things. The first thing you have to do, essentially; the real "good work" is, with respect to men, to enforce justice, and with respect to things, to enforce tidiness, and fruitfulness. And against these two great human deeds, justice and order, there are perpetually two great demons contending—the devil of iniquity, or inequity, and the devil of disorder, or of death; for death is only consummation of disorder. You have to fight these two fiends daily. So far as you don't fight against the fiend of iniquity, you work for him. You "work iniquity," and the judgment upon you, for all your "Lord, Lord's," will be "Depart from me, ye that work iniquity." And so far as you do not resist the fiend of disorder, you work disorder, and you yourself do the work of Death, which is sin, and has for its wages, Death himself.

Observe then, all wise work is mainly threefold in character. It is honest, useful, and cheerful.

I. It is HONEST. I hardly know anything more

strange than that you recognize honesty in play, and you do not in work. In your lightest games, you have always some one to see what you call "fair play." In boxing, you must hit fair; in racing, start fair. Your English watch-word is fair play, your English hatred, foul play. Did it ever strike you that you wanted another watch-word also, fair work, and another hatred also, foul work? Your prize-fighter has some honor in him yet; and so have the men in the ring round him: they will judge him to lose the match, by foul hitting. But your prize merchant gains his match by foul selling, and no one cries out against that. You drive a gambler out of the gambling-room who loads dice, but you leave a tradesman in flourishing business, who loads scales! For observe, all dishonest dealing *is* loading scales. What does it matter whether I get short weight, adulterate substance, or dishonest fabric? The fault in the fabric is incomparably the worst of the two. Give me short measure of food, and I only lose by you; but give me adulterate food, and I die by you. Here, then, is your chief duty, you workmen and tradesmen—to be true to yourselves, and to us who would help you. We can do nothing for you, nor you for yourselves, without honesty. Get that, you get all; without that, your suffrages, your reforms, your free-trade measures, your institutions of science, are all in vain. It is useless to put your heads together, if you can't put your hearts together.

Shoulder to shoulder, right hand to right hand among yourselves, and no wrong hand to anybody else, and you'll win the world yet.

II. Then, secondly, wise work is USEFUL. No man minds, or ought to mind, its being hard, if only it comes to something; but when it is hard, and comes to nothing; when all our bees' business turns to spiders'; and for honey-comb we have only resultant cobweb, blown away by the next breeze—that is the cruel tning for the worker. Yet do we ever ask ourselves, personally, or even nationally, whether our work is coming to anything or not? We don't care to keep what has been nobly done; still less do we care to do nobly what others would keep; and, least of all, to make the work itself useful instead of deadly to the doer, so as to use his life indeed, but not to waste it. Of all wastes, the greatest waste that you can commit is the waste of labor. If you went down in the morning into your dairy, and you found that your youngest child had got down before you; and that he and the cat were at play together, and that he had poured out all the cream on the floor for the cat to lap up, you would scold the child, and be sorry the milk was wasted. But if, instead of wooden bowls with milk in them, there are golden bowls with human life in them, and instead of the cat to play with—the devil to play with; and you yourself the player; and instead of leaving that golden bowl to be broken by God at the fountain, you break it in the dust yourself, and pour the human blood out on the ground for the fiend to lick up—that is no waste! What! you perhaps think, "to waste the labor of men is not to kill them." Is it not? I should like to know how you could kill them more utterly—kill them with second deaths, seventh deaths, hundredfold deaths? It is the slightest way of killing to stop a man's breath. Nay, the hunger, and the cold, and the little whistling bullets—or love-messengers between nation and nation—have brought pleasant messages from us to many a man before now; orders of sweet release, and leave at last to go where he will be most welcome and most happy. At the worst you do but shorten his life, you do not corrupt his life. But if you put him to base labor, if you bind his thoughts, if you blind his eyes, if you blunt his hopes, if you steal his joys, if you stunt his body, and blast his soul, and at last leave him not so much as to reap the poor fruit of his degradation, but gather that for yourself, and dismiss him to the grave, when you have done with him, having, so far as in you lay, made the walls of that grave everlasting (though, indeed, I fancy the goodly bricks of some of our family vaults will hold closer in the resurrection day than the sod over the laborer's head), this you think is no waste, and no sin!

III. Then, lastly, wise work is CHEERFUL, as a child's work is. And now I want you to take one thought home with you, and let it stay with you.

Everybody in this room has been taught to pray daily, "Thy kingdom come." Now, if we hear a man swear in the streets, we think it very wrong, and say he "takes God's name in vain." But there's a twenty times worse way of taking His name in vain than that. It is to *ask God for what we don't want.* He doesn't like that sort of prayer. If you don't want a thing, don't ask for it: such asking is the worst mockery of your King you can mock Him with; the soldiers striking Him on the head with the reed was nothing to that. If you do not wish for His kingdom, don't pray for it. But if you do, you must do more than pray for it; you must work for it. And, to work for it, you must know what it is: we have all prayed for it many a day without thinking. Observe, it is a kingdom that is to come to us; we are not to go to it. Also, it is not to be a kingdom of the dead, but of the living. Also, it is not to come all at once, but quietly; nobody knows how. "The kingdom of God cometh not with observation." Also, it is not to come outside of us, but in the hearts of us: "the kingdom of God is within you." And, being within us, it is not a thing to be seen, but to be felt; and though it brings all substance of good with it, it does not consist in that: "the kingdom of God is not meat and drink, but righteousness, peace, and joy in the Holy Ghost:" joy, that is to say, in the holy, healthful, and helpful Spirit. Now, if we want to work for this kingdom, and to bring it, and enter into it, there's just one condition to be first accepted. You must enter it as children, or not at all; "Whosoever will not receive it as a little child shall not enter therein." And again, "Suffer little children to come unto me, and forbid them not, for of such is the kingdom of heaven."

Of such, observe. Not of children themselves, but of such as children. I believe most mothers who read that text think that all heaven is to be full of babies. But that's not so. There will be children there, but the hoary head is the crown. "Length of days, and long life and peace," that is the blessing, not to die in babyhood. Children die but for their parents' sin; God means them to live, but He can't let them always; then they have their earlier place in heaven: and the little child of David, vainly prayed for; the little child of Jeroboam, killed by its mother's step on its own threshold—they will be there. But weary old David, and weary old Barzillai, having learned children's lessons at last, will be there too, and the one question for us all, young or old, is, have we learned our child's lesson? it is the *character of* children we want, and must gain at our peril; let us see, briefly, in what it consists.

The first character of right childhood is that it is Modest. A well-bred child does not think it can teach its parents, or that it knows everything. It may think its father and mother knows everything—perhaps that all grown-up people know everything; very certainly it is sure that *it* does not. And it is always asking questions, and wanting to know more. Well, that is the first character of a good and wise man at his work. To know that he knows very little—to perceive that there are many above him wiser than he; and to be always asking questions, wanting to learn, not to teach No one ever teaches well who wants to teach, or governs well who wants to govern; it is an old saying (Plato's, but I know not if his, first), and as wise as old.

Then, the second character of right childhood is to be Faithful. Perceiving that its father knows best what is good for it, and having found always, when it has tried its own way against his, that he was right and it was wrong, a noble child trusts him at last wholly, gives him its hand, and will walk blindfold with him, if he bids it. And that is the true character of all good men also, as obedient workers, or soldiers under captains. They must trust their captains—they are bound for their lives to choose none but those whom they *can* trust. Then, they are not always to be thinking that what seems strange to them, or wrong in what they are desired to do, *is* strange or wrong. They know their captain: where he leads they must follow, what he bids, they must do; and without this trust and faith, without this captainship and soldiership, no great deed, no great salvation, is possible to man. Among all the nations it is only when this faith is attained by them that they become great: the Jew, the Greek and the Mohammedan agree at least in testifying to this. It was a deed of this absolute trust which made Abraham the father of the f ith.al; it was the declaration of the power of God as captain over all men, and the acceptance of a leader appointed by Him as commander of the faithful, which laid the foundation of whatever national power yet exists in the East; and the deed of the Greeks, which has become the type of unselfish and noble soldiership to all lands, and to all times, was commemorated, on the tomb of those who gave their lives to do it, in the most pathetic, so far as I know, or can feel, of all human utterances: " Oh, stranger, go and tell our people that we are lying here, having *obeyed* their words."

Then the third character of right childhood is to be Loving and Generous. Give a little love to a child, and you get a great deal back. It loves everything near it, when it is a right kind of child—would hurt nothing, would give the best it has away, always, if you need it—does not lay plans for getting everything in the house for itself, and delights in helping people; you cannot please it so much as by giving it a chance of being useful, in ever so little a way.

And because of all these characters, lastly, it is Cheerful. Putting its trust in its father, it is careful for nothing—being full of love to every creature, it is happy always, whether in its play or in its duty. Well, that's the great worker's character also. Taking no thought for the morrow; taking thought only for the duty of the day; trusting somebody else to take care of to-morrow; knowing indeed what labor is, but not what sorrow is; and always ready for play —beautiful play—for lovely human play is like the play of the Sun. There's a worker for you. He, steady to his time, is set as a strong man to run his course, but also, he *rejoiceth* as a strong man to run his course. See how he plays in the morning, with the mists below, and the clouds above, with a ray here and a flash there, and a shower of jewels everywhere —that's the Sun's play; and great human play is like his—all various—all full of light and life, and tender, as the dew of the morning.

So then, you have the child's character in these four things—Humility, Faith, Charity, and Cheerfulness. That's what you have got to be converted to. "Except ye be converted and become as little children "— You hear much of conversion nowadays; but people always seem to think they have got to be made wretched by conversion—to be converted to long faces. No, friends, you have got to be converted to short ones; you have to repent into childhood, to repent into delight, and delightsomeness. You can't go into a conventicle but you'll hear plenty of talk of backsliding. Backsliding, indeed! I can tell you, on the ways most of us go, the faster we slide back the better. Slide back into the cradle, if going on is into the grave —back, I tell you; back—out of your long faces, and into your long clothes. It is among children only, and as children only, that you will find medicine for your healing and true wisdom for your teaching. There is poison in the counsels of the *men* of this world; the words they speak are all bitterness, "the poison of asps is under their lips," but, "the sucking child shall play by the hole of the asp." There is death in the looks of men. "Their eyes are privily set against the poor;" they are as the uncharmable serpent, the cockatrice, which slew, by seeing. But "the weaned child shall lay his hand on the cockatrice den." There is death in the steps of men: "their feet are swift to shed blood; they have compassed us in our steps like the lion that is greedy of his prey, and the young lion lurking in secret places," but, in that kingdom, the wolf shall lie down with the lamb, and the fatling with the lion, and "a little child shall lead them." There is death in the thoughts of men: the world is one wide riddle to them, darker and darker as it draws to a close; but the secret of it is known to the child, and the Lord of heaven and earth is most to be thanked in that "He has hidden these things from the wise and prudent, and has revealed them unto babes." Yes, and there is death—infinitude of death in the principalities and powers of men. As far as the east is from the west, so far our sins are—*not* set from us, but multiplied around us: the Sun himself, think you he *now* "rejoices" to run his course, when he plunges westward to the horizon, so widely red, not with clouds, but blood? And it will be red more widely yet. Whatever drought of the early and latter rain may be, there will be none of that red rain. You fortify yourselves, you arm yourselves against it in vain; the enemy and avenger will be upon you also, unless you learn that it is not out of the mouths of the knitted gun, or the smoothed rifle, but "out of the mouths of babes and sucklings" that the strength is ordained, which shall "still the enemy and avenger."

LECTURE II.

TRAFFIC.

(Delivered in the Town Hall, Bradford)

My good Yorkshire friends, you asked me down here among your hills that I might talk to you about this Exchange you are going to build: but earnestly and seriously asking you to pardon me, I am going to do nothing of the kind. I cannot talk, or at least can say very little, about this same Exchange. I must talk of quite other things, though not willingly; I could not deserve your pardon, if when you invited me to speak on one subject, I willfully spoke on another. But I cannot speak, to purpose, of anything about which I do not care; and most simply and sorrowfully I have to tell you, in the outset, that I do *not* care about this Exchange of yours.

If, however, when you sent me your invitation, I had answered, "I won't come, I don't care about the Exchange of Bradford," you would have been justly offended with me, not knowing the reasons of so blunt a carelessness. So I have come down, hoping that you will patiently let me tell you why, on this, and many other such occasions, I now remain silent, when formerly I should have caught at the opportunity of speaking to a gracious audience.

In a word, then, I do not care about this Exchange—because *you* don't; and because you know perfectly well I cannot make you. Look at the essential circumstances of the case, which you, as business men, know perfectly well, though perhaps you think I forget them. You are going to spend £30,000, which to you, collectively, is nothing; the buying a new coat is, as to the cost of it, a much more important matter of consideration to me than building a new Exchange is to you. But you think you may as well have the right thing for your money. You know there are a great many odd styles of architecture about; you don't want to do anything ridiculous; you hear of me, among others, as a respectable architectural man-milliner: and you send for me, that I may tell you the leading fashion; and what is, in our shops, for the moment, the newest and sweetest thing in pinnacles.

Now, pardon me for telling you frankly, you cannot have good architecture merely by asking people's advice on occasion. All good architecture is the expression of national life and character; and it is produced by a prevalent and eager national taste, or desire for beauty. And I want you to think a little of the deep significance of this word "taste;" for no statement of mine has been more earnestly or oftener controverted than that good taste is essentially a moral quality. "No," say many of my antagonists, "taste is one thing, morality is another. Tell us what is pretty; we shall be glad to know that; but preach no sermons to us."

Permit me, therefore, to fortify this old dogma of mine somewhat. Taste is not only a part and an index of morality—it is the ONLY morality. The first, and last, and closest trial question to any living creature is, "What do you like?" Tell me what you like, and I'll tell you what you are. Go out into the street, and ask the first man or woman you meet, what their "taste" is, and if they answer candidly, you know them, body and soul. "You, my friend in the rags, with the unsteady gait, what do *you* like?" "A pipe and a quartern of gin." I know you. "You, good woman, with the quick step and tidy bonnet, what do you like?" "A swept hearth and a clean tea-table, and my husband opposite me, and a baby at my breast." Good, I know you also. "You, little girl with the golden hair and the soft eyes, what do you like?" "My canary, and a run among the wood hyacinths." "You, little boy with the dirty hands and the low forehead, what do you like?" "A shy at the sparrows, and a game at pitch-farthing." Good; we know them all now. What more need we ask?

"Nay," perhaps you answer: "we need rather to ask what these people and children do, than what they like. If they *do* right, it is no matter that they like what is wrong; and if they *do* wrong, it is no matter that they like what is right. Doing is the great thing; and it does not matter that the man likes drinking, so that he does not drink; nor that the little girl likes to ke kind to her canary, if she will not learn her lessons; nor that the little boy likes throwing stones at the sparrows, if he goes to the Sunday-school." Indeed, for a short time, and in a provisional sense, this is true. For if, resolutely, people do what is right, in time they come to like doing it. But they only are in a right moral state when they *have* come to like doing it; and as long as they don't like it, they are still in a vicious state. The man is not in health of body who is always thirsting for the bottle in the cupboard, though he bravely bears his thirst; but the man who heartily enjoys water in the morning and wine in the evening, each in its proper quantity and time. And the entire object of true education is to make people not merely *do* the right things, but *enjoy* the right things—not merely industrious, but to love industry—not merely learned, but to love knowledge—not merely pure, but to love purity—not merely just, but to hunger and thirst after justice.

But you may answer or think, "Is the liking for outside ornaments—for pictures, or statues, or furniture, or architecture—a moral quality?" Yes, most surely, if a rightly set liking. Taste for *any* pictures or statues is not a moral quality, but taste for good ones is. Only here again we have to define the word "good." I don't mean by "good," clever—or learned —or difficult in the doing. Take a picture by Teniers, of sots quarreling over their dice: it is an entirely clever picture; so clever that nothing in its kind has ever been done equal to it; but it is also an entirely base and evil picture. It is an expression of delight in the prolonged contemplation of a vile thing, and delight in that is an "unmannered," or "immoral" quality. It is "bad taste" in the profoundest sense— it is the taste of the devils. On the other hand, a picture of Titian's, or a Greek statue, or a Greek coin, or a Turner landscape, expresses delight in the perpetual contemplation of a good and perfect thing. That is an entirely moral quality—it is the taste of the angels. And all delight in art, and all love of it, resolve themselves into simple love of that which deserves love. That deserving is the quality which we call "loveliness" (we ought to have an opposite word, hateliness, to be said of the things which deserve to be hated); and it is not an indifferent nor optional thing whether we love this or that; but it is just the vital function of all our being. What we *like* determines what we *are*, and is the sign of what we are; and to teach taste is inevitably to form character. As I was thinking over this, in walking up Fleet Street the other day, my eye caught the title of a book standing open in a bookseller's window. It was, "On the necessity of the diffusion of taste among all classes." "Ah," I thought to myself, "my classifying friend, when you have diffused your taste, where will your classes be? The man who likes what you like, belongs to the same class with you, I think. Inevitably so. You may put him to other work if you choose; but, by the condition you have brought him into, he will dislike the other work as much as you would yourself. You get hold of a scavenger, or a costermonger, who enjoyed the Newgate Calendar for literature, and 'Pop goes the Weasel' for music. You think you can make him like Dante and Beethoven? I wish you joy of your lessons; but if you do, you have made a gentleman of him—he won't like to go back to his costermongering."

And so completely and unexceptionally is this so, that, if I had time to-night, I could show you that a nation cannot be affected by any vice, or weakness, without expressing it, legibly, and forever, either in bad art, or by want of art; and that there is no national virtue, small or great, which is not manifestly expressed in all the art which circumstances enable the people possessing that virtue to produce. Take, for instance, your great English virtue of enduring and patient courage. You have at present in England only one art of any consequence—that is, iron-working. You know thoroughly well how to cast and hammer iron. Now, do you think in those masses of lava which you build volcanic cones to melt, and which you forge at the mouths of the Infernos you have created; do you think, on those iron plates, your courage and endurance are not written forever—not merely with an iron pen, but on iron parchment? And take also your great English vice—European vice—vice of all the world—vice of all other worlds that roll or shine in heaven, bearing with them yet the atmosphere of hell—the vice of jealousy, which brings competition into your commerce, treachery into your councils, and dishonor into your wars—that vice which has rendered for you, and for your next neighboring nation, the daily occupations of existence no longer possible, but with the mail upon your breasts and the sword loose in its sheath; so that, at last, you have realized for all the multitudes of the two great peoples who lead the so-called civilization of the earth—you have realized for them all, I say, in person and in policy, what was once true only of the rough Border riders of your Cheviot hills—

"They carved at the meal
With gloves of steel,
And they drank the red wine through the helmet barr'd;"

do you think that this national shame and dastardliness of heart are not written as legibly on every rivet of your iron armor as the strength of the right hands that forged it? Friends, I know not whether this thing be the more ludicrous or the more melancholy. It is quite unspeakably both. Suppose, instead of being now sent for by you, I had been sent for by some private gentleman, living in a suburban house, with his garden separated only by a fruit-wall from his next-door neighbor's; and he had called me to consult with him on the furnishing of his drawing-room. I begin looking about me, and find the walls rather bare; I think such and such a paper might be desirable—perhaps a little fresco here and there on the ceiling—a damask curtain or so at the windows. "Ah," says my employer, "damask curtains, indeed! That's all very fine, but you know I can't afford that kind of thing just now!" "Yet the world credits you with a splendid income!" "Ah, yes," says my friend, "but do you know, at present, I am obliged to spend it nearly all in steel-traps?" "Steel-traps! for whom?" "Why, for that fellow on the other side the wall, you know: we're very good friends, capital friends; but we are obliged to keep our traps set on both sides of the wall; we could not possibly keep on friendly terms without them, and our spring-guns. The worst of it is, we are both clever fellows enough; and there's never a day passes that we don't find out a new trap, or a new gun-barrel, or something; we spend about fifteen millions a year each in our traps, take it altogether; and I don't see how we're to do with less." A highly comic state of life for two private gentlemen; but for two nations, it seems to me, not wholly comic? Bedlam would be comic, perhaps, if there were only one madman in it; and your Christmas pantomime is comic, when there is only one clown in it; but when the whole world turns clown, and paints itself red with its own heart's-blood instead of vermilion, it is something else than comic, I think.

Mind, I know a great deal of this is play, and willingly allow for that. You don't know what to do with yourselves for a sensation: fox-hunting and cricketing will not carry you through the whole of this unendurably long mortal life: you liked pop-guns when you were school-boys, and rifles and Armstrongs are only the same things better made: but then the worst of it is, that what was play to you when boys, was not play to the sparrows; and what is play to you now, is not play to the small birds of State neither; and for the black eagles, you are somewhat shy of taking shots at them, if I mistake not.

I must get back to the matter in hand, however. Believe me, without further instance, I could show you, in all time, that every nation's vice, or virtue, was written in its art: the soldiership of early Greece; the sensuality of late Italy; the visionary religion of Tuscany; the splendid human energy and beauty of Venice. I have no time to do this to-night (I have done it elsewhere before now); but I proceed to apply the principle to ourselves in a more searching manner.

I notice that among all the new buildings that cover your once wild hills, churches and schools are mixed in due, that is to say, in large proportion, with your mills and mansions, and I notice also that the churches and schools are almost always Gothic, and the mansions and mills are never Gothic. Will you allow me to ask precisely the meaning of this? For, remember, it is peculiarly a modern phenomenon. When Gothic was invented, houses were Gothic as well as churches; and when the Italian style superseded the Gothic, churches were Italian as well as houses. If there is a Gothic spire to the cathedral of Antwerp, there is a Gothic belfry to the Hôtel de Ville at Brussels; if Inigo Jones builds an Italian Whitehall, Sir Christopher Wren builds an Italian St. Paul's. But now you live under one school of architecture, and worship under another. What do you mean by doing this? Am I to understand that you are thinking of changing your architecture back to Gothic; and that you treat your churches experimentally, because it does not matter what mistakes you make in a church? Or am I to understand that you consider Gothic a pre-eminently sacred and beautiful mode of building, which you think, like the fine frankincense, should be mixed for the tabernacle only, and reserved for your religious services? For if this be the feeling, though it may seem at first as if it were graceful and reverent, you will find that, at the root of the matter, it signifies neither more nor less than that you have separated your religion from your life.

For consider what a wide significance this fact has; and remember that it is not you only, but all the people of England, who are behaving thus just now.

You have all got into the habit of calling the church "the house of God." I have seen, over the doors of many churches, the legend actually carved, "*This* is the house of God, and this is the gate of heaven." Now, note where that legend comes from, and of what place it was first spoken. A boy leaves his father's house to go on a long journey on foot, to visit his uncle; he has to cross a wild hill-desert; just as if one of your own boys had to cross the wolds of Westmoreland, to visit an uncle at Carlisle. The second or third day your boy finds himself somewhere between Hawes and Brough, in the midst of the moors, at sunset. It is stony ground, and boggy; he cannot go one foot further that night. Down he lies, to sleep, on Wharnside, where best he may, gathering a few of the stones together to put under his head—so wild the place is, he cannot get anything but stones. And there, lying under the broad night, he has a dream; and he sees a ladder set up on the earth, and the top of it reaches to heaven, and the angels of God are ascending and descending upon it. And when he wakes out of his sleep, he says, "How dreadful is this place; surely, this is none other than the house of God, and this is the gate of heaven." This PLACE, observe; not this church; not this city; not this stone, even, which he puts up for a memorial—the piece of flint on which his head has lain. But this *place;* this windy slope of Wharnside; this moorland hollow, torrent-bitten, snow-blighted; this *any* place where God lets down the ladder. And how are you to know where that will be? or how are you to determine where it may be, but by being ready for it always? Do you know where the lightning is to fall next? You *do* know that, partly; you can guide the lightning; but you cannot guide the going forth of the Spirit, which is that lightning when it shines from the east to the west.

But the perpetual and insolent warping of that strong verse to serve a merely ecclesiastical purpose is only one of the thousand instances in which we sink back into gross Judaism. We call our churches "temples." Now, you know, or ought to know, they are *not* temples. They have never had, never can have, anything whatever to do with temples. They are "synagogues"—"gathering places"—where you gather yourselves together as an assembly; and by not calling them so, you again miss the force of another mighty text—"Thou, when thou prayest, shall not be as the hypocrites are; for they love to pray standing in the *churches*" [we should translate it], "that they may be seen of men. But thou, when thou prayest, enter into thy closet, and when thou hast shut thy door, pray to thy Father"—which is, not in chancel nor in aisle, but "in secret."

Now, you feel, as I say this to you—I know you feel—as if I were trying to take away the honor of your churches. Not so; I am trying to prove to you the honor of your houses and your hills; I am trying to show you—not that the Church is not sacred—but that the whole Earth is. I would have you feel, what careless, what constant, what infectious sin there is in all modes of thought, whereby, in calling your churches only "holy," you call your hearths and homes profane; and have separated yourselves from the heathen by casting all your household gods to the ground, instead of recognizing, in the place of their many and feeble Lares, the presence of your One and Mighty Lord and Lar.

"But what has all this to do with our Exchange?" you ask me, impatiently. My dear friends, it has just everything to do with it; on these inner and great questions depend all the outer and little ones; and if you have asked me down here to speak to you, because you had before been interested in anything I have written, you must know that all I have yet said about architecture was to show this. The book I called "The Seven Lamps" was to show that certain right states of temper and moral feeling were the magic powers by which all good architecture, without exception, had been produced. "The Stones of Venice" had, from beginning to end, no other aim than to show that the Gothic architecture of Venice had arisen out of, and indicated in all its features, a state of pure national faith, and of domestic virtue; and that its Renaissance architecture had arisen out of, and in all its features indicated, a state of concealed national infidelity, and of domestic corruption. And now, you ask me what style is best to build in; and how can I answer, knowing the meaning of the two styles, but by another question—do you mean to build as Christians or as Infidels? And still more—do you mean to build as honest Christians or as honest Infidels? as thoroughly and confessedly either one or the other? You don't like to be asked such rude questions. I cannot help it; they are of much more importance than this Exchange business; and if they can be at once answered, the Exchange business settles itself in a moment. But, before I press them further, I must ask leave to explain one point clearly. In all my past work, my endeavor has been to show that good architecture is essentially religious—the production of a faithful and virtuous, not of an infidel and corrupted people. But in the course of doing this, I have had also to show that good architecture is not *ecclesiastical*. People are so apt to look upon religion as the business of the clergy, not their own, that the moment they hear of anything depending on "religion," they think it must also have depended on the priesthood; and I have had to take what place was to be occupied between these two errors, and fight both, often with seeming contradiction. Good architecture is the work of good and believing men; therefore, you say, at least some people say, "Good architecture must essentially have been the work of the clergy, not of the laity." No—a thousand times no; good architecture has always been the work of the commonalty, *not* of the clergy. What, you say, those glorious cathedrals —the pride of Europe—did their builders not form Gothic architecture? No; they corrupted Gothic architecture. Gothic was formed in the baron's castle, and the burgher's street. It was formed by the thoughts, and hands, and powers of free citizens and soldier-kings. By the monk it was used as an instrument for the aid of his superstition; when that superstition became a beautiful madness, and the best hearts of Europe vainly dreamed and pined in the cloister, and vainly raged and perished in the crusade—through that fury of perverted faith and wasted war, the Gothic rose also to its loveliest, most fantastic, and, finally, most foolish dreams; and, in those dreams, was lost.

I hope, now, that there is no risk of your misunderstanding me when I come to the gist of what I want to say to-night—when I repeat, that every great national architecture has been the result and exponent of a great national religion. You can't have bits of it here, bits there—you must have it everywhere, or nowhere. It is not the monopoly of a clerical company—it is not the exponent of a theological dogma—it is not the hieroglyphic writing of an initiated priesthood; it is the manly language of a people inspired by resolute and common purpose, and rendering resolute and common fidelity to the legible laws of an undoubted God.

Now, there have as yet been three distinct schools of European architecture. I say, European, because Asiatic and African architectures belong so entirely to other races and climates, that there is no question of them here; only, in passing, I will simply assure you that whatever is good or great in Egypt, and Syria, and India, is just good or great for the same reasons as the buildings on our side of the Bosphorus. We Europeans, then, have had three great religions: the Greek, which was the worship of the God of Wisdom and power; the Mediæval, which was the Worship of the God of Judgment and Consolation; the Renaissance, which was the worship of the God of Pride and Beauty; these three we have had—they are past—and now, at last, we English have got a fourth religion, and a God of our own, about which I want to ask you. But I must explain these three old ones first.

I repeat, first, the Greeks essentially worshiped the God of Wisdom; so that whatever contended against their religion—to the Jews a stumbling-block—was, to the Greeks—*Foolishness.*

The first Greek idea of Deity was that expressed in the word, of which we keep the remnant in our words "*Di*-urnal" and "*Di*-vine"—the god of *Day*, Jupiter the revealer. Athena is his daughter, but especially daughter of the Intellect, springing armed from the head. We are only with the help of recent investigation beginning to penetrate the depth of meaning couched under the Athenaic symbols; but I may note rapidly, that her ægis, the mantle with the serpent fringes, in which she often, in the best statues, is represented as folding up her left hand for better guard, and the Gorgon on her shield, are both representative mainly of the chilling horror and sadness (turning men to stone, as it were), of the outmost and superficial spheres of knowledge—that knowledge which separates, in bitterness, hardness, and sorrow, the heart of the full-grown man from the heart of the child. For out of imperfect knowledge spring terror, dissension, danger, and disdain; but from perfect knowledge, given by the full-revealed Athena, strength and peace, in sign of which she is crowned with the olive spray, and bears the resistless spear.

This, then, was the Greek conception of purest Deity, and every habit of life, and every form of his art developed themselves from the seeking this bright, serene, resistless wisdom; and setting himself, as a

man, to do things evermore rightly and strongly ;*
not with any ardent affection or ultimate hope ; but
with a resolute and continent energy of will, as knowing that for failure there was no consolation, and for
sin there was no remission. And the Greek architecture rose unerring, bright, clearly defined, and self-
contained.

Next followed in Europe the great Christian faith,
which was essentially the religion of Comfort. Its
great doctrine is the remission of sins ; for which cause
it happens, too often, in certain phases of Christianity,
that sin and sickness themselves are partly glorified,
as if, the more you had to be healed of, the more
divine was the healing. The practical result of this
doctrine, in art, is a continual contemplation of sin
and disease, and of imaginary states of purification
from them ; thus we have an architecture conceived in
a mingled sentiment of melancholy and aspiration,
partly severe, partly luxuriant, which will bend itself
to every one of our needs, and every one of our fancies,

---

* It is an error to suppose that the Greek worship, or seeking, was chiefly of Beauty. It was essentially of Rightness and Strength, founded on Forethought: the principal character of Greek art is not Beauty, but Design: and the Dorian Apollo-worship and Athenian Virgin-worship are both expressions of adoration of divine Wisdom and Purity. Next to these great deities rank, in power over the national mind, Dionysus and Ceres, the givers of human strength and life: then, for heroic example, Hercules. There is no Venus-wor-ship among the Greeks in the great times: and the Muses are essen-tially teachers of Truth, and of its harmonies.

and be strong or weak with us, as we are strong or weak ourselves. It is, of all architecture, the basest, when base people build it—of all, the noblest, when built by the noble.

And now note that both these religions—Greek and Mediæval—perished by falsehood in their own main purpose. The Greek religion of Wisdom perished in a false philosophy—"Oppositions of science, falsely so-called." The Mediæval religion of Consolation perished in false comfort; in remission of sins given lyingly. It was the selling of absolution that ended the Mediæval faith; and I can tell you more, it is the selling of absolution which, to the end of time, will mark false Christianity. Pure Christianity gives her remission of sins only by *ending* them; but false Christianity gets her remission of sins by *compounding for* them. And there are many ways of compounding for them. We English have beautiful little quiet ways of buying absolution, whether in low Church or high, far more cunning than any of Tetzel's trading.

Then, thirdly, there followed the religion of Pleasure, in which all Europe gave itself to luxury, ending in death. First, *bals masqués* in every saloon, and then guillotines in every square. And all these three worships issue in vast temple-building. Your Greek worshiped Wisdom, and built you the Parthenon—the Virgin's temple. The

Mediæval worshiped Consolation, and built you Virgin temples also—but to our Lady of Salvation. Then the Revivalist worshiped beauty, of a sort, and built you Versailles, and the Vatican. Now, lastly, will you tell me what *we* worship, and what *we* build?

You know we are speaking always of the real, active, continual, national worship; that by which men act while they live; not that which they talk of when they die. Now, we have, indeed, a nominal religion, to which we pay tithes of property and sevenths of time; but we have also a practical and earnest religion, to which we devote nine-tenths of our property and sixth-sevenths of our time. And we dispute a great deal about the nominal religion; but we are all unanimous about this practical one, of which I think you will admit that the ruling goddess may be best generally described as the "Goddess of Getting-on," or "Britannia of the Market." The Athenians had an "Athena Agoraia," or Minerva of the Market; but she was a subordinate type of their goddess, while our Britannia Agoraia is the principal type of ours. And all your great architectural works, are, of course, built to her. It is long since you built a great cathedral; and how you would laugh at me, if I proposed building a cathedral on the top of one of these hills of yours, taking it for an Acropolis! But your railroad mounds, prolonged masses of Acropolis; your railroad stations, vaster than the Parthenon, and innumerable;

your chimneys, how much more mighty and costly than cathedral spires! your harbor piers; your warehouses; your exchanges!—all these are built to your great Goddess of "Getting-on;" and she has formed, and will continue to form, your architecture, as long as you worship her; and it is quite vain to ask me to tell you how to build to *her;* you know far better than I.

There might indeed, on some theories, be a conceivably good architecture for Exchanges—that is to say if there were any heroism in the fact or deed of exchange, which might be typically carved on the outside of your building. For, you know, all beautiful architecture must be adorned with sculpture or painting; and for sculpture or painting, you must have a subject. And hitherto it has been a received opinion among the nations of the world that the only right subjects for either, were *heroisms* of some sort. Even on his pots and his flagons, the Greek put a Hercules slaying lions, or an Apollo slaying serpents, or Bacchus slaying melancholy giants, and earth-born despondencies. On his temples, the Greek put contests of great warriors in founding states, or of gods with evil spirits. On his houses and temples alike, the Christian put carvings of angels conquering devils; or of hero-martyrs exchanging this world for another; subject inappropriate, I think, to our manner of exchange here. And the Master of Christians not only left his followers without any orders as to the sculpture of affairs of exchange on the outside of buildings, but gave some strong evidence of his dislike of affairs of exchange within them. And yet there might surely be a heroism in such affairs; and all commerce become a kind of selling of doves, not impious. The wonder has always been great to me, that heroism has never been supposed to be in anywise consistent with the practice of supplying people with food, or clothes; but rather with that of quartering one's self upon them for food, and stripping them of their clothes. Spoiling of armor is an heroic deed in all ages; but the selling of clothes, old, or new, has never taken any color of magnanimity. Yet one does not see why feeding the hungry and clothing the naked should ever become base businesses, even when engaged in on a large scale. If one could contrive to attach the notion of conquest to them anyhow? so that, supposing there were anywhere an obstinate race, who refused to be comforted, one might take some pride in giving them compulsory comfort; and as it were, "occupying a country" with one's gifts, instead of one's armies? If one could only consider it as much a victory to get a barren field sown, as to get an earned field stripped; and contend who should build villages, instead of who should "carry" them. Are not all forms of heroism, conceivable in doing these serviceable deeds? You doubt who is strongest?

It might be ascertained by push of spade, as well as push of sword. Who is wisest? There are witty things to be thought of in planning other business than campaigns. Who is bravest? There are always the elements to fight with stronger than men; and nearly as merciless. The only absolutely and unapproachably heroic element in the soldier's work seems to be—that he is paid little for it—and regularly: while you traffickers, and exchangers, and others occupied in presumably benevolent business, like to be paid much for it—and by chance. I never can make out how it is that a knight-errant does not expect to be paid for his trouble, but a peddler-errant always does—that people are willing to take hard knocks for nothing, but never to sell ribbons cheap—that they are ready to go on fervent crusades to recover the tomb of a buried God, never on any travels to fulfill the orders of a living God—that they will go anywhere barefoot to preach their faith, but must be well bribed to practice it, and are perfectly ready to give the Gospel gratis, but never the loaves and fishes. If you chose to take the matter up on any such soldierly principle, to do your commerce, and your feeding of nations, for fixed salaries; and to be as particular about giving people the best food, and the best cloth, as soldiers are about giving them the best gunpowder, I could carve something for you on your exchange worth looking at. But I can only at present suggest decorating its frieze with pendant purses; and making its pillars broad at the base for the sticking of bills. And in the innermost chambers of it there might be a statue of Britannia of the Market, who may have, perhaps advisably, a partridge for her crest, typical at once of her courage in fighting for noble ideas; and of her interest in game; and round its neck the inscription in golden letters, "Perdix fovit quæ non peperit."* Then, for her spear, she might have a weaver's beam; and on her shield, instead of her Cross, the Milanese boar, semi-fleeced, with the town of Gennesaret proper, in the field and the legend "In the best market," and her corslet, of leather, folded over her heart in the shape of a purse, with thirty slits in it for a piece of money to go in at, on each day of the month. And I doubt not but that people would come to see your exchange, and its goddess, with applause.

Nevertheless, I want to point out to you certain strange characters in this goddess of yours. She differs from the great Greek and Mediæval deities essentially in two things—first, as to the continuance of her presumed power; secondly, as to the extent of it.

I. As to the Continuance.

The Greek Goddess of Wisdom gave continual increase of wisdom, as the Christian Spirit of Comfort

---

* Jerem. xvii. 11 (best in Septuagint and Vulgate). "As the partridge, fostering what she brought not forth, so he that getteth riches, not by right shall leave them in the midst of his days, and at his end shall be a fool."

(or Comforter) continual increase of comfort. There was no question, with these, of any limit or cessation of function. But with your Agora Goddess, that is just the most important question. Getting on—but where to? Gathering together—but how much? Do you mean to gather always—never to spend? If so, I wish you joy of your goddess, for I am just as well off as you, without the trouble of worshiping her at all. But if you do not spend, somebody else will—somebody else must. And it is because of this (among many other such errors) that I have fearlessly declared your so-called science of Political Economy to be no science; because, namely, it has omitted the study of exactly the most important branch of the business—the study of *spending*. For spend you must, and as much as you make, ultimately. You gather corn: will you bury England under a heap of grain; or will you, when you have gathered, finally eat? You gather gold: will you make your house-roofs of it, or pave your streets with it? That is still one way of spending it. But if you keep it, that you may get more, I'll give you more; I'll give you all the gold you want—all you can imagine—if you can tell me what you'll do with it. You shall have thousands of gold-pieces; thousands of thousands—millions—mountains, of gold; where will you keep them? Will you put an Olympus of silver upon a golden Pelion—make Ossa like a wart? Do you think the rain and dew would then come down to you, in the streams from such mountains, more blessedly than they will down the mountains which God has made for you, of moss and whinstone? But it is not gold that you want to gather! What is it? greenbacks? No; not those neither. What is it then —is it ciphers after a capital I? Cannot you practice writing ciphers, and write as many as you want? Write ciphers for an hour every morning, in a big book, and say every evening, I am worth all those noughts more than I was yesterday. Won't that do? Well, what in the name of Plutus is it you want? Not gold, not greenbacks, not ciphers after a capital I? You will have to answer, after all, "No; we want, somehow or other, money's *worth*." Well, what is that? Let your Goddess of Getting-on discover it, and let her learn to stay therein.

II. But there is yet another question to be asked respecting this Goddess of Getting-on. The first was of the continuance of her power; the second is of its extent.

Pallas and the Madonna were supposed to be all the world's Pallas, and all the world's Madonna. They could teach all men, and they could comfort all men. But, look strictly into the nature of the power of your Goddess of Getting-on; and you will find she is the Goddess—not of everybody's getting on—but only of somebody's getting on. This is a vital, or rather deathful, distinction. Examine it in your own ideal of the state of national life which this Goddess is to evoke and maintain. I asked you what it was, when I was last here; you have never told me. Now, shall I try to tell you?

Your ideal of human life, then is, I think, that it should be passed in a pleasant undulating world, with iron and coal everywhere underneath it. On each pleasant bank of this world is to be a beautiful mansion with two wings; and stables, and coach-houses; a moderately sized park; a large garden and hot-houses; and pleasant carriage-drives through the shrubberies. In this mansion are to live the favored votaries of the Goddess; the English gentleman, with his gracious wife, and his beautiful family; always able to have the boudoir and the jewels for the wife, and the beautiful ball dresses for the daughters, and hunters for the sons, and a shooting in the Highlands for himself. At the bottom of the bank, is to be the mill; not less than a quarter of a mile long, with a steam-engine at each end, and two in the middle, and a chimney three hundred feet high. In this mill are to be in constant employment from eight hundred to a thousand workers, who never drink, never strike, always go to church on Sunday, and always express themselves in respectful language.

Is not that, broadly, and in the main features, the kind of thing you propose to yourselves? It is very pretty indeed seen from above; not at all so pretty, seen from below. For, observe, while to one family this deity is indeed the Goddess of Getting on, to a thousand families she is the Goddess of *not* Getting on. "Nay," you say, "they have all their chance." Yes, so has every one in a lottery, but there must always be the same number of blanks. " Ah! but in a lottery it is not skill and intelligence which take the lead, but blind chance." What then! do you think the old practice, that "they should take who have the power, and they should keep who can," is less iniquitous, when the power has become power of brains instead of fist? and that, though we may not take advantage of a child's or a woman's weakness, we may of a man's foolishness? "Nay, but finally, work must be done, and some one must be at the top, some one at the bottom." Granted, my friends. Work must always be, and captains of work must always be; and if you in the least remember the tone of any of my writings, you must know that they are thought unfit for this age, because they they are always insisting on need of government, and speaking with scorn of liberty. But I beg you to observe that there is wide difference between being captains or governors of work, and taking the profits of it. It does not follow, because you are general of an army, that you are to take all the treasure or land, it wins (if it fight for treasure or land); neither, because you are king of a nation, that you are to consume all the profits of the nation's work. Real kings, on the contrary, are known invariably by their doing quite the reverse of this—by their taking the least possible quantity of the nation's work for themselves. There is no test of real kinghood so infallible as that. Does the crowned creature live simply, bravely, unostentatiously? probably he *is* a King. Does he cover his body with jewels, and his table with delicates? in all probability he is *not* a King. It is possible he may be, as Solomon was; but that is when the nation shares his splendor with him. Solomon made gold, not only to be in his own palace as stones, but to be in Jerusalem as stones. But even so, for the most part, these splendid kinghoods expire in ruin, and only the true kinghoods live, which are of royal laborers governing loyal laborers; who, both leading rough lives, establish the true dynasties. Conclusively you will find that because you are king of a nation, it does not follow that you are to gather for yourself all the wealth of that nation; neither, because you are king of a small part of the nation, and lord over the means of its maintenance—over field, or mill, or mine, are you to take all the produce of that piece of the foundation of national existence for yourself.

You will tell me I need not preach against these

things, for I cannot mend them. No, good friends, I cannot; but you can, and you will; or something else can and will. Do you think these phenomena are to stay always in their present power or aspect? All history shows, on the contrary, that to be the exact thing they never can do. Change *must* come; but it is ours to determine whether change of growth, or change of death. Shall the Parthenon be in ruins on its rock, and Bolton priory in its meadow, but these mills of yours be the consummation of the buildings of the earth, and their wheels be as the wheels of eternity? Think you that "men may come, and men may go," but—mills—go on forever? Not so; out of these, better or worse shall come; and it is for you to choose which.

I know that none of this wrong is done with deliberate purpose. I know, on the contrary, that you wish your workmen well; that you do much for them, and that you desire to do more for them, if you saw your way to it safely. I know that many of you have done, and are every day doing whatever you feel to be in your power; and that even all this wrong and misery are brought about by a warped sense of duty, each of you striving to do his best, without noticing that this best is essentially and centrally the best for himself, not for others. And all this has come of the spreading of that thrice accursed, thrice impious doctrine of the modern economist, that "To do the best for yourself, is finally to do the best for others." Friends, our great Master said not so; and most absolutely we shall find this world is not made so. Indeed, to do the best for others, is finally to do the best for ourselves; but it will not do to have our eyes fixed on that issue. The Pagans had got beyond that. Hear what a Pagan says of this matter; hear what were, perhaps, the last written words of Plato—if not the last actually written (for this we cannot know), yet assuredly in fact and power his parting words—in which, endeavoring to give full crowning and harmonious close to all his thoughts, and to speak the sum of them by the imagined sentence of the Great Spirit, his strength and his heart fail him, and the words cease, broken off forever. It is the close of the dialogue called "Critias," in which he describes, partly from real tradition, partly in ideal dream, the early state of Athens; and the genesis, and order, and religion, of the fabled isle of Atlantis; in which genesis he conceives the same first perfection and final degeneracy of man, which in our own Scriptural tradition is expressed by saying that the Sons of God intermarried with the daughters of men, for he supposes the earliest race to have been indeed the children of God; and to have corrupted themselves, until "their spot was not the spot of his children." And this, he says, was the end; that indeed "through many generations, so long as the God's nature in them yet was full, they were submissive to the sacred laws, and carried themselves lovingly to all that had kindred with them in divineness; for their uttermost spirit was faithful and true, and in every wise great; so that, in all meekness of wisdom, they dealt with each other, and took all the chances of life; and despising all things except virtue, they cared little what happened day by day, and *bore lightly the burden* of gold and of possessions: for they saw that, if only their common love and virtue increased, all these things would be increased together with them; but to set their esteem and ardent pursuit upon material possession would be to lose that first, and their virtue and affection together with it. And by such reasoning, and what of the divine nature remained in them, they gained all this greatness of which we have already told; but when the God's part of them faded and became extinct, being mixed again and again, and effaced by the prevalent mortality; and the human nature at last exceeded, they then became unable to endure the courses of fortune; and fell into shapelessness of life, and baseness in the sight of him who could see, having lost everything that was fairest of their honor; while to the blind hearts which could not discern the true life, tending to happiness, it seemed that they were then chiefly noble and happy, being filled with an iniquity of inordinate possession and power. Whereupon, the God of Gods, whose Kinghood is in laws, beholding a once just nation thus cast into misery, and desiring to lay such punishment upon them as might make them repent into restraining, gathered together all the gods into his dwelling-place, which from heaven's center overlooks whatever has part in creation; and having assembled them, he said"——

The rest is silence. So ended are the last words of the chief wisdom of the heathen, spoken of this idol of riches; this idol of yours; this golden image high by measureless cubits, set up where your green fields of England are furnace-burnt into the likeness of the plain of Dura: this idol, forbidden to us, first of all idols, by our own Master and faith; forbidden to us also by every human lip that has ever, in any age or people, been accounted of as able to speak according to the purposes of God. Continue to make that forbidden deity your principal one, and soon no more art, no more science, no more pleasure will be possible. Catastrophe will come; or worse than catastrophe, slow moldering and withering into Hades. But if you can fix some conception of a true human state of life to be striven for—life for all men as for yourselves if you can determine some honest and simple order of existence; following those trodden ways of wisdom, which are pleasantness, and seeking her quiet and withdrawn paths, which are peace; then, and so sanctifying wealth unto "commonwealth," all your art, your literature, your daily labors, your domestic affection, and citizen's duty, will join and increase into one magnificent harmony. You will know then how to build, well enough; you will build with stone well but with flesh better; temples not made with hands, but riveted of hearts; and that kind of marble, crimson-veined, is indeed eternal.

LECTURE III.

WAR.

(Delivered at the Royal Military Academy, Woolwich.)

YOUNG SOLDIERS—I do not doubt but that many of you came unwillingly to-night, and many in merely contemptuous curiosity, to hear what a writer on painting could possibly say, or would venture to say, respecting your great art of war. You may well think within yourselves, that a painter might, perhaps without immodesty, lecture younger painters upon painting, but not young lawyers upon law, nor young physicians upon medicine—least of all, it may seem to you, young warriors upon war. And, indeed, when I was asked to address you, I declined at first, and declined long; for I felt that you would not be interested in my special business, and would certainly think there was small need for me to come to teach you yours. Nay, I knew that there ought to to be *no* such need, for the great veteran soldiers of England are now men every way so thoughtful, so noble, and so good, that no other teaching than their knightly example, and their few words of grave and tried counsel should be either necessary for you, or even, without assurance of due modesty in the offerer, endured by you.

But being asked, not once nor twice, I have not ventured persistently to refuse; and I will try, in very few words, to lay before you some reason why you should accept my excuse, and hear me patiently. You may imagine that your work is wholly foreign to, and separate from mine. So far from that, all the pure and noble arts of peace are founded on war; no great art ever yet rose on earth, but among a nation of soldiers. There is no art among a shepherd people, if it remains at peace. There is no art among an agricultural people, if it remains at peace. Commerce is barely consistent with fine art; but cannot produce it. Manufacture not only is unable to produce it, but invariably destroys whatever seeds of it exist. There is no great art possible to a nation but that which is based on battle.

Now, though I hope you love fighting for its own sake, you must, I imagine, be surprised at my assertion that there is any such good fruit of fighting. You supposed, probably, that your office was to defend the works of peace, but certainly not to found them: nay, the common course of war, you may have thought, was only to destroy them. And truly, I who tell you this of the use of war, should have been the last of men to tell you so, had I trusted my own experience only. Hear why: I have given a considerable part of my life to the investigation of Venetian painting, and the result of that inquiry was my fixing upon one man as the greatest of all Venetians, and therefore, as I believed, of all painters whatsoever. I formed this faith (whether right or wrong matters at present nothing), in the supremacy of the painter Tintoret, under a roof covered with his pictures; and of those pictures, three of the noblest were then in the form of shreds of ragged canvas, mixed up with the laths of the roof, rent through by three Austrian shells. Now it is not every lecturer who *could* tell you that he had seen three of his favorite pictures torn to rags by bombshells. And after such a sight, it is not every lecturer who *would* tell you that, nevertheless, war was the foundation of all great art.

Yet the conclusion is inevitable, from any careful comparison of the states of great historic races at different periods. Merely to show you what I mean, I will sketch for you, very briefly, the broad steps of the advance of the best art of the world. The first dawn of it is in Egypt; and the power of it is founded on the perpetual contemplation of death, and of future judgment, by the mind of a nation of which the ruling caste were priests, and the second, soldiers. The greatest works produced by them are sculptures of their kings going out to battle, or receiving the homage of conquered armies. And you must remember also, as one of the great keys to the splendor of the Egyptian nation, that the priests were not occupied in theology only. Their theology was the basis of practical government and law, so that they were not so much priests as religious judges, the office of Samuel, among the Jews, being as nearly as possible correspondent to theirs.

All the rudiments of art then, and much more than the rudiments of all science, are laid first by this great warrior-nation, which held in contempt all mechanical trades, and in absolute hatred the peaceful life of shepherds. From Egypt art passes directly into Greece, where all poetry, and all painting, are nothing else than the description, praise, or dramatic representation of war, or of the exercises which prepare for it, in their connection with offices of religion. All Greek institutions had first respect to war; and their conception of it, as one necessary office of all human and divine life, is expressed simply by the images of their guiding gods. Apollo is the god of all wisdom of the intellect; he bears the arrow and the bow, before he bears the lyre. Again, Athena is the goddess of all wisdom in conduct. It is by the helmet and the shield, oftener than by the shuttle, that she is distinguished from other deities.

There were, however, two great differences in principle between the Greek and the Egyptian theories of policy. In Greece there was no soldier caste; every citizen was necessarily a soldier. And, again, while the Greeks rightly despised mechanical arts as much as the Egyptians, they did not make the fatal mistake of despising agricultural and pastoral life; but perfectly honored both. These two conditions of truer thought raise them quite into the highest rank of wise manhood that has yet been reached; for all our great arts, and nearly all our great thoughts, have been borrowed or derived from them. Take away from us what they have given; and I hardly can imagine how low the modern European would stand.

Now, you are to remember, in passing to the next phase of history, that though you *must* have war to produce art—you must also have much more than war; namely, an art-instinct or genius in the people; and that, though all the talent for painting in the world won't make painters of you, unless you have a gift for fighting as well, you may have the gift for fighting, and none for painting. Now, in the next great dynasty of soldiers, the art-instinct is wholly wanting. I have not yet investigated the Roman character enough to tell you the causes of this; but I believe, paradoxical as it may seem to you, that, however truly the Roman might say of himself that he was born of Mars, and suckled by the wolf, he was nevertheless, at heart, more of a farmer than a soldier. The exercises of war were with him practical, not poetical; his poetry was in domestic life only, and the object of battle, "pacis imponere morem." And the arts are extinguished in his hands, and do not rise again, until, with Gothic chivalry, there comes back into the mind of Europe a passionate delight in war itself, for the sake of war. And then, with the romantic knighthood which can imagine no other noble employment—under the fighting kings of France, England, and Spain; and under the fighting dukeships and citizenships of Italy, art is born again, and rises to her height in the great valleys of Lombardy and Tuscany, through which there flows not a single stream, from all their Alps or Appennines, that did not once run dark red from battle: and it reaches its culminating glory in the city which gave to history the most intense type of soldiership yet seen among men; the city whose armies were led in their assault by their king, led through it to victory by their king, and so led, though that king of theirs was blind, and in the extremity of his age.

And from this time forward, as peace is established or extended in Europe, the arts decline. They reach an unparalleled pitch of costliness, but lose their life, enlist themselves at last on the side of luxury and various corruption, and, among wholly tranquil nations, wither utterly away; remaining only in partial practice among races who, like the French and us, have still the minds, though we cannot all live the lives, of soldiers.

"It may be so," I can suppose that a philanthropist might exclaim. "Perish then the arts, if they can flourish only at such a cost. What worth is there in toys of canvas and stone, if compared to the joy and peace of artless domestic life?" And the answer is—truly, in themselves, none. But as expressions of the highest state of the human spirit, their worth is infinite. As results they may be worthless, but, as signs, they are above price. For it is an assured truth that, whenever the faculties of men are at their fulness, they *must* express themselves by art; and to say that a state is without such expression, is to say that it is sunk from its proper level of manly nature. So that, when I tell you that war is the foundation of all the arts, I mean also that it is the foundation of all the high virtues and faculties of men.

It was very strange to me to discover this; and very dreadful—but I saw it to be quite an undeniable fact. The common notion that peace and the virtues of civil life flourished together, I found, to be wholly untenable. Peace and the *vices* of civil life only flourish together. We talk of peace and learning, and of peace and plenty, and of peace and civilization; but I found that those were not the words which the Muse of History coupled together: that on her lips, the words were—peace and sensuality, peace and selfishness, peace and corruption, peace and death. I found, in brief, that all great nations learned their truth of word, and strength of thought, in war; that they were nourished in war, and wasted by peace;

taught by war, and deceived by peace; trained by war, and betrayed by peace—in a word, that they were born in war and expired in peace.

Yet, now note carefully, in the second place, it is not *all* war of which this can be said—nor all dragon's teeth, which, sown, will start up into men. It is not the ravage of a barbarian wolf-flock, as under Genseric or Suwarrow; nor the habitual restlessness and rapine of mountaineers, as on the old borders of Scotland: nor the occasional struggle of a strong peaceful nation for its life, as in the wars of the Swiss with Austria; nor the contest of merely ambitious nations for extent of power, as in the wars of France under Napoleon, or the just-terminated war in America. None of these forms of war builds anything but tombs. But the creative or foundational war is that in which the natural restlessness and love of contest among men are disciplined by consent, into modes of beautiful— though it may be fatal—play: in which the natural ambition and love of power of men are disciplined into the aggressive conquest of surrounding evil: and in which the natural instincts of self-defense are sanctified by the nobleness of the institutions, and purity of the households, which they are appointed to defend. To such war as this all men are born; in such war as this any man may happily die; and forth from such war as this have arisen throughout the extent of past ages, all the highest sanctities and virtues of humanity.

I shall therefore divide the war of which I would speak to you into three heads. War for exercise or play; war for dominion; and, war for defense.

I. And first, of war for exercise or play. I speak of it primarily in this light, because, through all past history, manly war has been more an exercise than anything else, among the classes who cause, and proclaim it. It is not a game to the conscript, or the pressed sailor; but neither of these is the causer of it. To the governor who determines that war shall be, and to the youths who voluntarily adopt it as their profession, it has always been a grand pastime; and chiefly pursued because they had nothing else to do. And this is true without any exception. No king whose mind was fully occupied with the development of the inner resources of his kingdom, or with any other sufficing subject of thought, ever entered into war but on compulsion. No youth who was earnestly busy with any peaceful subject of study, or set on any serviceable course of action, ever voluntarily became a soldier. Occupy him early, and wisely, in agriculture or business, in science or in literature, and he will never think of war otherwise than as a calamity. But leave him idle; and, the more brave and active and capable he is by nature, the more he will thirst for some appointed field for action; and find, in the passion and peril of battle, the only satisfying fulfillment of his unoccupied being. And from the earliest incipient civilization until now, the population of the earth divides itself, when you look at it widely, into two races; one of workers, and the other of players—one tilling the ground, manufacturing, building, and otherwise providing for the necessities of life; the other part proudly idle, and continually therefore needing recreation, in which they use the productive and laborious orders partly as their cattle, and partly as their puppets or pieces in the game of death.

Now, remember, whatever virtue or godliness there may be in this game of war, rightly played, there is none when you thus play it with a multitude of small human pawns.

If you, the gentlemen of this or any other kingdom, choose to make your pastime of contest, do so, and welcome; but set not up these unhappy peasant-pieces upon the green-fielded board. If the wager is to be of death, lay it on your own heads, not theirs. A goodly struggle in the Olympic dust, though it be the dust of the grave, the gods will look upon, and be with you in; but they will not be with you, if you sit on the sides of the amphitheater, whose steps are the mountains of earth, whose arena its valleys, to urge your peasant millions into gladiatorial war. You also, you tender and delicate women, for whom, and by whose command, all true battle has been, and must ever be; you would perhaps shrink now, though you need not, from the thought of sitting as queens above set lists where the jousting game might be mortal. How much more, then, ought you to shrink from the thought of sitting above a theater pit in which even a few condemned slaves were slaying each other only for your delight! And do you *not* shrink from the *fact* of sitting above a theater, pit, where—not condemned slaves—but the best and bravest of the poor sons of your people, slay each other—not man to man—as the coupled gladiators; but race to race, in duel of generations? You would tell me, perhaps, that you do not sit to see this; and it is indeed true, that the women of Europe—those who have no heart-interest of their own at peril in the contest—draw the curtains of their boxes, and muffle the openings; so that from the pit of the circus of slaughter there may reach them only at intervals a half-heard cry and a murmur as of the wind's sighing, when myriads of souls expire. They shut out the death-cries; and are happy, and talk wittily among themselves. That is the utter literal fact of what our ladies do in their pleasant lives.

Nay, you might answer, speaking for them—"We do not let these wars come to pass for our play, nor by our carelessness; we cannot help them. How can any final quarrel of nations be settled otherwise than by war?" I cannot now delay, to tell you how political quarrels might be otherwise settled. But grant that they cannot. Grant that no law of reason can be understood by nations; no law of justice submitted to by them : and that, while questions of a few acres, and of petty cash, can be determined by truth and equity, the questions which are to issue in the perishing or saving of kingdoms can be determined only by the truth of the sword, and the equity of the rifle. Grant this, and even then, judge if it will always be necessary for you to put your quarrel into the hearts of your poor, and sign your treaties with peasants' blood. You would be ashamed to do this in your own private position and power. Why should you not be ashamed also to do it in public place and power? If you quarrel with your neighbor, and the quarrel be indeterminable by law, and mortal, you and he do not send your footmen to Battersea fields to fight it out; nor do you set fire to his tenants' cottages, nor spoil their goods. You fight out your quarrel yourselves, and at your own danger, if at all. And you do not think it materially affects the arbitrament that one of you has a larger household than the other; so that, if the servants or tenants were brought into the field with their masters, the issue of the contest could not be doubtful? You either refuse the private duel, or you practice it under laws of honor, not of physical force; that so it may be, in a manner, justly concluded. Now the just or unjust conclusion of the private feud is of little moment, while the just or unjust conclusion of the public feud is of eternal moment: and yet, in this public quarrel, you take your servants' sons from their arms to fight for it, and your servants' food from their lips to support it; and the black seals on the parchment of your treaties of peace are the deserted hearth and the fruitless field. There is a ghastly ludicrousness in this, as there is mostly in these wide and universal crimes. Hear the statement of the very fact of it in the most literal words of the greatest of our English thinkers:

"What, speaking in quite unofficial language, is the net purport and upshot of war? To my own knowledge, for example, there dwell and toil, in the British village of Dumdrudge, usually some five hundred souls. From these, by certain 'natural enemies' of the French, there are successively selected, during the French war, say thirty able-bodied men. Dumdrudge, at her own expense, has suckled and nursed them; she has, not without difficulty and sorrow, fed them up to manhood, and even trained them to crafts, so that one can weave, another build, another hammer, and the weakest can stand under thirty stone avoirdupois. Nevertheless, amid much weeping and swearing, they are selected; all dressed in red; and shipped away, at the public charge, some two thousand miles, or say only to the south of Spain; and fed there till wanted.

"And now to that same spot in the south of Spain are thirty similar French artisans, from a French Dumdrudge, in like manner wending; till at length, after infinite effort, the two parties come into actual juxtaposition; and Thirty stand fronting Thirty, each with a gun in his hand.

"Straightway the word 'Fire!' is given, and they blow the souls out of one another, and in place of sixty brisk useful craftsmen, the world has sixty dead carcasses, which it must bury, and anon shed tears for. Had these men any quarrel? Busy as the devil is, not the smallest! They lived far enough apart; were the entirest strangers; nay, in so wide a universe, there was even, unconsciously, by commerce, some mutual helpfulness between them. How then? Simpleton! their governors had fallen out; and instead of shooting one another, had the cunning to make these poor blockheads shoot." (Sartor Resartus.)

Positively, then, gentlemen, the game of battle must not, and shall not, ultimately be played this way. But should it be played any way? Should it, if not by your servants, be practiced by yourselves? I think, yes. Both history and human instinct seem alike to say, yes. All healthy men like fighting, and like the sense of danger; all brave women like to hear of their fighting, and of their facing danger. This is a fixed instinct in the fine race of them; and I cannot help fancying that fair fight is the best play for them; and that a tournament was a better game than a steeple-chase. The time may perhaps come in France as well as here, for universal hurdle-races and cricketing: but I do not think universal "crickets" will bring out the best qualities of the nobles of either country. I use, in such question, the test which I have adopted, of the connection of war with other arts; and I reflect how, as a sculptor, I should feel, if I were asked to design a monument for a dead knight, in Westminster abbey, with a carving of a bat at one end, and a ball at the other. It may be the remains in me only of savage Gothic prejudice; but I had rather carve it with a shield at one end, and a sword at the other. And this observe, with no reference whatever to any story of duty done, or cause defended. Assume the knight merely to have ridden out occasionally to fight his neighbor for exercise; assume him even a soldier of fortune, and to have gained his bread, and filled his purse, at the sword's point. Still, I feel as if it were, somehow, grander and worthier in him to have made his bread by sword play than any other play; I had rather he had made it by thrusting than by batting; much more, than by betting. Much rather that he should ride war-horses, than back race-horses; and—I say it sternly and deliberately—much rather would I have him slay his neighbor, than cheat him.

But remember, so far as this may be true, the game of war is only that in which the *full personal power of the human creature* is brought out in management of its weapons. And this for three reasons:

First, the great justification of this game is that it truly when well played, determines *who is the best man;* who is the highest bred, the most self-denying, the most fearless, the coolest of nerve, the swiftest of eye and hand. You cannot test these qualities wholly, unless there is a clear possibility of the struggle's ending in death. It is only in the fronting of that condition that the full trial of the man, soul and body, comes out. You may go to your game of wickets, or of hurdles, or of cards, and any knavery that is in you may stay unchallenged all the while. But if the play may be ended at any moment by a lance-thrust, a man will probably make up his accounts a little before he enters it. Whatever is rotten and evil in him will weaken his hand more in holding a sword-hilt, than in balancing a billiard-cue; and on the whole, the habit of living lightly hearted, in daily presence of death, always has had, and must have, a tendency both to the making and testing of honest men. But for the final testing, observe, you must make the issue of battle strictly dependent on fineness of frame, and firmness of hand. You must not make it the question, which of the combatants has the longest gun, or which has got behind the biggest tree, or which has the wind in his face, or which has gunpowder made by the best chemists, or iron smelted with the best coal, or the angriest mob at his back. Decide your battle, whether of nations, or individuals, on *those* terms; and you have only multiplied confusion, and added slaughter to iniquity. But decide your battle by pure trial which has the strongest arm, and steadiest heart —and you have gone far to decide a great many matters besides, and to decide them rightly.

And the other reasons for this mode of decision of cause, are the diminution both of the material destructiveness, or cost, and of the physical distress of war. For you must not think that in speaking to you in this (as you may imagine) fantastic praise of battle, I have overlooked the conditions weighing against me. I pray all of you, who have not read, to read with the most earnest attention, Mr. Helps' two essays on War and Government, in the first volume of the last series of "Friends in Council." Everything that can be urged against war is there simply, exhaustively, and most graphically stated. And all, there urged, is true. But the two great counts of evil alleged against war by that most thoughtful writer, hold only against modern war. If you have to take away masses of men from all industrial employment—to feed them by the labor of others—to move them and provide them with destructive machines, varied daily in national rivalship of inventive cost; if you have to ravage the country which you attack—to destroy for a score of future years, its roads, its woods, its cities, and its harbors; and if, finally, having brought masses of men, counted by hundreds of thousands, face to face, you tear those masses to pieces with jagged shot, and leave the fragments of living creatures, countlessly beyond all help of surgery, to starve and parch, through days of torture, down into clots of clay—what book of accounts shall record the cost of your work; what book of judgment sentence the guilt of it?

That, I say, is *modern* war—scientific war—chemical and mechanic war, worse even than the savage's poisoned arrow. And yet you will tell me, perhaps, that any other war than this is impossible now. It may be so; the progress of science cannot, perhaps, be otherwise registered than by new facilities of destruction; and the brotherly love of our enlarging Christianity be only proved by multiplication of murder. Yet hear, for a moment, what war was, in Pagan and ignorant days; what war might yet be, if we could extinguish our science in darkness, and join the heathen's practice to the Christian's theory. I read you this from a book which probably most of you know well, and all ought to know—Muller's "Dorians;" but I have put the points I wish you to remember in closer connection than in his text.

"The chief characteristic of the warriors of Sparta was great composure and subdued strength; the violence of Aristodemus and Isadas being considered as deserving rather of blame than praise; and these qualities in general distinguished the Greeks from the northern Barbarians, whose boldness always consisted in noise and tumult. For the same reason the Spartans *sacrificed to the Muses* before an action, these goddesses being expected to produce regularity and order in battle; as they *sacrificed on the same occasion in Crete to the god of love,* as the confirmer of mutual esteem and shame. Every man put on a crown, when the band of flute-players gave the signal for attack; all the shields of the line glittered with their high polish, and mingled their splendor with the dark red of the purple mantles, which were meant both to adorn the combatant, and to conceal the blood of the wounded; to fall well and decorously being an incentive the more to the most heroic valor. The conduct of the Spartans in battle denotes a high and noble disposition, which rejected all the extremes of brutal rage. The pursuit of the enemy ceased when the victory was completed; and after the signal for retreat had been given, all hostilities ceased. The spoiling of arms, at least during the battle, was also interdicted; and the consecration of the spoils of slain enemies to the gods, as, in general, all rejoicings for victory, were considered as ill omened."

Such was the war of the greatest soldiers who prayed to heathen gods. What Christian war is, preached by Christian ministers, let any one tell you, who saw the sacred crowning, and heard the sacred flute-playing, and was inspired and sanctified by the divinely-measured and musical language, of any North American regiment preparing for its charge. And what is the relative cost of life in pagan and Christian wars, let this one fact tell you—the Spartans won the decisive battle of Corinth with the loss of eight men; the victors at indecisive Gettysburg confess to the loss of 30,000.

II. I pass now to our second order of war, the commonest among men, that undertaken in desire of dominion. And let me ask you to think for a few moments what the real meaning of this desire of dominion is—first in the minds of kings—then in that of nations.

Now, mind you this first—that I speak either about kings or masses of men, with a fixed conviction that human nature is a noble and beautiful thing; not a foul nor a base thing. All the sin of men I esteem as their disease, not their nature; as a folly which may be prevented, not a necessity which must be accepted. And my wonder, even when things are at their worst, is always at the height which this human nature can attain. Thinking it high, I find it always a higher thing than I thought it; while those who think it low, find it, and will find it, always lower than they thought it: the fact being that it is infinite, and capable of infinite height and infinite fall; but the nature of it—and here is the faith which I would have you hold with me—the *nature* of it is in the nobleness, not in the catastrophe.

Take the faith in its utmost terms. When the captain of the "London" shook hands with his mate, saying "God speed you! I will go down with my passengers," *that* I believe to be "human nature." He does not do it from any religious motive—from any hope of reward, or any fear of punishment; he does it because he is a man. But when a mother, living among the fair fields of merry England, gives her two-year-old child to be suffocated under a mattress in her inner room, while the said mother waits and talks outside; *that* I believe to be *not* human nature. You have the two extremes there, shortly. And you men, and mothers, who are here face to face with me to-night, I call upon you to say which of these is human, and which inhuman which "natural" and which "unnatural?" Choose your creed at once, I beseech you—choose it with unshaken choice—choose it forever. Will you take for foundation of act and hope, the faith that this man was such as God made him, or that this woman was such as God made her? Which of them has failed from their nature—from their present, possible, actual nature—not their nature of long ago, but their nature of now? Which has betrayed it, falsified it? Did the guardian who died in his trust, die inhumanly, and as a fool; and did the murderess of her child fulfill the law of her being? Choose, I say; infinitude of choices hang upon this. You have had false prophets among you—for centuries you have had them—solemnly warned against them though you were; false prophets, who have told you that all men are nothing but fiends or wolves, half beast, half devil. Believe that and indeed you may sink to that. But refuse that, and have faith that God "made you upright," though *you* have sought out many inventions; so, you will strive daily to become more what your Maker meant and means you to be, and daily gives you also the power to be—and you will cling more and more to the nobleness and virtue that is in you, saying, "My righteousness I hold fast, and will not let it go."

I have put this to you as a choice, as if you might hold either of these creeds you liked best. But there is in reality no choice for you; the facts being quite easily ascertainable. You have no business to *think* about this matter, or to choose in it. The broad fact is, that a human creature of the highest race, and most perfect as a human thing, is invariably both kind and true; and that as you lower the race, you get cruelty and falseness, as you get deformity: and this so steadily and assuredly, that the two great words which, in their first use, meant only perfection of race, have come, by consequence of the invariable connection of virtue with the fine human nature, both to signify benevolence of disposition. The word generous, and the word gentle, both, in their origin, meant only "of pure race," but because charity and tenderness are inseparable from this purity of blood, the words which once stood only for pride, now stand as synonyms for virtue.

Now, this being the true power of our inherent humanity, and seeing that all the aims of education should be to develop this; and seeing also what magnificent self-sacrifice the higher classes of men are capable of, for any cause that they understand or feel, it is wholly inconceivable to me how well-educated princes, who ought to be of all gentlemen the gentlest, and of all nobles the most generous, and whose title of royalty means only their function of doing every man "*right*"—how these, I say, throughout history, should so rarely pronounce themselves on the side of the poor and of justice, but continually maintain themselves and their own interests by oppression of the poor, and by wresting of justice; and how this should be accepted as so natural, that the word loyalty, which means faithfulness to law, is used as if it were only the duty of a people to be loyal to their king, and not the duty of a king to be infinitely more loyal to his people. How comes it to pass that a captain will die with his passengers, and lean over the gunwale to give the parting boat its course; but that a king will not usually die with, much less *for*, his passengers—thinks it rather incumbent on his passengers, in any number, to die for *him?* Think, I beseech you, of the wonder of this. The sea-captain, not captain by divine right, but only by company's appointment; not a man of royal descent, but only a plebeian who can steer; not with the eyes of the world upon him, but with feeble chance, depending on one poor boat, of his name being ever heard above the wash of the fatal waves; not with the cause of a nation resting on his act, but helpless to save so much as a child from among the lost crowd with whom he resolves to be lost, yet goes down quietly to his grave, rather than break his faith to those few emigrants. But your captain by divine right—your captain with the hues of a hundred shields of kings upon his breast—your captain whose every deed, brave or base, will be illuminated or branded forever before unescapable eyes of men—your captain whose every thought and act are beneficent, or fatal, from sunrising to setting, blessing as the sunshine, or shadowing as the night—this captain, as you find him in history, for the most part thinks only how he may tax his passengers, and sit at most ease in his state cabin!

For observe, if there had been indeed in the hearts of the rulers of great multitudes of men any such conception of work for the good of those under their command, as there is in the good and thoughtful masters of any small company of men, not only wars for the sake of mere increase of power could never take place, but our idea of power itself would be entirely altered. Do you suppose that to think and act even for a million of men, to hear their complaints, watch their weaknesses, restrain their vices, make laws for them, lead them, day by day, to purer life, is not enough for one man's work? If any of us were absolute lord only of a district of a hundred miles square, and were resolved on doing our utmost for it; making it feed as large a number of people as possible; making every clod productive, and every rock defensive, and every human being happy; should we not have enough on our hands think you? But if the ruler has any other aim than this; if, careless of the result of his interference, he desire only the authority to interfere; and, regardless of what is ill-done or well-done, cares only that it shall be done at his bidding; if he would rather do two hundred miles' space of mischief, than one hundred miles' space of good, of course he will try to add to his territory; and to add illimitably. But does he add to his power? Do you call it power in a child, if he is allowed to play with the wheels and bands of some vast engine, pleased with their murmur and whirl, till his unwise touch, wandering where it ought not, scatters beam and wheel into ruin? Yet what machine is so vast, so incognizable, as the working of the mind of a nation; what child's touch so wanton, as the word of a selfish king? And yet, how long have we allowed the historian to speak of the extent of the calamity a man causes, as a just ground for his pride; and to extol him as the greatest prince, who is only the center of the widest error. Follow out this thought by yourselves; and you will find that all power, properly so-called, is wise and benevolent. There may be capacity in a drifting fire-ship to destroy a fleet; there may be venom enough in a dead body to infect a nation: but which of you, the most ambitious, would desire a drifting kinghood, robed in consuming fire, or a poison-dipped scepter whose touch was mortal? There is no true potency, remember, but that of help; nor true ambition, but ambition to save.

And then, observe further, this true power, the power of saving, depends neither on multitude of men, nor on extent of territory. We are continually assuming that nations become strong according to their numbers. They indeed become so, if those numbers can be made of one mind; but how are you sure you can stay them in one mind, and keep them from having north and south minds? Grant them unanimous, how know you they will be unanimous in right? If they are unanimous in wrong, the more they are, essentially the weaker they are. Or, suppose that they can neither be of one mind, nor of two minds, but can only be of *no* mind? Suppose they are a mere helpless mob; tottering into precipitant catastrophe, like a wagon-load of stones when the wheel comes off. Dangerous enough for their neighbors, certainly, but not "powerful."

Neither does strength depend on extent of territory, any more than upon number of population. Take up your maps when you go home this evening—put the cluster of British Isles beside the mass of South America; and then consider whether any race of men need care how much ground they stand upon. The strength is in the men, and in their unity and virtue, not in their standing-room: a little group of wise hearts is better than a wilderness full of fools; and only that nation gains true territory, which gains itself.

And now for the brief practical outcome of all this.

Remember, no government is ultimately strong, but in proportion to its kindness and justice; and that a nation does not strengthen, by merely multiplying and diffusing itself. We have not strengthened us yet, by multiplying into America. Nay, even when it has not to encounter the separating conditions of emigration, a nation need not boast itself of multiplying on its own ground, if it multiplies only as flies or locusts do, with the god of flies for its god. It multiplies its strength only by increasing as one great family, in perfect fellowship and brotherhood. And lastly, it does not strengthen itself by seizing dominion over races whom it cannot benefit. Austria is not strengthened, but weakened, by her grasp of Lombardy; and whatever apparent increase of majesty and of wealth may have accrued to us from the possession of India, whether these prove to us ultimately power or weakness, depends wholly on the degree in which our influence on the native race shall be benevolent and exalting. But, as it is at their own peril that any race extends their dominion in mere desire of power, so it is at their own still greater peril that they refuse to undertake aggressive war, according to their force, whenever they are assured that their authority would be helpful and protective. Nor need you listen to any sophistical objection of the impossibility of knowing when a people's help is needed, or when not. Make your national conscience clean, and your national eyes will soon be clear.

No man who is truly ready to take part in a noble
quarrel will ever stand long in doubt by whom, or in
what cause, his aid is needed. I hold it my duty to
make no political statement of any special bearing in
this presence; but I tell you broadly and boldly, that,
within these last ten years, we English have, as a
knightly nation, lost our spurs: we have fought where
we should not have fought, for gain; and we have
been passive where we should not have been passive,
for fear. I tell you that the principle of non-interven-
tion, as now preached among us, is as selfish and cruel
as the worst frenzy of conquest, and differs from it
only by being not only malignant, but dastardly.

I know, however, that my opinions on this subject
differ too widely from those ordinarily held, to be any
further intruded upon you; and therefore I pass lastly
to examine the conditions of the third kind of noble
war—war waged simply for defense of the country
in which we were born, and for the maintenance and
execution of her laws, by whomsoever threatened or de-
fied. It is to this duty that I suppose most men entering
the army consider themselves in reality to be bound,
and I want you now to reflect what the laws of mere
defense are; and what the soldier's duty, as now
understood, or supposed to be understood. You have
selemnly devoted yourselves to be English soldiers, for
the guardianship of England. I want you to feel
what this vow of yours indeed means, or is gradually

coming to mean. You take it upon you, first, while you are sentimental school-boys; you go into your military convent, or barracks, just as a girl goes into her convent while she is a sentimental school-girl; neither of you then know what you are about, though both the good soldiers and good nuns make the best of it afterward. You don't understand perhaps why I call you "sentimental" school-boys, when you go into the army? Because, on the whole, it is love of adventure, of excitement, of fine dress and of the pride of fame, all which are sentimental motives, which chiefly make a boy like going into the Guards better than into a counting-house. You fancy, perhaps, that there is a severe sense of duty mixed with these peacocky motives? And in the best of you, there is; but do not think that it is principal. If you cared to do your duty to your country in a prosaic and unsentimental way, depend upon it, there is now truer duty to be done in raising harvests, than in burning them; more in building houses, than in shelling them—more in winning money by your own work, wherewith to help men, than in taxing other people's work, for money wherewith to slay men; more duty finally, in honest and unselfish living than in honest and unselfish dying, though that seems to your boys' eyes the bravest. So far then, as for your own honor, and the honor of your families, you choose **brave** death in a red coat before brave life in a black one, you are sentimental; and now see what this passionate vow of yours comes to. For a little while you ride, and you hunt tigers or savages, you shoot and are shot; you are happy, and proud, always, and honored and wept if you die; and you are satisfied with your life, and with the end of it; believing, on the whole, that good rather than harm of it comes to others, and much pleasure to you. But as the sense of duty enters into your forming minds, the vow takes another aspect. You find that you have put yourselves into the hand of your country as a weapon. You have vowed to strike, when she bids you, and to stay scabbarded when she bids you; all that you need answer for is, that you fail not in her grasp. And there is goodness in this, and greatness, if you can trust the hand and heart of the Britomart who has braced you to her side, and are assured that when she leaves you sheathed in darkness, there is no need for your flash to the sun. But remember, good and noble as this state may be, it is a state of slavery. There are different kinds of slaves and different masters. Some slaves are scourged to their work by whips, others are scourged to it by restlessness or ambition. It does not matter what the whip is; it is none the less a whip, because you have cut thongs for it out of your own souls: the fact, so far, of slavery, is in being driven to your work without thought, at another's bidding. Again, some slaves are bought with money, and others with praise. It matters not what the purchase-money is. The distinguishing sign of slavery is to have a price, and be bought for it. Again, it matters not what kind of work you are set on; some slaves are set to forced diggings, others to forced marches; some dig furrows, others field-works, and others graves. Some press the juice of reeds, and some the juice of vines, and some the blood of men. The fact of the captivity is the same whatever work we are set upon, though the fruits of the toil may be different. But, remember, in thus vowing ourselves to be the slaves of any master, it ought to be some subject of forethought with us, what work he is likely to put us upon. You may think that the whole duty of a soldier is to be passive, that it is the country you have left behind who is to command, and you have only to obey. But are you sure that you have left *all* your country behind, or that the part of it you have so left is indeed the best part of it? Suppose—and, remember, it is quite conceivable—that you yourselves are indeed the best part of England; that you, who have become the slaves, ought to have been the masters; and that those who are the masters, ought to have been the slaves! If it is a noble and whole-hearted England, whose bidding you are bound to do, it is well; but if you are yourselves the best of her heart, and the England you have left be but a half-hearted England, how say you of your obedience? You were too proud to become shopkeepers: are you satisfied then to become the servants of shopkeepers? You were too proud to become merchants or farmers yourselves: will you have merchants or farmers then for your field marshals? You had no gifts of special grace for Exeter Hall: will you have some gifted person thereat for your commander-in-chief, to judge of your work, and reward it? You imagine yourselves to be the army of England: how if you should find yourselves, at last, only the police of her manufacturing towns, and the beadles of her little Bethels?

It is not so yet, nor will be so, I trust, forever; but what I want you to see, and to be assured of, is, that the ideal of soldiership is not mere passive obedience and bravery; that, so far from this, no country is in a healthy state which has separated, even in a small degree, her civil from her military power. All states of the world, however great, fall at once when they use mercenary armies; and although it is a less instant form of error (because involving no national taint of cowardice), it is yet an error no less ultimately fatal—it is the error especially of modern times of which we cannot yet know all the calamitous consequences—to take away the best blood and strength of the nation, all the soul-substance of it that is brave, and careless of reward, and scornful of pain, and faithful in trust; and to cast that into steel, and make a mere sword of it; taking away its voice and will; but to keep the worst part of the nation—whatever is cowardly, avaricious, sensual, and faithless—and to give to this the voice, to this the authority, to this the chief privilege, where there is least capacity, of thought. The fulfillment of your vow for the defense of England will by no means consist in carrying out such a system. You are not true soldiers, if you only mean to stand at a shop-door, to protect shop-boys who are cheating inside. A soldier's vow to his country is that he will die for the guardianship of her domestic virtue, of her righteous laws, and of her any way challenged or endangered honor. A state without virtue, without laws, and without honor, he is bound *not* to defend; nay, bound to redress by his own right hand that which he sees to be base in her. So sternly is this the law of Nature and life, that a nation once utterly corrupt can only be redeemed by a military despotism—never by talking, nor by its free effort. And the health of any state consists simply in this: that in it, those who are wisest shall also be strongest; its rulers should be also its soldiers; or, rather, by force of intellect more than of sword, its soldiers its rulers. Whatever the hold which the aristocracy of England has on the heart of

England, in that they are still always in front of her battles, this hold will not be enough, unless they are also in front of her thoughts. And truly her thoughts need good captain's leading now, if ever! Do you know what, by this beautiful division of labor (her brave men fighting, and her cowards thinking), she has come at last to think? Here is a bit of paper in my hand,* a good one too, and an honest one; quite representative of the best common public thought of England at this moment; and it is holding forth in one of its leaders upon our "social welfare," upon our "vivid life," upon the "political supremacy of Great Britain." And what do you think all these are owing to? To what our English sires have done for us, and taught us, age after age? No: not to that. To our honesty of heart, or coolness of head, or steadiness of will? No: not to these. To our thinkers, or

---

* I do not care to refer to the journal quoted, because the article was unworthy of its general tone, though in order to enable the audience to verify the quoted sentence, I left the number containing it on the table, when I delivered this lecture. But a saying of Baron Liebig's, quoted at the head of a leader on the same subject in the *Daily Telegraph* of January 11, 1866, summarily digests and presents the maximum folly of modern thought in this respect. "Civilization," says the Baron, "is the economy of power, and English power is coal." Not altogether so, my chemical friend. Civilization is the making of civil persons, which is a kind of distillation of which alembics are incapable, and does not at all imply the turning of a small company of gentlemen into a large company of iron-mongers. And English power (what little of it may be left), is by no means coal, but, indeed, of that which, "when the whole world turns to coal, then chiefly lives."

our statesmen, or our poets, or our captains, or our martyrs, or the patient labor of our poor? No: not to these; or at least not to these in any chief measure. Nay, says the journal, "more than any agency, it is the cheapness and abundance of our coal which have made us what we are." If it be so, then "ashes to ashes" be our epitaph! and the sooner the better. I tell you, gentlemen of England, if ever you would have your country breathe the pure breath of heaven again, and receive again a soul into her body, instead of rotting into a carcass, blown up in the belly with carbonic acid (and great *that* way), you must think, and feel, for your England, as well as fight for her: you must teach her that all the true greatness she ever had, or ever can have, she won while her fields were green and her faces ruddy; that greatness is still possible for Englishmen, even though the ground be not hollow under their feet, nor the sky black over their heads; and that, when the day comes for their country to lay her honors in the dust, her crest will not rise from it more loftily because it is dust of coal. Gentlemen, I tell you, solemnly, that the day is coming when the soldiers of England must be her tutors and the captains of her army, captains also of her mind.

And now, remember, you soldier youths, who are thus in all ways the hope of your country; or must be, if she have any hope: remember that your fitness for all future trust depends upon what you are now. No good soldier in his old age was ever careless or indolent in his youth. Many a giddy and thoughtless boy has become a good bishop, or a good lawyer, or a good merchant; but no such an one ever became a good general. I challenge you, in all history, to find a record of a good soldier who was not grave and earnest in his youth. And, in general, I have no patience with people who talk about "the thoughtlessness of youth" indulgently. I had infinitely rather hear of thoughtless old age, and the indulgence due to *that*. When a man has done his work, and nothing can any way be materially altered in his fate, let him forget his toil, and jest with his fate, if he will; but what excuse can you find for willfulness of thought, at the very time when every crisis of future fortune hangs on your decisions? A youth thoughtless! when all the happiness of his home forever depends on the chances, or the passions, of an hour! A youth thoughtless! when the career of all his days depends on the opportunity of a moment! A youth thoughtless! when his every act is a foundation-stone of future conduct, and every imagination a fountain of life or death! Be thoughtless in *any* after-years, rather than now—though, indeed, there is only one place where a man may be nobly thoughtless—his death-bed. No thinking should ever be left to be done there.

Having, then, resolved that you will not waste recklessly, but earnestly use, these early days of yours, remember that all the duties of her children to England may be summed in two words—industry, and honor. I say first, industry, for it is in this that soldier youth are especially tempted to fail. Yet, surely, there is no reason, because your life may possibly or probably be shorter than other men's, that you should therefore waste more recklessly the portion of it that is granted you; neither do the duties of your profession, which require you to keep your bodies strong, in anywise involve the keeping of your minds weak. So far from that, the experience, the hardship, and the activity of a soldier's life render his powers of thought more accurate than those of other men; and while, for others, all knowledge is often little more than a means of amusement, there is no form of science which a soldier may not at some time or other find bearing on business of life and death. A young mathematician may be excused for languor in studying curves to be described only with a pencil; but not in tracing those which are to be described with a rocket. Your knowledge of a wholesome herb may involve the feeding of an army; and acquaintance with an obscure point of geography, the success of a campaign. Never waste an instant's time, therefore; the sin of idleness is a thousandfold greater in you than in other youths; for the fates of those who will one day be under your command hang upon your knowledge; lost moments now will be lost lives then, and every instant which you carelessly take for play, you buy with blood. But there is one way of wasting time, of all the vilest, because it wastes, not time only, but the interest and energy of your minds. Of all the ungentlemanly habits into which you can fall, the vilest is betting, or interesting yourselves in the issues of betting. It unites nearly every condition of folly and vice: you concentrate your interest upon a matter of chance, instead of upon a subject of true knowledge; and you back opinions which you have no grounds for forming, merely because they are your own. All the insolence of egotism is in this; and so far as the love of excitement is complicated with the hope of winning money, you turn yourselves into the basest sort of tradesmen —those who live by speculation. Were there no other ground for industry, this would be a sufficient one; that it protected you from the temptation to so scandalous a vice. Work faithfully, and you will put yourselves in possession of a glorious and enlarging happiness; not such as can be won by the speed of a horse, or marred by the obliquity of a ball.

First, then, by industry you must fulfill your vow to your country; but all industry and earnestness will be useless unless they are consecrated by your resolution, to be in all things men of honor: not honor in the common sense only, but in the highest. Rest on the force of the two main words in the great verse, *integer* vitæ, scelerisque *purus*. You have vowed your life to England; give it her wholly—a bright, stainless, perfect life—a knightly life. Because you have to fight with machines instead of lances, there may be a necessity for more ghastly danger, but there is none for less worthiness of character, than in olden time. You may be true knights yet, though perhaps not *equites ;* you may have to call yourselves "cannonry" instead of "chivalry," but that is no reason why you should not call yourselves true men. So the first thing you have to see to in becoming soldiers is that you make yourselves wholly true. Courage is a mere matter of course among any ordinarily well-born youths; but neither truth nor gentleness is matter of course. You must bind them like shields about your necks; you must write them on the tablets of your hearts. Though it be not exacted of you, yet exact it of yourselves, this vow of stainless truth. Your hearts are, if you leave them unstirred, as tombs in which a god lies buried. Vow yourselves crusaders to redeem that sacred sepulcher. And remember, before all things—for no other memory will be so protective of you—that the highest law of this knightly truth is that under which it is vowed to women. Whomsoever else you deceive, whomsoever you injure, whomsoever you leave unaided, you must not deceive, nor injure, nor leave unaided, according to your power, any woman of whatever rank. Believe me, every virtue of the higher phases of manly character begins in this—in truth and modesty before the face of all maidens; in truth and pity, or truth and reverence, to all womanhood.

And now let me turn for a moment to you—wives and maidens, who are the souls of soldiers; to you—mothers, who have devoted your children to the great hierarchy of war. Let me ask you to consider what part you have to take for the aid of those who love you; for if you fail in your part they cannot fulfill theirs; such absolute helpmates you are that no man can stand without that help, nor labor in his own strength.

I know your hearts, and that the truth of them never fails when an hour of trial comes which you recognize for such. But you know not when the hour of trial first finds you, nor when it verily finds you. You imagine that you are only called upon to wait and to suffer; to surrender and to mourn. You know that you must not weaken the hearts of your husbands and lovers, even by the one fear of which those hearts are capable—the fear of parting from you, or of causing you grief. Through weary years of separation, through fearful expectancies of unknown fate; through the tenfold bitterness of the sorrow which might so easily have been joy, and the tenfold yearning for glorious life struck down in its prime—through all these agonies you fail not, and never will fail. But your trial is not in these. To be heroic in danger is little—you are Englishwomen. To be heroic in change and sway of fortune is little—for do you not love? To be patient through the great chasm and pause of loss is little—for do you not still love in heaven? But to be heroic in happiness; to bear yourselves gravely and righteously in the dazzling of the sunshine of morning; not to forget the God in whom you trust, when He gives you most; not to fail those who trust you, when they seem to need you least; this is the difficult fortitude. It is not in the pining of absence, not in the peril of battle, not in the wasting of sickness, that your prayer should be most passionate, or your guardianship most tender. Pray, mothers and maidens, for your young soldiers in the bloom of their pride; pray for them, while the only dangers round them are in their own wayward wills; watch you, and pray, when they have to face, not death but temptation. But it is this fortitude also for which there is the crowning reward. Believe me, the whole course and character of your lovers' lives is in your hands; what you would have them be, they shall be, if you not only desire to have them so, but deserve to have them so; for they are but mirrors in which you will see yourselves imaged. If you are frivolous, they will be so also; if you have no understanding of the scope of their duty, they also will forget it; they will listen—they *can* listen—to no other interpretation of it than that uttered from your lips. Bid them be brave—they will be brave for you; bid them be cowards; and how noble soever they be—they will quail for you. Bid them be wise, and they will be wise for you; mock at their counsel, they will be fools for you: such and so absolute is your rule over them. You fancy, perhaps, as you have been told so often, that a wife's rule should only be over her husband's house, not over his mind. Ah, no! the true rule is just the reverse of that; a true wife, in her husband's house, is his servant; it is in his heart that she is queen. Whatever of the best he can conceive, it is her part to be; whatever of highest he can hope, it is hers to promise; all that is dark in him she must purge into purity; all that is failing in him she must strengthen into truth: from her, through all the world's clamor, he must win his praise; in her, through all the world's warfare, he must find his peace.

And, now, but one word more. You may wonder, perhaps, that I have spoken all this night in praise of war. Yet, truly, if it might be, I, for one, would fain join in the cadence of hammer-strokes that should beat swords into plowshares: and that this cannot be, is not the fault of us men. It is *your* fault.

Wholly yours. Only by your command, or by your permission, can any contest take place among us. And the real, final, reason for all the poverty, misery, and rage of battle, throughout Europe, is simply that you women, however good, however religious, however self-sacrificing for those whom you love, are too selfish and too thoughtless to take pains for any creature out of your own immediate circles. You fancy that you are sorry for the pain of others. Now I just tell you this, that if the usual course of war, instead of unroofing peasants' houses, and ravaging peasants' fields, merely broke the china upon your own drawing-room tables, no war in civilized countries would last a week. I tell you more, that at whatever moment you choose to put a period to war, you could do it with less trouble than you take any day to go out to dinner. You know, or at least you might know if you would think, that every battle you hear of has made many widows and orphans. We have, none of us, heart enough truly to mourn with these. But at least we might put on the outer symbols of mourning with them. Let but every Christian lady who has conscience toward God, vow that she will mourn, at least outwardly, for His killed creatures. Your praying is useless, and your church-going mere mockery of God, if you have not plain obedience in you enough for this. Let every lady in the upper classes of civilized Europe simply vow that, while any cruel war proceeds, she will wear *black;* a mute's black—with no jewel, no ornament, no excuse for, or evasion into, prettiness. I tell you again, no war would last a week.

And lastly. You women of England are all now shrieking with one voice—you and your clergymen together—because you hear of your Bibles being attacked. If you choose to obey your Bibles, you will never care who attacks them. It is just because you never fulfill a single downright precept of the Book, that you are so careful for its credit: and just because you don't care to obey its whole words, that you are so particular about the letters of them. The Bible tells you to dress plainly—and you are mad for finery; the Bible tells you to have pity on the poor—and you crush them under your carriage-wheels; the Bible tells you to do judgment and justice—and you do not know, nor care to know, so much as what the Bible word "justice" means. Do but learn so much of God's truth as that comes to; know what He means when He tells you to be just: and teach your sons, that their bravery is but a fool's boast, and their deeds but a firebrand's tossing, unless they are indeed Just men, and Perfect in the Fear of God; and you will soon have no more war, unless it be indeed such as is willed by Him, of whom, though Prince of Peace, it is also written, "In Righteousness He doth judge, and make war."

LECTURES ON ART.

SEVEN LECTURES.

1. INAUGURAL.
2. THE RELATION OF ART TO RELIGION.
3. THE RELATION OF ART TO MORALS.
4. THE RELATION OF ART TO USE.
5. LINE.
6. LIGHT.
7. COLOR.

LECTURE 1.

INAUGURAL.

THE DUTY which is to-day laid on me, of introducing, among the elements of education appointed in this great university, one not only new, but such as to involve in its possible results some modification of the rest, is, as you well feel, so grave, that no man could undertake it without laying himself open to the imputation of a kind of insolence; and no man could undertake it rightly, without being in danger of having his hands shortened by dread of his task, and mistrust of himself.

And it has chanced to me, of late, to be so little acquainted either with pride, or hope, that I can scarcely recover so much as I now need of the one for strength and of the other for foresight, except by remembering that noble persons, and friends of the high temper that judges most clearly where it loves best, have desired that this trust should be given me; and by resting also in the conviction that the goodly tree, whose roots, by God's help, we set in earth to-day, will not fail of its height because the planting of it is under poor auspices, or the first shoots of it enfeebled by ill gardening.

2. The munificence of the English gentleman to whom we owe the founding of this professorship at once in our three great universities, has accomplished the first great group of a series of changes now taking gradual effect in our system of public education; and which, as you well know, are the sign of a vital change in the national mind, respecting both the principles on which that education should be conducted, and the ranks of society to which it should extend. For, whereas it was formerly thought that the discipline necessary to form the character of youth was best given in the study of abstract branches of literature and philosophy, it is now thought that the same, or a better, discipline may be given by informing men in early years of things it cannot but be of chief practical advantage to them afterward to know; and by permitting to them the choice of any field of study which they may feel to be best adapted to their personal dispositions. I have always used what poor influence I possessed in advancing this change; nor can anyone rejoice more than I in its practical results. But the completion—I will not venture to say, correction—of a system established by the highest wisdom of noble ancestors, cannot be too reverently undertaken; and it is necessary for the English people, who are sometimes violent in change in proportion to the reluctance with

which they admit its necessity, to be now oftener than at other times reminded that the object of instruction here is not primarily attainment, but discipline; and that a youth is sent to our universities, not (hitherto at least) to be apprenticed to a trade, nor even always to be advanced in a profession; but, always, to be made a gentleman and a scholar.

3. To be made these—if there is in him the making of either. The populace of all civilized countries have lately been under a feverish impression that it is possible for all men to be both; and that having once become, by passing through certain mechanical processes of instruction, gentle and learned, they are sure to attain in the sequel the consummate beatitude of being rich.

Rich, in the way and measure in which it is well for them to be so, they may, without doubt, *all* become. There is indeed a land of Havilah open to them, of which the wonderful sentence is literally true—"The gold of *that* land is good." But they must first understand, that education, in its deepest sense, is not the equalizer, but the discerner, of men; and that, so far from being instruments for the collection of riches, the first lesson of wisdom is to disdain them, and of gentleness, to diffuse.

It is not therefore, as far as we can judge, yet possible for all men to be gentlemen and scholars. Even under the best training some will remain too selfish to refuse wealth, and some too dull to desire leisure. But many more might be so than are now; nay, perhaps all men in England might one day be so, if England truly desired her supremacy among the nations to be in kindness and in learning. To which good end, it will indeed contribute that we add some practice of the lower arts to our scheme of university education; but the thing which is vitally necessary is, that we should extend the spirit of university education to the practice of the lower arts.

4. And, above all, it is needful that we do this by redeeming them from their present pain of self-contempt, and by giving them rest. It has been too long boasted as the pride of England, that out of a vast multitude of men confessed to be in evil case, it was possible for individuals, by strenuous effort, and singular good fortune, occasionally to emerge into the light and look back with self-gratulatory scorn upon the occupations of their parents, and the circumstances of their infancy. Ought we not rather to aim at an ideal of national life, when, of the employments of Englishmen, though each shall be distinct, none shall be unhappy or ignoble; when mechanical operations acknowledged to be debasing in their tendency, shall be deputed to less fortunate and more covetous races; when advance from rank to rank, though possible to all men, may be rather shunned than desired by the best; and the chief object in the mind of every citizen

may not be extrication from a condition admitted to be disgraceful, but fulfillment of a duty which shall be also a birthright?

5. And then, the training of all these distinct classes will not be by universities of all knowledge, but by distinct schools of such knowledge as shall be most useful for every class: in which, first the principles of their special business may be perfectly taught, and whatever higher learning, and cultivation of the faculties for receiving and giving pleasure, may be properly joined with that labor, taught in connection with it. Thus, I do not despair of seeing a School of Agriculture, with its fully endowed institutes of zoölogy, botany, and chemistry; and a School of Mercantile Seamanship, with its institutes of astronomy, meteorology, and natural history of the sea: and, to name only one of the finer, I do not say higher, arts, we shall, I hope, in a little time, have a perfect school of metal-work, at the head of which will be, not the ironmasters, but the goldsmiths; and therein, I believe, that artists, being taught how to deal wisely with the most precious of metals, will take into due government the uses of all others; having in connection with their practical work splendid institutes of chemistry and mineralogy, and of ethical and imaginative literature.

And thus I confess myself more interested in the final issue of the change in our system of central education, which is to-day consummated by the admission of the manual arts into its scheme, than in any direct effect likely to result upon ourselves from the innovation. But I must not permit myself to fail in the estimate of my immediate duty, while I debate what that duty may hereafter become in the hands of others; and I will therefore now, so far as I am able, lay before you a brief general view of the existing state of the arts in England, and of the influence which her universities, through these newly-founded lectureships, may, I think, bring to bear upon it for good.

6. And first, we have to consider the impulse which has been given to the practice of all the arts of which the object is the production of beautiful things, by the extension of our commerce, and of the means of intercourse with foreign nations, by which we now become more familiarly acquainted with their works in past and in present times. The immediate result of this new knowledge has been, I regret to say, to make us more jealous of the genius of others, than conscious of the limitations of our own; and to make us rather desire to enlarge our wealth by the sale of art, than to elevate our enjoyments by its acquisition.

Now, whatever efforts we make, with a true desire to produce, and possess, as themselves a constituent part of true wealth, things that are intrinsically beautiful, have in them at least one of the essential elements of success. But efforts having origin only in the hope of enriching ourselves by the sale of our productions, are assuredly condemned to dishonorable failure; not because, ultimately a well-trained nation may not profit by the exercise of its peculiar art-skill; but because that peculiar art-skill can never be developed with a view to profit. The right fulfillment of national power in art depends always on the direction of its aim by the experience of ages. Self-knowledge is not less difficult, nor less necessary for the direction of its genius, to a people than to an individual, and it is neither to be acquired by the eagerness of unpractised pride, nor during the anxieties of improvident distress. No nation ever had, or will have, the power of suddenly developing, under the pressure of necessity, faculties it had neglected when it was at ease; nor of teaching itself in poverty, the skill to produce, what it has never in opulence had the sense to admire.

7. Connected also with some of the worst parts of our social system, but capable of being directed to better result than this commercial endeavor, we see lately a most powerful impulse given to the production of costly works of art by the various causes which promote the sudden accumulation of wealth in the hands of private persons. We have thus a vast and new patronage, which, in its present agency, is injurious to our schools; but which is nevertheless in a great degree earnest and conscientious, and far from being influenced chiefly by motives of ostentation.

Most of our rich men would be glad to promote the true interests of art in this country; and even those who buy for vanity, found their vanity on the possession of what they suppose to be best.

It is therefore in a great measure the fault of artists themselves if they suffer from this partly unintelligent, but thoroughly well-intended patronage. If they seek to attract it by eccentricity, to deceive it by superficial qualities, or take advantage of it by thoughtless and facile production, they necessarily degrade themselves and it together, and have no right to complain afterward that it will not acknowledge better-grounded claims. But if every painter of real power would do only what he knew would be worthy of himself, and refuse to be involved in the contention for undeserved or accidental success, there is indeed, whatever may have been thought or said to the contrary, true instinct enough in the public mind to follow such firm guidance. It is one of the facts which the experience of thirty years enables me to assert without qualification, that a really good picture is ultimately always approved and bought, unless it is willfully rendered offensive to the public by faults which the artist has been either too proud to abandon, or too weak to correct.

8. The development of whatever is healthful and serviceable in the two modes of impulse which we have been considering, depends however, ultimately,

on the direction taken by the true interest in art which has lately been aroused by the great and active genius of many of our living, or but lately lost, painters, sculptors, and architects. It may perhaps surprise but I think it will please you to hear me, or (if you will forgive me, in my own Oxford, the presumption of fancying that some may recognize me by an old name) to hear the author of "Modern Painters" say, that his chief error in earlier days was not in over-estimating, but in too slightly acknowledging the merit of living men. The great painter whose power, while he was yet among us, I was able to perceive, was the first to reprove me for my disregard of the skill of his fellow-artists; and, with this inauguration of the study of the art of all time—a study which can only by true modesty end in wise admiration—it is surely well that I connect the record of these words of his, spoken then too truly to myself and true always more or less for all who are untrained in that toil—"You don't know how difficult it is."

You will not expect me, within the compass of this lecture, to give you any analysis of the many kinds of excellent art (in all the three great divisions) which the complex demands of modern life, and yet more varied instincts of modern genius, have developed for pleasure or service. It must be my endeavor, in conjunction with my colleagues in other universities, hereafter to enable you to appreciate these worthily;

in the hope that also the members in the Royal Academy, and those of the Institute of British Architects, may be induced to assist, and guide, the efforts of the universities, by organizing such a system of art education for their own students as shall in future prevent the waste of genius in any mistaken endeavors; especially removing doubt as to the proper substance and the use of materials; and requiring compliance with certain elementary principles of right, in every picture and design exhibited with their sanction. It is not indeed possible for talent so varied as that of English artists to be compelled into the formalities of a determined school; but it must certainly be the function of every academical body to see that their younger students are guarded from what must in every school be error; and that they are practised in the best methods of work hitherto known, before their ingenuity is directed to the invention of others.

9. I need scarcely refer, except for the sake of completeness in my statement, to one form of demand for art which is wholly unenlightened, and powerful only for evil: namely, the demand of the classes occupied solely in the pursuit of pleasure, for objects and modes of art that can amuse indolence or satisfy sensibility. There is no need for any discussion of these requirements, or of their forms of influence, though they are very deadly at present in their operation on sculpture, and on jewelers' work. They cannot be

checked by blame, nor guided by instruction; they are merely the necessary results of whatever defects exist in the temper and principles of a luxurious society; and it is only by moral changes, not by art-criticism, that their action can be modified.

10. Lastly, there is a continually increasing demand for popular art, multipliable by the printing press, illustrative of daily events, of general literature, and of natural science. Admirable skill, and some of the best talent of modern times, are occupied in supplying this want; and there is no limit to the good which may be effected by rightly taking advantage of the powers we now possess of placing good and lovely art within the reach of the poorest classes. Much has been already accomplished; but great harm has been done also—first, by forms of art definitely addressed to depraved tastes; and, secondly, in a more subtle way, by really beautiful and useful engravings which are yet not good enough to retain their influence on the public mind; which weary it by redundant quantity of monotonous average excellence, and diminish or destroy its power of accurate attention to work of a higher order.

Especially this is to be regretted in the effect produced on the schools of line engraving, which had reached in England an executive skill of a kind before unexampled, and which of late have lost much of their more sterling and legitimate methods. Still, I have seen plates produced quite recently, more beautiful, I think, in some qualities than anything ever before attained by the burin; and I have not the slightest fear that photography, or any other adverse or competitive operation, will in the least ultimately diminish,—I believe they will, on the contrary, stimulate and exalt—the grand old powers of the wood and the steel.

11. Such are, I think, briefly the present conditions of art with which we have to deal; and I conceive it to be the function of this professorship, with respect to them, to establish both a practical and critical school of fine art for English gentlemen; practical, so that if they draw at all, they may draw rightly; and critical, so that they may both be directed to such works of existing art as will best reward their study; and enabled to make the exercise of their patronage, if living artists delightful to themselves by their consciousness of its justice, and, to the utmost, beneficial to their country, by being given only to the men who deserve it; and, to those, in the early period of their lives, when they both need it most, and can be influenced by it to the best advantage.

12. And especially with reference to this function of patronage, I believe myself justified in taking into account future probabilities as to the character and range of art in England; and I shall endeavor at once to organize with you a system of study calculated to develop chiefly the knowledge of those branches in

which the English schools have shown, and are likely to show, peculiar excellence. Now, in asking your sanction both for the nature of the general plans I wish to adopt, and for what I conceive to be necessary limitations of them, I wish you to be fully aware of my reasons for both; and I will therefore risk the burden of your patience while I state the directions of effort in which I think English artists are liable to failure, and those also in which past experience has shown they are secure of success.

13. I referred, but now, to the effort we are making to improve the designs of our manufactures. Within certain limits I believe this improvement may indeed take effect; so that we may no more humor momentary fashions by ugly results of chance instead of design; and may produce both good tissues, of harmonious colors, and good forms and substance of pottery and glass. But we shall never excel in decorative design. Such design is usually produced by people of great natural powers of mind, who have no variety of subjects to employ themselves on, no oppressive anxieties, and are in circumstances, either of natural scenery or of daily life, which cause pleasurable excitement. We cannot design because we have too much to think of, and we think of it too anxiously. It has long been observed how little real anxiety exists in the minds of the partly savage races which excel in decorative art; and we must not suppose that

the temper of the middle ages was a troubled one, because every day brought its dangers or its changes. The very eventfulness of the life rendered it careless, as generally is still the case with soldiers and sailors. Now, when there are great powers of thought, and little to think of, all the waste energy and fancy are thrown into the manual work, and you have as much intellect as would direct the affairs of a large mercantile concern for a day, spent all at once, quite unconsciously, in drawing an ingenious spiral.

Also, powers of doing fine ornamental work are only to be reached by a perpetual discipline of the hand as well as of the fancy; discipline as attentive and painful as that which a juggler has to put himself through, to overcome the more palpable difficulties of his profession. The execution of the best artists is always a splendid *tour-de-force* and much that in painting is supposed to be dependent on material is indeed only a lovely and quite inimitable legerdemain. Now, when powers of fancy, stimulated by this triumphant precision of manual dexterity, descend uninterruptedly from generation to generation, you have at last, what is not so much a trained artist as a new species of animal, with whose instinctive gifts you have no chance of contending. And thus all our imitations of other peoples' work are futile. We must learn first to make honest English wares, and afterward to decorate them as may please the then approving Graces.

14. Secondly—and this is an incapacity of a graver kind, yet having its own good in it also—we shall never be successful in the highest fields of ideal or theological art. For there is one strange, but quite essential, character in us; ever since the Conquest, if not earlier: a delight in the forms of burlesque which are connected in some degree with the foulness in evil. I think the most perfect type of a true English mind in its best possible temper, is that of Chaucer; and you will find that, while it is for the most part full of thoughts of beauty, pure and wild like that of an April morning, there are even in the midst of this, sometimes momentarily jesting passages which stoop to play with evil—while the power of listening to and enjoying the jesting of entirely gross persons, whatever the feeling may be which permits it, afterward degenerates into forms of humor which render some of quite the greatest, wisest, and most moral of English writers now almost useless for our youth. And yet you will find that whenever Englishmen are wholly without this instinct, their genius is comparatively weak and restricted.

15. Now, the first necessity for the doing of any great work in ideal art, is the looking upon all foulness with horror, as a contemptible though dreadful enemy. You may easily understand what I mean, by comparing the feelings with which Dante regards any form of obscenity or of base jest, with the temper in

which the same things are regarded by Shakespeare. And this strange earthly instinct of ours, coupled as it is, in our good men, with great simplicity and common sense, renders them shrewd and perfect observers and delineators of actual nature low or high; but precludes them from that speciality of art which is properly called sublime. If ever we try anything in the manner of Michael Angelo or of Dante, we catch a fall, even in literature, as Milton in the battle of the angels, spoiled from Hesiod: while in art, every attempt in this style has hitherto been the sign either of the presumptuous egotism of persons who had never really learned to be workmen, or it has been connected with very tragic forms of the contemplation of death, it has always been partly insane, and never once wholly successful.

But we need not feel any discomfort in these limitations of our capacity. We can do much that others cannot, and more than we have ever yet ourselves completely done. Our first great gift is in the portraiture of living people—a power already so accomplished in both Reynolds and Gainsborough, that nothing is left for future masters but to add the calm of perfect workmanship to their vigor and felicity of perception. And of what value a true school of portraiture may become in the future, when worthy men will desire only to be known, and others will not fear to know them for what they truly were, we cannot from any past records of art influence yet conceive. But in my next address it will be partly my endeavor to show you how much more useful, because more humble, the labor of great masters might have been, had they been content to bear record of the souls that were dwelling with them on earth, instead of striving to give a deceptive glory to those they dreamed of in heaven.

16. Secondly, we have an intense power of invention and expression in domestic drama (King Lear and Hamlet being essentially domestic in their strongest motives of interest). There is a tendency at this moment toward a noble development of our art in this direction, checked by many adverse conditions which may be summed in one—the insufficiency of generous civic or patriotic passion in the heart of the English people; a fault which makes its domestic affections selfish, contracted, and, therefore, frivolous.

17. Thirdly, in connection with our simplicity, and good-humor, and partly with that very love of the grotesque which debases our ideal, we have a sympathy with the lower animals which is peculiarly our own; and which, though it has already found some exquisite expression in the works of Bewick and Landseer, is yet quite undeveloped. This sympathy, with the aid of our now authoritative science of physiology, and in association with our British love of adventure, will, I hope, enable us to give to the future inhabitants

of the globe an almost perfect record of the present forms of animal life upon it, of which many are on the point of being extinguished.

Lastly, but not as the least important of our special powers, I have to note our skill in landscape, of which I will presently speak more particularly.

18. Such, I conceive to be the directions in which principally, we have the power to excel; and you must at once see how the consideration of them must modify the advisable methods of our art study. For if our professional painters were likely to produce pieces of art loftily ideal in their character, it would be desirable to form the taste of the students here by setting before them only the purest examples of Greek, and the mightiest of Italian art. But I do not think you will yet find a single instance of a school directed exclusively to these higher branches of study in England, which has strongly, or even definitely, made impression on its younger scholars. While, therefore, I shall endeavor to point out clearly the characters to be looked for and admired in the great masters of imaginative design, I shall make no special effort to stimulate the imitation of them; and, above all things, I shall try to probe in you, and to prevent, the affectation into which it is easy to fall, even through modesty—of either endeavoring to admire a grandeur with which we have no natural sympathy, or losing the pleasure we might take in the study of familiar things,

by considering it a sign of refinement to look for what is of higher class, or rarer occurrence.

19. Again, if our artisans were likely to attain any distinguished skill in ornamental design, it would be incumbent upon me to make my class here accurately acquainted with the principles of earth and metal work, and to accustom them to take pleasure in conventional arrangements of color and form. I hope, indeed, to do this, so far as to enable them to discern the real merit of many styles of art which are at present neglected; and, above all, to read the minds of semi-barbaric nations in the only language by which their feelings were capable of expression: and those members of my class whose temper inclines them to take pleasure in the interpretation of mythic symbols, will not probably be induced to quit the profound fields of investigation which early art, examined carefully, will open to them, and which belong to it alone; for this is a general law, that, supposing the intellect of the workman the same, the more imitatively complete his art, the less he will mean by it; and the ruder the symbol, the deeper is its intention. Nevertheless, when I have once sufficiently pointed out the nature and value of this conventional work, and vindicated it from the contempt with which it is too generally regarded, I shall leave the student to his own pleasure in its pursuit; and even, so far as I may, discourage all admiration founded on quaintness

or peculiarity of style; and repress any other modes of feeling which are likely to lead rather to fastidious collection of curiosities, than to the intelligent appreciation of work, which being executed in compliance with constant laws of right, cannot be singular, and must be distinguished only by excellence in what is always desirable.

20. While, therefore, in these and such other directions, I shall endeavor to put every adequate means of advance within reach of the members of my class, I shall use my own best energy to show them what is consummately beautiful and well done, by men who have passed through the symbolic or suggestive stage of design, and have enabled themselves to comply, by truth of representation, with the strictest or most eager demands of accurate science, and of disciplined passion. I shall therefore direct your observation, during the greater part of the time you may spare to me, to what is indisputably best, both in painting and sculpture; trusting that you will afterward recognize the nascent and partial skill of former days both with greater interest and greater respect, when you know the full difficulty of what it attempted, and the complete range of what it foretold.

21. And with this view, I shall at once endeavor to do what has for many years been in my thoughts, and now, with the advice and assistance of the curators of

the university galleries, I do not doubt may be accomplished here in Oxford, just where it will be pre-eminently useful—namely, to arrange an educational series of examples of excellent art, standards to which you may at once refer on any questionable point, and by the study of which you may gradually attain an instinctive sense of right, which will afterward be liable to no serious error. Such a collection may be formed, both more perfectly, and more easily, than would commonly be supposed. For the real utility of the series will depend on its restricted extent—on the severe exclusion of all second-rate, superfluous, or even attractively varied examples—and on the confining the students' attention to a few types of what is insuperably good. More progress in power of judgment may be made in a limited time by the examination of one work, than by the review of many; and a certain degree of vitality is given to the impressiveness of every characteristic, by its being exhibited in clear contrast, and without repetition.

The greater number of the examples I shall choose will at first not be costly; many of them, only engravings or photographs; they shall be arranged so as to be easily accessible, and I will prepare a catalogue pointing out my purpose in the selection of each. But in process of time, I have good hope that assistance will be given me by the English public in making the series here no less splendid than serviceable; and in placing minor collections, arranged on a similar principle, at the command also of the students in our public schools.

22. In the second place, I shall endeavor to prevail upon all the younger members of the university who wish to attend the art lectures, to give at least so much time to manual practice as may enable them to understand the nature and difficulty of executive skill. The time so spent will not be lost, even as regards their other studies at the university, for I will prepare the practical exercises in a double series, one illustrative of history, the other of natural science. And whether you are drawing a piece of Greek armor, or a hawk's beak, or a lion's paw, you will find that the mere necessity of using the hand compels attention to circumstances which would otherwise have escaped notice, and fastens them in the memory without farther effort. But were it even otherwise, and this practical training did really involve some sacrifice of your time, I do not fear but that it will be justified to you by its felt results: and I think that general public feeling is also tending to the admission that accomplished education must include, not only full command of expression by language, but command of true musical sound by the voice, and of true form by the hand.

23. While I myself hold this professorship, I shall direct you in these exercises very definitely to natural

history, and to landscape; not only because in these two branches I am probably able to show you truths which might be despised by my successors; but because I think the vital and joyful study of natural history quite the principal element requiring introduction not only into university, but into national education, from highest to lowest; and I even will risk incurring your ridicule by confessing one of my fondest dreams, that I may succeed in making some of you English youths like better to look at a bird than to shoot it; and even desire to make wild creatures tame, instead of tame creatures wild. And for the study of landscape, it is, I think, now calculated to be of use in deeper, if not more important modes, than that of natural science, for reasons which I will ask you to let me state at some length.

24. Observe first—no race of men which is entirely bred in wild country, far from cities, ever enjoys landscape. They may enjoy the beauty of animals, but scarcely even that: a true peasant cannot see the beauty of cattle; but only the qualities expressive of their serviceableness. I waive discussion of this to-day; permit my assertion of it, under my confident guarantee of future proof. Landscape can only be enjoyed by cultivated persons and it is only by music, literature and painting, that cultivation can be given. Also the faculties which are thus received are hereditary; so that the child of an educated race has an innate instinct for

beauty, derived from arts practiced hundreds of years before its birth. Now farther note this, one of the loveliest things in human nature. In the children of noble races, trained by surrounding art, and at the same time in the practice of great deeds, there is an intense delight in the landscape of their country as *memorial*; a sense not taught to them, nor teachable to any others; but, in them, innate; and the seal and reward of persistence in great national life;—the obedience and the peace of ages having extended gradually the glory of the revered ancestors also to the ancestral land; until the motherhood of the dust, the mystery of the Demeter from whose bosom we came, and to whose bosom we return, surrounds and inspires, everywhere, the local awe of field and fountain; the sacredness of landmark that none may remove, and of wave that none may pollute; while records of proud days, and of dear persons, make every rock monumental with ghostly inscription, and every path lovely with noble desolateness.

25. Now, however, checked by lightness of temperament, the instinctive love of landscape in us has this deep root, which, in your minds, I will pray you to disencumber from whatever may oppress or mortify it, and to strive to feel with all the strength of your youth that a nation is only worthy of the soil and the scenes that it has inherited, when, by all its acts and arts, it is making them more lovely for its children.

And now, I trust, you will feel that it is not in mere yielding to my own fancies that I have chosen, for the first three subjects in your educational series, landscape scenes—two in England, and one in France —the association of these not being without purpose; and for the fourth, Albert Dürer's dream of the spirit of Labor. And of the landscape subjects, I must tell you this much. The first is an engraving only; the original drawing by Turner was destroyed by fire twenty years ago. For which loss I wish you to be sorry, and to remember, in connection with this first example, that whatever remains to us of possession in the arts is, compared to what we might have had if we had cared for them, just what that engraving is to the lost drawing. You will find also that its subject has meaning in it which will not be harmful to you. The second example is a real drawing by Turner, in the same series, and very nearly of the same place; the two scenes are within a quarter of a mile of each other. It will show you the character of the work that was destroyed. It will show you, in process of time, much more; but chiefly, and this is my main reason for choosing both, it will be a permanent expression to you of what English landscape was once; and must, if we are to remain a nation, be again.

I think it farther right to tell you, for otherwise you might hardly pay regard enough to work apparently so simple, that by a chance which is not altogether displeasing to me, this drawing, which it has become, for these reasons, necessary for me to give you, is—not indeed the best I have (I have several as good, though none better)—but, of all I have, the one I had least mind to part with.

The third example is also a Turner drawing—a scene on the Loire—never engraved. It is an introduction to the series of the Loire, which you have already; it has in its present place a due concurrence with the expressionable purpose of its companions; and though small, it is very precious, being a faultless, and, I believe, unsurpassable example of water-color painting.

Chiefly, however, remember the object of these three first examples is to give you an index to your truest feelings about European, and especially about your native landscape, as it is pensive and historical; and so far as you yourselves make any effort at its representation, to give you a motive for fidelity in handwork more animating than any connected with mere success in the art itself.

26. With respect to actual methods of practice I will not incur the responsibility of determining them for you. We will take Lionardo's treatise on training for our first text-book; and I think you need not fear being misled by me if I ask you to do only what Lionardo bids, or what will be necessary to enable you to do his bidding. But you need not possess the book,

nor read it through. I will translate the pieces to the authority of which I shall appeal; and, in process of time, by analysis of this fragmentary treatise, show you some characters not usually understood of the simplicity as well as subtlety common to most great workmen of that age. Afterward we will collect the instructions of other undisputed masters, till we have obtained a code of laws clearly resting on the consent of antiquity.

While, however, I thus in some measure limit for the present the methods of your practice, I shall endeavor to make the courses of my university lectures as wide in their range as my knowledge will permit. The range so conceded will be narrow enough; but I believe that my proper function is not to acquaint you with the general history, but with the essential principles of art; and with its history only when it has been both great and good or where some special excellence of it requires examination of the causes to which it must be ascribed.

27. But if either our work, or our inquiries, are to be indeed successful in their own field, they must be connected with others of a sterner character. Now listen to me, if I have in these past details lost or burdened your attention; for this is what I have chiefly to say to you. The art of any country is the exponent of its social and political virtues. I will show you

that it is so in some detail, in the second of my subsequent course of lectures; meantime accept this as one of the things, and the most important of all things, I can positively declare to you. The art, or general productive and formative energy, of any country, is an exact exponent of its ethical life. You can have noble art only from noble persons, associated under laws fitted to their time and circumstances. And the best skill that any teacher of art could spend here in your help, would not end in enabling you even so much as rightly to draw the water-lilies in the Cherwell (and though it did, the work when done would not be worth the lilies themselves) unless both he and you were seeking, as I trust we shall together seek, in the laws which regulate the finest industries, the clue to the laws which regulate *all* industries, and in better obedience to which we shall actually have henceforward to live, not merely in compliance with our own sense of what is right, but under the weight of quite literal necessity. For the trades by which the British people has believed it to be the highest of destinies to maintain itself, cannot now long remain undisputed in its hands; its unemployed poor are daily becoming more violently criminal; and a searching distress in the middle classes, arising partly from their vanity in living always up to their incomes, and partly from their folly in imagining that they can subsist in idleness upon usury, will at last compel the sons and daughters of English families to acquaint themselves with the principles of providential economy; and to learn that food can only be got out of the ground, and competence only secured by frugality; and that although it is not possible for all to be occupied in the highest arts, nor for any, guiltlessly, to pass their days in a succession of pleasures, the most perfect mental culture possible to men is founded on their useful energies, and their best arts and brightest happiness are consistent, and consistent only, with their virtue.

28. This I repeat, gentlemen, will soon become manifest to those among us, and there are yet many, who are honest hearted. And the future fate of England depends upon the position they then take, and on their courage in maintaining it.

There is a destiny now possible to us—the highest ever set before a nation to be accepted or refused. We are still undegenerate in race; a race mingled of the best northern blood. We are not yet dissolute in temper, but still have the firmness to govern, and the grace to obey. We have been taught a religion of pure mercy, which we must either now finally betray, or learn to defend by fulfilling. And we are rich in an inheritance of honor, bequeathed to us through a thousand years of noble history, which it should be our daily thirst to increase with splendid avarice, so that Englishmen, if it be a sin to covet honor, should be the most offending souls alive. Within the last few years we have had the laws of natural science opened to us with a rapidity which has been blinding by its brightness; and means of transit and communication given to us, which have made but one kingdom of the habitable globe. One kingdom—but who is to be its king? Is there to be no king in it, think you, and every man to do that which is right in his own eyes? Or only kings of terror, and the obscene empires of Mammon and Belial? Or will you, youths of England, make your country again a royal throne of kings; a sceptred isle, for all the world a source of light, a center of peace; mistress of Learning and of the Arts; faithful guardian of great memories in the midst of irreverent and ephemeral visions—faithful servant of time-tried principles, under temptation from fond experiments and licentious desires; and amidst the cruel and clamorous jealousies of the nations worshiped in her strange valor, of good-will toward men?

29. *Vexilla regis prodeunt.* Yes, but of which king? There are the two oriflammes; which shall we plant on the farthest islands—the one that floats in heavenly fire, or that hangs heavy with foul tissue of terrestrial gold? There is indeed a course of beneficent glory open to us, such as never was yet offered to any poor group of mortal souls. But it must be—it *is* with us, now, "Reign or die." And if it shall be said of this country, *Fece per viltate, il gran rifiuto*; that

refusal of the crown will be, of all yet recorded in history, the shamefullest and most untimely.

And this is what she must either do, or perish: she must found colonies as fast and as far as she is able, formed of her most energetic and worthiest men; seizing every piece of fruitful waste ground she can set her foot on, and there teaching these her colonists that their chief virtue is to be fidelity to their country and that their first aim is to be to advance the power of England by land and sea; and that, though they live on a distant plot of ground, they are no more to consider themselves therefore disfranchised from their native land than the sailors of her fleets do, because they float on distant waves. So that literally, these colonies must be fastened fleets, and every man of them must be under authority of captains and officers, whose better command is to be over fields and streets instead of ships of the line; and England, in these her motionless navies (or, in the true and mightiest sense, motionless churches, ruled by pilots on the Galilean lake of all the world) is to "expect every man to do his duty;" recognizing that duty is indeed possible no less in peace than war; and that if we can get men, for little pay, to cast themselves against cannon-mouths for love of England, we may find men also who will plow and sow for her, who will behave kindly and righteously for her, who will bring up their children to love her, and who will gladden themselves in the brightness of her glory, more than in all the light of tropic skies.

But that they may be able to do this, she must make her own majesty stainless; she must give them thoughts of their home of which they can be proud. The England who is to be mistress of half the earth cannot remain herself a heap of cinders, trampled by contending and miserable crowds; she must yet again become the England she was once, and in all beautiful ways more; so happy, so secluded, and so pure, that in her sky—polluted by no unholy clouds—she may be able to spell rightly of every star that heaven doth show; and in her fields, ordered and wide and fair, of every herb that sips the dew; and under the green avenues of her enchanted garden, a sacred Circe, true daughter of the Sun, she must guide the human arts, and gather the divine knowledge, of distant nations, transformed from savageness to manhood, and redeemed from despairing into Peace.

30. You think that an impossible ideal. Be it so; refuse to accept it if you will; but see that you form your own in its stead. All that I ask of you is to have a fixed purpose of some kind for your country and yourselves; no matter how restricted, so that it be fixed and unselfish. I know what stout hearts are in you, to answer acknowledged need; but it is the fatallest form of error in English youth to hide their best hardihood till it fades for lack of sunshine, and to act

in disdain of purpose, till all purpose is vain. It is not by deliberate, but by careless selfishness; not by compromise with evil, but by dull following of good, that the weight of national evil increases upon us daily. Break through at least this pretence of existence; determine what you will be, and what you would win. You will not decide wrongly if you resolve to decide at all. Were even the choice between lawless pleasure and loyal suffering, you would not, I believe, choose basely. But your trial is not so sharp. It is between drifting in confused wreck among the castaways of Fortune, who condemns to assured ruin those who know not either how to resist her, or obey; between this, I say, and the taking your appointed part in the heroism of Rest; the resolving to share in the victory which is to the weak rather than the strong; and the binding yourselves by that law, which, thought on through lingering night and laboring day, makes a man's life to be as a tree planted by the water-side, that bringeth forth his fruit in his season—

"ET FOLIUM EJUS NON DEFLUET,

ET OMNIA, QUÆCUNQUE FACIET, PROSPERABUNTUR."

LECTURE II.

THE RELATION OF ART TO RELIGION.

31. It was stated, and I trust partly with your acceptance, in my opening lecture, that the study on which we are about to enter cannot be rightly undertaken except in furtherance of the grave purposes of life with respect to which the rest of the scheme of your education here is designed. But you can scarcely have at once felt all that I intended in saying so— you cannot but be still partly under the impression that the so-called fine arts are merely modes of graceful recreation, and a new resource for your times of rest. Let me ask you, forthwith, so far as you can trust me, to change your thoughts in this matter. All the great arts have for their object either the support or exaltation of human life—usually both; and their dignity, and ultimately their very existence, depend on their being '$μετὰ λόθογου ἀληῦς$,' that is to say, apprehending, with right reason, the nature of the materials they work with, of the things they relate or represent, and of the faculties to which they are addressed. And farther, they form one united system from which it is

impossible to remove any part without harm to the rest. They are founded first in mastery, by strength of *arm*, of the earth and sea, in agriculture and seamanship; then their inventive power begins, with the clay in the hand of the potter, whose art is the humblest, but truest type of the forming of the human body and spirit; and in the carpenter's work, which probably was the early employment of the Founder of our religion. And until men have perfectly learned the laws of art in clay and wood, they can consummately know no others. Nor is it without the strange significance which you will find in what at first seemed chance, in all noble histories, as soon as you can read them rightly—that the statue of Athena Polias was of olive wood, and that the Greek temple and Gothic spire are both merely the permanent representations of useful wooden structures. On these two first arts follow building in stone, sculpture, metal work, and painting; every art being properly called "fine" which demands the exercise of the full faculties of heart and intellect. For though the fine arts are not necessarily imitative or representative, for their essence is being '$\pi\varepsilon\rho\grave{\iota}\ \gamma\acute{\varepsilon}\nu\varepsilon\sigma\iota\nu$'—occupied in the actual production of beautiful form or color—still, the highest of them are appointed also to relate to us the utmost ascertainable truth respecting visible things and moral feelings; and this pursuit of fact is the vital element of the art power—that in which alone it can develop itself to its utmost. And I will anticipate by an assertion which you will at present think too bold, but which I am willing that you should think so, in order that you may well remember it—the highest thing that art can do is to set before you the true image of the presence of a noble human being. It has never done more than this, and it ought not to do less.

32. The great arts—forming thus one perfect scheme of human skill, of which it is not right to call one division more honorable, though it may be more subtle, than another—have had, and can have, but three principal directions of purpose—first that of enforcing the religion of men: secondly, that of perfecting their ethical stated; thirdly, that of doing them material service.

33. I do not doubt but that you are surprised at my saying the arts can in their second function only be directed to the perfecting of ethical state, it being our usual impression that they are often destructive of morality. But it is impossible to direct fine art to an immoral end, except by giving it characters unconnected with its fineness, or by addressing it to persons who cannot perceive it to be fine. Whosoever recognizes it is exalted by it. On the other hand, it has been commonly thought that art was a most fitting means for the enforcement of religious doctrines and emotions; whereas there is, as I must presently try to show you room for

grave doubt whether it has not in this function hitherto done evil rather than good.

24. In this and the two next following lectures, I shall endeavor therefore to show you the grave relations of human art, in these three functions, to human life. I can do this but roughly, as you may well suppose—since each of these subjects would require for its right treatment years instead of hours. Only, remember, I have already given years, not a few, to each of them; and what I try to tell you now will be only so much as is absolutely necessary to set our work on a clear foundation. You may not, at present, see the necessity for *any* foundation, and may think that I ought to put pencil and paper in your hands at once. On that point I must simply answer, "Trust me a little while," asking you however also to remember, that—irrespectively of what you do last or first—my true function here is not that of your master in painting, or sculpture, or pottery; but my real duty is to show you what it is that makes any of these arts fine, or the contrary of fine; essentially good, or essentially base. You need not fear my not being pratical enough for you; all the industry you choose to give me I will take; but far the better part of what you may gain by such industry would be lost, if I did not first lead you to see what every form of art-industry intends, and why some of it is justly called right, and some wrong.

35. It would be well if you were to look over, with respect to this matter, the end of the second, and what interests you of the third book of Plato's Republic; noting therein these two principal things, of which I have to speak in this and my next lecture: first, the power which Plato so frankly, and quite justly, attributes to art, of falsifying our conceptions of Deity: which power he by fatal error partly implies may be used wisely for good, and that the feigning is only wrong when it is of evil, 'ἐάν τις μὴ καλῶς ψεύδηται;' and you may trace through all that follows the beginning of the change of Greek ideal art into a beautiful expediency, instead of what it was in the days of Pindar, the statement of what "could not be otherwise than so." But, in the second place, you will find in those books of the Polity, stated with far greater accuracy of expression than our English language admits, the essential relations of art to morality; the sum of these being given in one lovely sentence, which, considering that we have to-day grace done us by fair companionship, you will pardon me for translating. "Must it be then only with our poets that we insist they shall either create for us the image of a noble morality, or among us create none? or shall we not also keep guard over all other workers for the people, and forbid them to make what is ill customed, and unrestrained, and and ungentle, and without order or shape, either in likenesses of living things, or in buildings, or in any

other thing whatsoever that is made for the people?
and shall we not rather seek for workers who can
track the inner nature of all that may be sweetly
schemed; so that the young men, as living in a wholesome place, may be profited by everything that, in
work fairly wrought, may touch them through hearing or sight—as if it were a breeze bringing health to
them from places strong for life?"

36. And now—but one word, before we enter on
our task, as to the way you must understand what I
may endeavor to tell you.

Let me beg you—now and always—not to think that
I mean more than I say. In all probability, I mean
just what I say, and only that. At all events I do
fully mean that, and if there is anything reserved in
my mind, it will be probably different from what you
would guess. You are perfectly welcome to know all
that I think, as soon as I have put before you all my
grounds for thinking it; but by the time I have
done so, you will be able to form an opinion of your
own; and mine will then be of no consequence to
you.

37. I use then to-day, as I shall in future use the
word "religion," as signifying the feelings of love, reverence, or dread with which the human mind is affected by its conceptions of spiritual being; and you
know well how necessary it is, both to the rightness of
our own life, and to the understanding the lives of

others, that we should always keep clearly distinguished our ideas of religion, as thus defined, and of morality, as the law of rightness in human conduct. For there are many religions, but there is only one morality. There are moral and immoral religions, which differ as much in precept as in emotion; but there is only one morality, which has been, is, and must be forever, an instinct in the hearts of all civilized men, as certain and unalterable as their outward bodily form, and which receives from religion neither law, nor peace; but only hope, and felicity.

38. The pure forms or states of religion hitherto known, are those in which a healthy humanity, finding in itself many foibles and sins, has imagined, or been made conscious of, the existence of higher spiritual personality, liable to no such fault or stain; and has been assisted in effort, and consoled in pain, by reference to the will or sympathy of such more pure spirits, whether imagined or real. I am compelled to use these painful latitudes of expression, because no analysis has hitherto sufficed to distinguish accurately, in historical narrative, the difference between impressions resulting from the imagination of the worshiper, and those made, if any, by the actually local and temporary presence of another spirit. For instance, take the vision, which of all others has been since made most frequently the subject of physical representation—the appearance to Ezekiel and St. John of the

four living creatures, which throughout Christendom have been used to symbolize the Evangelists.* Supposing such interpretation just, one of those figures was either the mere symbol to St. John of himself, or it was the power which inspired him manifesting itself in an independent form. Which of these it was, or whether neither of these, but a vision of other powers, or a dream, of which neither the prophet himself knew, nor can any other person yet know, the interpretation, I suppose no modestly-tempered and accurate thinker would now take upon himself to decide. Nor is it therefore anywise necessary for you to decide on that, or any other such question; but it is necessary that you should be bold enough to look every opposing question steadily in its face; and modest enough, having done so, to know when it is too hard for you. But above all things, see that you be modest in your thoughts, for of this one thing we may be absolutely sure, that all our thoughts are but degrees of darkness. And in these days you have to guard against the fatallest darkness of the two opposite Prides: the Pride of Faith, which imagines that the Nature of the Deity can be defined by its convictions; and the Pride of Science, which imagines that the Energy of Deity can be explained by its analysis.

39. Of these, the first, the Pride of Faith, is now, as it has been always, the most deadly, because the

---

* Only the Gospels "IV. Evangelia," according to St. Jerome.

most complacent and subtle ; because it invests every evil passion of our nature with the aspect of an angel of light, and enables the self-love, which might otherwise have been put to wholesome shame, and the cruel carelessness of the ruin of our fellow-men, which might otherwise have been warmed into human love, or at least checked by human intelligence, to congeal themselves into the mortal intellectual disease of imagining that myriads of the inhabitants of the world for four thousand years have been left to wander and perish, many of them everlastingly, in order that, in fullness of time, divine truth might be preached sufficiently to ourselves ; with this farther ineffable mischief for direct result, that multitudes of kindly-disposed, gentle, and submissive persons, who might else by their true patience have alloyed the hardness of the common crowd, and by their activity for good, balanced its misdoing, are withdrawn from all such true service of man, that they may pass the best part of their lives in what they are told is the service of God ; namely, desiring what they cannot obtain, lamenting what they could avoid, and reflecting on what they cannot understand.

40. This, I repeat, is the deadliest; but for you, under existing circumstances, it is becoming daily, almost hourly, the least probable form of pride. That which you have chiefly to guard against consists in the over-valuing of minute though correct discovery ; the

groundless denial of all that seems to you to have been groundlessly affirmed; and the interesting yourselves too curiously in the progress of some scientific minds, which in their judgment of the universe can be compared to nothing so accurately as to the woodworms in the panel of a picture by some great painter, if we may conceive them as tasting with discrimination of the wood, and with repugnance of the color, and declaring that even this unlooked-for and undesirable combination is a normal result of the action of molecular forces.

41. Now, I must very earnestly warn you, in the beginning of my work with you here, against allowing either of these forms of egotism to interfere with your judgment or practice of art. On the one hand, you must not allow the expression of your own favorite religious feelings by any particular form of art to modify your judgment of its absolute merit; nor allow the art itself to become an illegitimate means of deepening and confirming your convictions, by realizing to your eyes what you dimly conceive with the brain; as if the greater clearness of the image were a stronger proof of its truth. On the other hand, you must not allow your scientific habit of trusting nothing but what you have ascertained, to prevent you from appreciating, or at least endeavoring to qualify yourselves to appreciate, the work of the highest faculty of the human mind—its imagination—when it is toil-

ing in the presence of things that cannot be dealt with by any other power.

42. These are both vital conditions of your healthy progress. On the one hand, observe that you do not willfully use the realistic power of art to convince yourselves of historical or theological statements which you cannot otherwise prove; and which you wish to prove. On the other hand, that you do not check your imagination and conscience while seizing the truths of which they alone are cognizant, because you value too highly the scientific interest which attaches to the investigation of second causes.

For instance, it may be quite possible to show the conditions in water and electricity which necessarily produce the craggy outline, the apparently self-contained silvery light, and the sulphurous blue shadow of a thunder cloud, and which separate these from the depth of the golden peace in the dawn of a summer morning. Similarly, it may be possible to show the necessities of structure which groove the fangs and depress the brow of the asp, and which distinguish the character of its head from that of the face of a young girl. But it is the function of the rightly-trained imagination to recognize, in these, and such other relative aspects, the unity of teaching which impresses, alike on our senses and our conscience, the eternal difference between good and evil: and the rule, over the clouds of heaven and over the creatures in the earth, of the same Spirit which teaches to our own hearts the bitterness of death, and strength of love.

43. Now, therefore, approaching our subject in this balanced temper, which will neither resolve to see only what it would desire, nor expect to see only what it can explain, we shall find our inquiry into the relation of art to religion is distinctly threefold; first, we have to ask how far art may have been literally directed by spiritual powers; secondly, how far, if not inspired, it may have been exalted by them; lastly, how far, in any of its agencies, it has advanced the cause of the creeds it has been used to recommend.

44. First: What ground have we for thinking that art has ever been inspired as a message or revelation? What internal evidence is there in the work of great artists of their having been under the authoritative guidance of supernatural powers?

It is true that the answer to so mysterious a question cannot rest alone upon internal evidence; but it is well that you should know what might, from that evidence alone, be concluded. And the more impartially you examine the phenomena of imagination, the more firmly you will be led to conclude that they are the result of the influence of the common and vital, but not, therefore, less divine spirit, of which some portion is given to all living creatures in such manner as may be adapted to their rank in creation; and that everything which men rightly accomplish is indeed done by divine help, but under a consistent law which is never departed from.

The strength of this spiritual life within us may be increased or lessoned by our own conduct; it varies from time to time, as physical strength varies; it is summoned on different occasions by our will, and dejected by our distress, or our sin; but it is always equally human, and equally divine. We are men, and not mere animals, because a special form of it is with us always; we are nobler and baser men, as it is with us more or less; but it is never given to us in any degree which can make us more than men.

45. Observe: I give you this general statement doubtfully, and only as that toward which an impartial reasoner will, I think, be inclined by existing data. But I shall be able to show you, without any doubt, in the course of our studies, that the achievements of art which have been usually looked upon as the results of peculiar inspiration, have been arrived at only through long courses of wisely directed labor, and under the influence of feelings which are common to all humanity.

But of these feelings and powers which in different degrees are common to humanity, you are to note that there are three principal divisions: first, the instincts of construction or melody, which we share with lower animals, and which are in us as native as the instinct of the bee or nightingale; secondly, the faculty of vision, or of dreaming, whether in sleep or in conscious trance, or by voluntary exerted fancy; and lastly, the power of rational inference and collection, of both the laws and forms of beauty.

46. Now the faculty of vision, being closely associated with the innermost spiritual nature, is the one which has by most reasoners been held for the peculiar channel of divine teaching; and it is a fact that great part of purely didactic art has been the record, whether in language, or by linear representation, of actual vision involuntarily received at the moment, though cast on a mental retina blanched by the past course of faithful life. But it is also true that these visions, where most distinctly received, are always—I speak deliberately—*always*, the sign of some mental limitation or derangement; and that the persons who most clearly recognize their value, exaggeratedly estimate it, choosing what they find to be useful, and calling that "inspired," and disregarding what they perceive to be useless, though presented to the visionary by an equal authority.

47. Thus it is probable that no work of art has been more widely didactic than Albert Dürer's engraving, known as the "Knight and Death."* But that is only one of a series of works representing similarly vivid dreams, of which some are uninteresting, except

---

* Standard Series, No. 9.

for the manner of their representation, as the "St. Hubert," and others are unintelligible; some frightful, and wholly unprofitable; so that we find the visionary faculty in that great painter, when accurately examined, to be a morbid influence, abasing his skill more frequently than encouraging it, and sacrificing the greater part of his energies upon vain subjects, two only being produced, in the course of a long life, which are of high didactic value, and both of these capable only of giving sad courage.* Whatever the value of these two, it bears more the aspect of a treasure obtained at great cost of suffering, than of a directly granted gift from heaven.

48. On the contrary, not only the highest, but the most consistent results have been attained in art by men whom the faculty of vision, however strong, was subordinate to that of deliberative design, and tranquilized by a measured, continual, not feverish, but affectionate, observance of the quite unvisionary facts of the surrounding world.

And so far as we can trace the connection of their powers with the moral character of their lives, we shall find that the best art is the work of good, but of not distinctively religious men, who, at least, are conscious of no inspiration, and often so unconscious of their

---

* The meaning of the "Knight and Death," even in this respect, has lately been questioned on good grounds. See note on the plate in Catalogue.

superiority to others, that one of the very greatest of them, deceived by his modesty, has asserted that "all things are possible to well-directed labor."

49. The second question, namely, how far art, if not inspired, has yet been ennobled by religion, I shall not touch upon to-day; for it both requires technical criticism, and would divert you too long from the main question of all—How far religion has been helped by art?

You will find that the operation of formative art (I will not speak to-day of music) the operation of formative art on religious creed is essentially twofold; the realization, to the eyes, of imagined spiritual persons; and the limitation of their imagined presence to certain places. We will examine these two functions of it successively.

50. At first, consider accurately what the agency of art is, in realizing, to the sight, our conceptions of spiritual persons.

For instance. Assume that we believe that the Madonna is always present to hear and answer our prayers. Assume also that this is true. I think that persons in a perfectly honest, faithful, and humble temper would in that case desire only to feel so much of the divine presence as the spiritual power herself chose to make felt; and, above all things, not to think they saw, or knew, anything except what might be truly perceived or known.

But a mind imperfectly faithful, and impatient in its distress, or craving in its dullness for a more distinct and convincing sense of the Divinity, would endeavor to complete, or perhaps we should rather say to contract its conception, into the definite figure of a woman wearing a blue or crimson dress, and having fair features, dark eyes, and gracefully arranged hair.

Suppose, after forming such a conception, that we have the power to realize and preserve it, this image of a beautiful figure with a pleasant expression cannot but have the tendency of afterward leading us to think of the Virgin as present, when she is not actually present, or as pleased with us, when she is not actually pleased; or if we resolutely prevent ourselves from such imagination, nevertheless the existence of the image beside us will often turn our thoughts toward subjects of religion, when otherwise they would have been differently occupied; and, in the midst of other occupations, will familiarize more or less, and even mechanically associate with common or faultful states of mind, the appearance of the supposed divine person.

51. There are thus two distinct operations upon our mind: first, the art makes us believe what we would not otherwise have believed; and secondly, it makes us think of subjects we should not otherwise have thought of, intruding them amid our ordinary thoughts in a confused and familiar manner. We can-

not with any certainty affirm the advantage or the harm of such accidental pieties, for their effect will be very different on different characters: but without any question, the art, which makes us believe what we would not have otherwise believed, is misapplied, and in most instances very dangerously so. Our duty is to believe in the existence of divine, or any other, persons, only upon rational proofs of their existence; and not because we have seen pictures of them. And since the real relations between us and higher spirits are, of all facts concerning our being those which it is most important to know accurately, if we know at all, it is a folly so great as to amount to real, though most unintentional sin, to allow our conceptions of those relations to be modified by our own undisciplined fancy.

52. But now observe, it is here necessary to draw a distinction, so subtle that in dealing with facts it is continually impossible to mark it with precision, yet so vital, that not only your understanding of the power of art, but the working of your minds in matters of primal moment to you, depends on the effort you make to affirm this distinction strongly. The art which realizes a creature of the imagination is only mischievous when that realization is conceived to imply, or does practically induce a belief in, the real existence of the imagined personage, contrary to, or unjustified by the other evidence of its existence. But

if the art only represents the personage on the understanding that its form is imaginary, then the effort at realization is healthful and beneficial.

For instance. I shall place in your standard series a Greek design of Apollo crossing the sea to Delphi, which is an example of one of the highest types of Greek or any other art. So far as that design is only an expression, under the symbol of a human form, of what may be rightly imagined respecting the solar power, the art is right and ennobling; but so far as it conveyed to the Greek the idea of there being a real Apollo, it was mischievous, whether there be, or be not a real Apollo. If there is no real Apollo, then the art was mischievous because it deceived; but if there is a real Apollo, then it was still more mischievous, for it not only began the degradation of the image of that true god into a decoration for niches, and a device for seals; but prevented any true witness being borne to his existence. For if the Greeks, instead of multiplying representations of what they imagined to be the figure of the god, had given us accurate drawings of the heroes and battles of Marathon and Salamis, and had simply told us in plain Greek what evidence they had of the power of Apollo, either through his oracles, his help or chastisement, or by immediate vision, they would have served their religion more truly than by all the vase-paintings and fine statues that ever were buried or adored.

53. Now in this particular instance, and in many other examples of fine Greek art, the two conditions of thought, symbolic and realistic, are mingled; and the art is helpful, as I will hereafter show you, in one function, and in the other so deadly, that I think no degradation of conception of Deity has ever been quite so base as that implied by the designs of Greek vases in the period of decline, say about 250 B.C.

But though among the Greeks it is thus nearly always difficult to say what is symbolic and what realistic, in the range of Christian art, the distinction is clear. In that, a vast division of imaginative work is occupied in the symbolism of virtues, vices, or natural powers or passions; and in the representation of personages who, though nominally real, become in conception symbolic. In the greater part of this work there is no intention of implying the existence of the represented creature; Dürer's "Melencolia" and Giotto's "Justice" are accurately characteristic examples. Now all such art is wholly good and useful when it is the work of good men.

54. Again, there is another division of Christian work in which the persons represented, though nominally real, are treated only as *dramatis-personæ* of a poem, and so presented confessedly as subjects of imagination. All this poetic art is also good when it is the work of good men.

55. There remains only therefore to be considered, as truly religious, the work which definitely implies and modifies the conception of the existence of a real person. There is hardly any great art which entirely belongs to this class; but Raphael's "Madonna della Seggiola" is as accurate a type of it as I can give you; Holbein's *Madonna at Dresden,* the "Madonna di San Sisto," and the *Madonna of Titian's Assumption," all belong mainly to this class, but are removed somewhat from it (as I repeat, nearly all great art is) into the poetical one. It is only the bloody crucifixes and gilded virgins and other such lower forms of imagery (by which, to the honor of the English Church, it has been truly claimed for her, that "she has never appealed to the madness or dullness of her people") which belong to the realistic class in strict limitation, and which properly constitute the type of it.

There is indeed an important school of sculpture in Spain, directed to the same objects, but not demanding at present any special attention. And finally, there is the vigorous and most interesting realistic school of our own, in modern times, mainly known to the public by Holman Hunt's picture the "Light of the World," though, I believe, deriving its first origin from the genius of the painter to whom you owe also the revival of interest, first here in Oxford, and then universally, in the cycle of early English legend—Dante Rossetti.

56. The effect of this realistic art on the religious mind of Europe varies in scope more than any other art power; for in its higher branches it touches the most sincere religious minds, affecting an earnest class of persons who cannot be reached by merely poetical design; while in its lowest, it addresses itself not only to the most vulgar desires for religious excitement, but to the mere thirst for sensation of horror which characterizes the uneducated orders of partially civilized countries; nor merely to the thirst for horror, but to the strange love of death, as such, which has sometimes in Catholic countries showed itself peculiarly by the endeavor to paint the images in the chapels of the Sepulchre so as to look deceptively like corpses. The same morbid instinct has also affected the minds of many among the more imaginative and powerful artists with a feverish gloom which distorts their finest work; and lastly—and this is the worst of all its effects—it has occupied the sensibility of Christian women, universally, in lamenting the sufferings of Christ, instead of preventing those of His people.

57. When any of you next go abroad, observe, and consider the meaning of the sculptures and paintings, which of every rank in art, and in every chapel and cathedral, and by every mountain path, recall the hours, and represent the agonies, of the Passion of Christ: and try to form some estimate of the efforts that have been made by the four art of eloquence,

music, painting, and sculpture, since the twelfth century, to wring out of the hearts of women the last drops of pity that could be excited for this merely physical agony : for the art nearly always dwells on the physical wounds or exhaustion chiefly, and degrades, far more than it animates, the conception of pain.

Then try to conceive the quantity of time, and of excited and thrilling emotion, which have been wasted by the tender and delicate women of Christendom during these last six hundred years, in thus picturing to themselves, under the influence of such imagery, the bodily pain, long since passed, of One Person— which, so far as they indeed conceived it to be sustained by a divine nature, could not for that reason have been less endurable than the agonies of any simple human death by torture: and then try to estimate what might have been the better result, for the righteousness and felicity of mankind, if these same women had been taught the deep meaning of the last words that were ever spoken by their Master to those who had ministered to Him of their substance: "Daughters of Jerusalem, weep not for me, but weep for yourselves, and for your children." If they had but been taught to measure with their pitiful thoughts the tortures of battlefields; the slowly consuming plagues of death in the starving children, and wasted age, of the innumerable desolate those battles left; nay, in our own life of peace, the agony of unnurtured, untaught, unhelped creatures, awaking at the grave's edge to know how they should have lived; and the worse pain of those whose existence, not the ceasing of it, is death; those to whom the cradle was a curse, and for whom the words they cannot hear, "ashes to ashes," are all that they have ever received of benediction. These—you who would fain have wept at His feet, or stood by his cross—these you have always with you, Him you have not always.

58. The wretched in death you have always with you. Yes, and the brave and good in life you have always; these also needing help, though you supposed they had only to help others; these also claiming to be thought for, and remembered. And you will find, if you look into history with this clue, that one of quite the chief reasons for the continual misery of mankind is that they are always divided in their worship between angels or saints, who are out of their sight, and need no help, and proud and evil-minded men, who are too definitely in their sight, and ought not to have their help. And consider how the arts have thus followed the worship of the crowd. You have paintings of saints and angels, innumerable—of petty courtiers, and contemptible or cruel kings, innumerable. Few, how few you have (but these, observe, almost always by great painters) of the best men, or of their actions. But think for yourselves—I have no time now to enter upon the mighty field, nor

imagination enough to guide me beyond the threshold of it—think, what history might have been to us now; nay, what a different history that all of Europe might have become, if it had but been the object both of the people to discern, and of their arts to honor and bear record of the great deeds of their worthiest men. And if, instead of living, as they have always hitherto done, in a hellish cloud of contention and revenge, lighted by fantastic dreams of cloudy sanctities, they had sought to reward and punish justly, wherever reward and punishment were due, but chiefly to reward; and at least rather to bear testimony to the human acts which deserved God's anger or His blessing, than only in presumptuous imagination to display the secrets of Judgment, or the beatitudes of Eternity.

59. Such I conceive generally, though indeed with good arising out of it, for every great evil brings some good in its backward eddies—such I conceive to have been the deadly function of art in its ministry to what, whether in heathen or Christian lands, and whether in the pageantry of words, or colors, or fair forms, is truly, and in the deep sense, to be called idolatry—the serving with the best of our hearts and minds, some dear or sad fantasy which we have made for ourselves, while we disobey the present call of the Master, who is not dead, and who is not now fainting under His cross, but requiring us to take up ours.

60. I pass to the second great function of religious

art, the limitation of the idea of divine presence to particular localities. It is of course impossible within my present limits to touch upon this power of art, as employed on the temples of the gods of various religions; we will examine that on future occasions. To-day, I want only to map out main ideas, and I can do this best by speaking exclusively of this localizing influence as it affects our own faith.

Observe first, that the localization is almost entirely dependent upon human art. You must at least take a stone and set it up for a pillar, if you are to mark the place, so as to know it again, where a vision appeared. A persecuted people, needing to conceal their places of worship, may perform every religious ceremony first under one crag of the hill-side, and then under another, without invalidating the sacredness of the rites or sacraments thus administered. It is, therefore, we all acknowledge, inessential that a particular spot should be surrounded with a ring of stones, or inclosed within walls of a certain style of architecture, and so set apart as the only place where such ceremonies may be properly performed; and it is thus less by any direct appeal to experience or to reason, but in consequence of the effect upon our senses produced by the architecture, that we receive the first strong impressions of what we afterward contend for as absolute truth. I particularly wish you to notice how it is always by help of human art that such a result is attained, because, remember always, I am neither disputing nor asserting the truth of any theological doctrine—that is not my province—I am only questioning the expediency of enforcing that doctrine by the help of architecture. Put a rough stone for an altar under the hawthorn on a village green—separate a portion of the green itself with an ordinary paling from the rest—then consecrate, with whatever form you choose, the space of grass you have inclosed, and meet within the wooden fence as often as you desire to pray or preach; yet you will not easily fasten an impression in the minds of the villagers, that God inhabits the space of grass inside the fence, and does not extend His presence to the common beyond it; and that the daisies and violets on one side of the railing are holy, on the other profane. But, instead of a wooden fence, build a wall; pave the interior space; roof it over, so as to make it comparatively dark, and you may persuade the villagers with ease that you have built a house which Deity inhabits, or that you have become, in the old French phrase, a "*logeur du Bon Dieu.*"

61. And farther, though I have no desire to introduce any question as to the truth of what we thus architecturally teach, I would desire you most strictly to determine what is intended to be taught.

Do not think I underrate—I am among the last men living who would underrate—the importance of the sentiments connected with their church to the population of a pastoral village. I admit, in its fullest extent, the moral value of the scene, which is almost always one of perfect purity and peace; and of the sense of supernatural love and protection, which fills and surrounds the low aisles and homely porch. But the question I desire earnestly to leave with you is, whether all the earth ought not to be peaceful and pure, and the acknowledgment of the divine protection as universal, as its reality? That in a mysterious way the presence of Deity is vouchsafed where it is sought, and withdrawn where it is forgotten, must of course be granted as the first postulate in the inquiry: but the point for our decision is just this, whether it ought always to be sought in one place only, and forgotten in every other.

It may be replied, that since it is impossible to consecrate the entire space of the earth, it is better thus to secure a portion of it than none: but surely, if so, we ought to make some effort to enlarge the favored ground, and even look forward to a time when in English villages there may be a God's acre tenanted by the living, not the dead; and when we shall rather look with aversion and fear to the remnant of ground that is set apart as profane, than with reverence to a narrow portion of it enclosed as holy.

62. But now, farther. Suppose it be admitted that by inclosing ground with walls, and performing certain ceremonies there habitually, some kind of

sanctity is indeed secured within that space—still the question remains open whether it be advisable for religious purposes to decorate the enclosure. For separation the mere walls would be enough. What is the purpose of your decoration?

Let us take an instance—the most notable with which I am acquainted, the Cathedral of Chartres. You have there the most splendid colored glass, and the richest sculpture, and the grandest proportions of building, united to produce a sensation of pleasure and awe. We profess that this is to honor the Deity ; or in other words, that it is pleasing to Him that we should delight our eyes with blue and golden colors, and solemnize our spirits by the sight of large stones laid one on another, and ingeniously carved.

63. I do not think that it can be doubted that it *is* pleasing to Him when we do this; for He has Himself prepared for us, nearly every morning and evening, windows painted with divine art, in blue and gold and vermilion; windows lighted from within by the luster of that heaven which we may assume, at least with more certainty than any consecrated ground, to be one of His dwelling-places. Again, in every mountain side, and cliff of rude sea-shore, He has heaped stones one upon another of greater magnitude than those of Chartres Cathedral, and sculptured them with floral ornament—surely not less sacred because living?

64. Must it not then be only because we love our own work better than His, that we respect the lucent glass, but not the lucent clouds; that we weave embroidered robes with ingenious fingers, and make bright the gilded vaults we have beautifully ordained—while yet we have not considered the heavens the work of His fingers; nor the stars of the strange vault which He has ordained. And do we dream that by carving fonts and lifting pillars in His honor, who cuts the way of the rivers among the rocks, and at whose reproof the pillars of the earth are astonished, we shall obtain pardon for the dishonor done to the hills and streams by which He has appointed our dwelling-place —for the infection of their sweet air with poison—for the burning up of their tender grass and flowers with fire, and for spreading such a shame of mixed luxury and misery over our native land, as if we labored only that, at least here in England, we might be able to give the lie to the song, whether of the Cherubim above, or Church beneath—" Holy, holy, Lord God of all creatures; Heaven—*and Earth*—are full of Thy glory?"

65. And how much more there is that I long to say to you; and how much, I hope, that you would like to answer to me, or to question me of! But I can say no more to-day. We are not, I trust at the end of our talks or thoughts together; but, if it were so, and I never spoke to you more, this that I have

said to you I should have been glad to have been permitted to say; and this, farther, which is the sum of it—That we *may* have splendor of art again, and with that, we may truly praise and honor our Maker, and with that set forth the beauty and holiness of all that He has made: but only after we have striven with our whole hearts first to sanctify the temple of the body and spirit of every child that has no roof to cover its head from the cold, and no walls to guard its soul from corruption, in this our English land.

One word more.

What I have suggested hitherto, respecting the relations of Art to Religion, you must receive throughout as merely motive of thought; though you must have well seen that my own convictions were established finally on some of the points in question. But I must in conclusion, tell you something that I *know*—which if you truly labor, you will one day know also; and which I trust some of you will believe, now.

During the minutes in which you have been listening to me, I suppose that almost at every other sentence those whose habit of mind has been one of veneration for established forms and faiths, must have been in dread that I was about to say, or in pang of regret at my having said, what seemed to them an irreverent or reckless word touching vitally important things.

So far from this being the fact, it is just because the feelings that I most desire to cultivate in your minds are those of reverence and admiration, that I am so earnest to prevent you from being moved to either by trivial or false semblances. *This* is the thing which I KNOW—and which, if you labor faithfully, you shall know also—that in reverence is the chief joy and power of life—reverence for what is pure and bright in your own youth; for what is true and tried in the age of others; for all that is gracious among the living, great among the dead, and marvelous in the powers that cannot die.

LECTURE III.

THE RELATION OF ART TO MORALS.

66. You probably recollect that, in the beginning of my last lecture, it was stated that fine art had, and could have, but three functions: the enforcing of the religious sentiments of men, the perfecting their ethical state, and the doing them material service. We have to day to examine the mode of its action in the second power, that of perfecting the morality or ethical state of men.

Perfecting, observe—not producing.

You must have the right moral state first, or you cannot have the art. But when the art is once obtained, its reflected action, enhances and completes the moral state out of which it arose, and, above all, communicates the exaltation to other minds which are already morally capable of the like.

67. For instance, take the art of singing, and the simplest perfect master of it (up to the limits of his nature) whom can you find—a skylark. From him you may learn what it is to "sing for joy." You must get the moral state first, the pure gladness, then

give it finished expression; and it is perfected in itself, and made communicable to other creatures capable of such joy. But it is incommunicable to those who are not prepared to receive it.

Now, all right human song is, similarly, the finished expression, by art, of the joy or grief of noble persons, for right causes. And accurately in proportion to the rightness of the cause, and purity of the emotion, is the possibility of the fine art. A maiden may sing of her lost love, but a miser cannot sing of his lost money. And with absolute precision from highest to lowest, the fineness of the possible art is an index of the moral purity and majesty of the emotion it expresses. You may test it practically at any instant. Question with yourselves respecting any feeling that has taken strong possession of your mind, "Could this be sung by a master, and sung nobly, with a true melody and art?" Then it is a right feeling. Could it not be sung at all, or only sung ludicrously? It is a base one. And that is so in all the arts; so that with mathematical precision, subject to no error or exception, the art of a nation, so far as it exists, is an exponent of its ethical state.

68. An exponent, observe, and exalting influence; but not the root or cause. You cannot paint or sing yourselves into being good men; you must be good men before you can either paint or sing, and then the color and sound will complete in you all that is best.

And this it was that I called upon you to hear, saying, "listen to me at least now," in the first lecture, namely, that no art-teaching could be of use to you, but would rather be harmful, unless it was grafted on something deeper than all art. For indeed not only with this, of which it is my function to show you the laws, but much more with the art of all men, which you came here chiefly to learn, that of language, the chief vices of education have arisen from the one great fallacy of supposing that noble language is a communicable trick of grammar and accent, instead of simply the careful expression of right thought. All the virtues of language are, in their roots, moral; it becomes accurate if the speaker desires to be true; clear, if he speaks with sympathy and a desire to be intelligible; powerful, if he has earnestness; pleasant if he has sense of rythm and order. There are no other virtues of language producible by art than these: but let me mark more deeply for an instant the significance of one of them. Language, I said, is only clear when it is sympathetic. You can, in truth, understand a man's word only by understanding his temper. Your own word is also as of an unknown tongue to him unless he understands yours. And it is this which makes the art of language, if any one is to be chosen separately from the rest, that which is fittest for the instrument of a gentleman's education. To teach the meaning of a word thoroughly is to teach the nature of the spirit that coined it; the secret of language is the secret of sympathy, and its full charm is possible only to the gentle. And thus the principles of beautiful speech have all been fixed by sincere and kindly speech. On the laws which have been determined by sincerity, false speech, apparently beautiful, may afterward be constructed ; but all such utterance, whether in oration or poetry, is not only without permanent power, but it is destructive of the principles it has usurped. So long as no words are uttered but in faithfulness, so long the art of language goes on exalting itself; but the moment it is shaped and chiseled on external principles, it falls into frivolity, and perishes. And this truth would have been long ago manifest, had it not been that in periods of advanced academical science there is always a tendency to deny the sincerity of the first masters of language. Once learn to write gracefully in the manner of an ancient author, and we are apt to think that he also wrote in the manner of some one else. But no noble nor right style was ever yet founded but out of a sincere heart.

No man is worth reading to form your style, who does not mean what he says ; nor was any great style ever invented but by some man who meant what he said. Find out the beginner of a great manner of writing, and you have also found the declarer of some true facts or sincere passions; and your whole method of reading will thus be quickened, for, being sure that your author really meant what he said, you will be much more careful to ascertain what it is that he means.

69. And of yet greater importance is it deeply to know that every beauty possessed by the language of a nation is significant of the innermost laws of its being. Keep the temper of the people stern and manly; make their associations grave, courteous, and for worthy objects; occupy them in just deeds; and their tongue must needs be a grand one. Nor is it possible, therefore—observe the necessary reflected action—that any tongue should be a noble one, of which the words are not so many trumpet-calls to action. All great languages invariably utter great things, and command them; they cannot be mimicked but by obedience; the breath of them is inspiration because it is not only vocal, but vital; and you can only learn to speak as these men spoke, by becoming what these men were.

70. Now for direct confirmation of this, I want you to think over the relation of expression to character in two great masters of the absolute art of language, Virgil and Pope. You are perhaps surprised at the last name; and indeed you have in English much higher grasp and melody of language from more passionate minds, but you have nothing else, in its range, so perfect. I name, therefore, these two men, because they are the two most accomplished

Artists, merely as such, whom I know in literature; and because I think you will be afterward interested in investigating how the infinite grace in the words of the one, the severity in those of the other, and the precision in those of both, arise wholly out of the moral elements of their minds—out of the deep tenderness in Virgil which enabled him to write the stories of Nisus and Lausus; and the serene and just benevolence which placed Pope, in his theology, two centuries in advance of his time, and enabled him to sum the law of noble life in two lines which, so far as I know, are the most complete, the most concise, and the most lofty expression of moral temper existing in English words:

> "Never elated, while one man's oppress'd;
> Never dejected, while another's bless'd.'

I wish you also to remember these lines of Pope, and and to make yourselves entirely masters of his system of ethics; because, putting Shakespeare aside as rather the world's than ours, I hold Pope to be the most perfect representative we have, since Chaucer, of the true English mind; and I think the Dunciad is the most absolutely chiseled and monumental work "exacted" in our country. You will find, as you study Pope, that he has expressed for you, in the strictest language and within the briefest limits every law of art, of criticism, of economy, of policy, and, finally, of a benevolence, humble, rational, and resigned, contented with its allotted share of life, and trusting the problem of its salvation to Him in whose hand lies that of the universe.

71. And now I pass to the arts with which I have special concern, in which, though the facts are exactly the same, I shall have more difficulty in proving my assertion, because very few of us are as cognizant of the merit of painting as we are of that of language; and I can only show you whence that merit springs from, after having thoroughly shown you in what it consists. But, in the meantime, I have simply to tell you, that the manual arts are as accurate exponents of ethical state, as other modes of expression; first, with absolute precision, of that of the workman, and then with precision disguised by many distorting influences, of that of the nation to which he belongs.

And, first, they are a perfect exponent of the mind of the workman; but, being so, remember, if the mind be great or complex, the art is not an easy book to read; for we must ourselves possess all the mental characters of which we are to read the signs. No man can read the evidence of labor who is not himself laborious, for he does not know what the work cost; nor can he read the evidence of true passion if he is not passionate; nor of gentleness if he is not gentle: and the most subtle signs of fault and weakness of character, he can only judge by having had the same faults to fight with. I myself, for instance, know impatient work, and tired work, better than most critics, because I am myself always impatient, and often tired : so also, the patient and indefatigable touch of a mighty master becomes more wonderful to me than to others. Yet, wonderful in no mean measure it will be to you all, when I make it manifest; and as soon as we begin our real work, and you have learned what it is to draw a true line, I shall be able to make manifest to you—and undisputably so—that the day's work of a man like Mantegna or Paul Veronese consists of an unfaltering, uninterrupted succession of movements of the hand more precise than those of the finest fencer; the pencil leaving one point and arriving at another, not only with unerring precision at the extremity of the line, but with an unerring, and yet varied course—sometimes over spaces a foot or more in extent—yet a course so determined everywhere that either of these men could, and Veronese often does, draw a finished profile, or any other portion of the contour of a face, with one line, not afterward changed. Try, first, to realize to yourselves the muscular precision of that action, and the intellectual strain of it; for the movement of a fencer is perfect in practised monotony; but the movement of the hand of a great painter is at every instant governed by direct and new intention. Then imagine that muscular firmness and subtlety, and the instantaneously selective and ordinant energy or the brain, sustained all day long, not only without fatigue, but with a visible joy in the exertion, like that which an eagle seems to take in the wave of his wings; and this all life long, and through long life, not only without failure of power, but with visible increase of it, until the actually organic changes of old age. And then consider, so far as you know anything of physiology, what sort of an ethical state of body and mind that means—ethic through ages past! What fineness of race there must be to get it, what exquisite balance and symmetry of the vital powers! And then, finally determine for yourselves whether a manhood like that is consistent with any viciousness of soul, with any mean anxiety, any gnawing lust, any wretchedness of spite or remorse, any consciousness of rebellion against law of God or man, or any actual, though unconscious, violation of even the least law to which obedience is essential for the glory of life, and the pleasing of its Giver.

72. It is, of course, true that many of the strong masters had deep faults of character, but their faults always show in their work. It is true that some could not govern their passions; if so, they died young, or they painted ill when old. But the greater part of our misapprehension in the whole matter is from our not having well known who the great painters were, and taking delight in the petty skill that was bred in

the fumes of the taverns of the north, instead of theirs who breathed empyreal air, sons of the morning, underneath the woods of Assisi and the crags of Cadore.

73. It is true, however also, as I have pointed out long ago, that the strong masters fall into two great divisions, one leading simple and natural lives, the other restrained in a Puritanism of the worship of beauty; and these two manners of life you may recognize in a moment by their work. Generally the naturalists are the strongest; but there are two of the Puritans, whose work if I can succeed in making clearly understandable to you during my three years here, it is all I need care to do. But of these two Puritans one I cannot name to you, and the other I at present will not. One I cannot, for no one knows his name, except the baptismal one, Bernard, or "dear little Bernard"—Bernardino, called, from his birthplace (Luino, on the lago Maggiore), Bernard of Luino. The other is a Venetian, of whom many of you probably have never heard, and of whom, through me, you shall not hear until I have tried to get some picture by him over to England.

74. Observe then, this Puritanism in the worship of beauty, though sometimes weak, is always honorable and amiable, and the exact reverse of the false Puritanism, which consists in the dread or disdain of beauty. And in order to treat my subject rightly, I ought to

proceed from the skill of art to the choice of its subject, and show you how the moral temper of the workman is shown by his seeking lovely forms and thoughts to express, as well as by the force of his hand in expression. But I need not now urge this part of the proof on you, because you are already, I believe, sufficiently conscious of the truth in this matter, and also I have already said enough of it in my writings; whereas I have not at all said enough of the infallibleness of fine technical work as a proof of every other good power. And indeed it was long before I myself understood the true meaning of the pride of the greatest men in their mere execution, shown, for a permanent lesson to us, in the stories which, whether true or not, indicate with absolute accuracy the general conviction of great artists; the stories of the contest of Apelles and Protogenes in a line only (of which I can promise you, you shall know the meaning to some purpose in a little while)—the story of the circle of Giotto, and especially, which you may perhaps not have observed, the expression of Dürer in his inscription on the drawings sent him by Raphael. "These figures," he says, "Raphael drew and sent to Albert Dürer in Nürnberg, to show him"—what? Not his invention, nor his beauty of expression, but "*sein Hand zu weisen*," "to show him his *hand*." And you will find, as you examine farther, that all inferior artists are continually trying to escape from the necessity of sound work, and either indulging themselves in their delights in subject, or pluming themselves on their noble motives for attempting what they cannot perform (and observe, by the way, that a great deal of what is mistaken for conscientious motive is nothing but a very pestilent, because very subtle, condition of vanity); whereas the great men always understand at once that the first morality of a painter, as of everybody else, is to know his business; and so earnest are they in this, that many, whose lives you would think, by the results of their work, had been passed in strong emotion, have in reality subdued themselves, though capable of the very strongest passions, into a calm as absolute as that of a deeply sheltered mountain lake, which reflects every agitation of the clouds in the sky, and every change of the shadows on the hills, but is itself motionless.

75. Finally, you must remember that great obscurity has been brought upon the truth in this matter by the want of integrity and simplicity in our modern life. I mean integrity in the Latin sense, wholeness. Everything is broken up, and mingled in confusion, both in our habits and thoughts; besides being in great part imitative: so that you not only cannot tell what a man is, but sometimes you cannot tell whether he *is*, at all!—whether you have indeed to do with a spirit, or only with an echo. And thus the same inconsistencies appear now, between the work of artists

of merit and their personal characters, as those which you find continually disappointing expectation in the the lives of men of modern literary power—the same conditions of society having obscured or misdirected the best qualities of the imagination, both in our literature and art. Thus there is no serious question with any of us as to the personal character of Dante and Giotto, of Shakespeare and Holbein; but we pause timidly in the attempt to analyze the moral laws of the art skill in recent poets, novelists, and painters.

76. Let me assure you once for all, that as you grow older, if you enable yourselves to distinguish by the truth of your own lives, what is true in those of other men you will gradually perceive that all good has its origin in good, never in evil; that the fact of either literature or painting being truly fine of their kind, whatever their mistaken aim or partial error, is proof of their noble origin: and that, if there is indeed sterling value in the thing done, it has come of a sterling worth in the soul that did it, however alloyed or defiled by conditions of sin which are sometimes more appalling or more strange than those which all may detect in their own hearts, because they are part of a personality altogether larger than ours, and as far beyond our judgment in its darkness as beyond our following in its light. And it is sufficient warning against what some might dread as the probable effect of such a conviction on your own minds, namely, that you might permit

yourselves in the weaknesses which you imagined to be allied to genius, when they took the form of personal temptations—it is surely, I say, sufficient warning against so mean a folly, to discern, as you may with little pains, that, of all human existences, the lives of men of that distorted and tainted nobility of intellect are probably the most miserable.

77. I pass to the second, and for us the more practically important question, What is the effect of noble art upon other men; what has it done for national morality in time past; and what effect is the extended knowledge or possession of it likely to have upon us now? And here we are at once met by the facts, which are as gloomy as indisputable, that, while many peasant populations, among whom scarcely the rudest practice of art has ever been attempted, have lived in comparative innocence, honor, and happiness, the worst foulness and cruelty of savage tribes have been frequently associated with fine ingenuities of decorative design; also, that no people has ever attained the higher stages of art skill, except at a period of its civilization which was sullied by frequent, violent, and even monstrous crime; and lastly, that the attaining of perfection in art power, has been hitherto, in every nation, the accurate signal of the beginning of its ruin.

78. Respecting which phenomena, observe first, that although good never springs out of evil, it is de-

veloped to its highest by contention with evil. There are some groups of peasantry, in far away nooks of Christian countries who are nearly as innocent as lambs; but the morality which gives power to art is the morality of men, not of cattle.

Secondly, the virtues of the inhabitants of many country districts are apparent, not real; their lives are indeed artless, but not innocent; and it is only the monotony of circumstances, and the absence of temptation, which prevent the exhibition of evil passions not less real because often dormant, nor less foul because shown only in petty faults, or inactive malignities.

79. But you will observe also that *absolute* artlessness, to men in any kind of moral health, is impossible; they have always, at least, the art by which they live —agriculture or seamanship; and in these industries, skillfully practised, you will find the law of their moral training; while, whatever the adversity of circumstances, every rightly-minded peasantry, such as that of Sweden, Denmark, Bavaria, or Switzerland, has associated with its needful industry a quite studied school of pleasurable art in dress; and generally also in song, and simple domestic architecture.

80. Again, I need not repeat to you here what I endeavored to explain in the first lecture in the book I called " The Two Paths," respecting the arts of savage races: but I may now note briefly that such arts are the result of an intellectual activity which has

found no room to expand, and which the tyranny of nature or of man has condemned to disease through arrested growth. And where neither Christianity, nor any other religion conveying some moral help, has reached, the animal energy of such races necessarily flames into ghastly conditions of evil, and the grotesque or frightful forms assumed by their art are precisely indicative of their distorted moral nature.

81. But the truly great nations nearly always begin from a race possessing this imaginative power; and for some time their progress is very slow, and their state not one of innocence, but of feverish and faultful animal energy. This is gradually subdued and exalted into bright human life; the art instinct purifying itself with the rest of the nature, until social perfectness is nearly reached; and then comes the period when conscience and intellect are so highly developed, that new forms of error begin in the inability to fulfill the demands of the one, or to answer the doubts of the other. Then the wholeness of the people is lost; all kinds of hypocrisies and oppositions of science devolop themselves; their faith is questioned on one side, and compromised with on the other; wealth commonly increases at the same period to a destructive extent; luxury follows; and the ruin of the nation is then certain; while the arts, all this time, are simply, as I said at first, the exponents of each phase of its moral state, and no more control it in its politi-

cal career than the gleam of the firefly guides its oscillation. It is true that their most splendid results are usually obtained in the swiftness of the power which is hurrying to the precipice; but to lay the charge of the catastrophe to the art by which it is illumined, is to find a cause for the cataract in the hues of its iris. It is true that the colossal vices belonging to periods of great national wealth (for wealth, you will find, is the real root of all evil) can turn every good gift and skill of nature or of man to evil purpose. If, in such times, fair pictures have been misused, how much more fair realities? And if Miranda is immoral to Caliban is that Miranda's fault?

82. And I could easily go on to trace for you what at the moment I speak, is signified, in our own national character, by the forms of art, and unhappily also by the forms of what is not art, but $\dot{\alpha}\tau\epsilon\chi\nu\iota\alpha$, that exist among us. But the more important question is, What *will* be signified by them; what is there in us now of worth and strength which, under our new and partly accidental impulse toward formative labor, may be by that expressed, and by that fortified?

Would it not be well to know this? Nay, irrespective of all future work, is it not the first thing we should want to know, what stuff we are made of—how far we are $\dot{\alpha}\gamma\alpha\theta o\iota$ or $\kappa\alpha\kappa o\iota$—good, or good for nothing? We may all know that, each of ourselves, easily enough, if we like to put one grave question well home.

83. Supposing it were told any of you by a physician whose word you could not but trust, that you had not more than seven days to live. And suppose also that, by the manner of your education it had happened to you, as it has happened to many, never to have heard of any future state, or not to have credited what you heard; and therefore that you had to face this fact of the approach of death in its simplicity: fearing no punishment for any sin that you might have before committed, or in the coming days might determine to commit; and having similarly no hope of reward for past, or yet possible, virtue; nor even of any consciousness whatever to be left to you, after the seventh day had ended, either of the results of your acts to those whom you loved, or of the feelings of any survivors toward you. Then the manner in which you would spend the seven days is an exact measure of the morality of your nature.

84. I know that some of you, and I believe the greater number of you, would, in such a case, spend the granted days entirely as you ought. Neither in numbering the errors, or deploring the pleasures of the past; nor in grasping at vile good in the present, nor vainly lamenting the darkness of the future; but in instant and earnest execution of whatever it might be possible for you to accomplish in the time, in setting your affairs in order, and in providing for the future comfort, and—so far as you might by any message or

record of yourself, for the consolation—of those whom you loved, and by whom you desired to be remembered, not for your good, but for theirs. How far you might fail through human weakness, in shame for the past, despair at the little that could in the remnant of life be accomplished, or the intolerable pain of broken affection, would depend wholly on the degree in which your nature had been depressed or fortified by the manner of your past life. But I think there are few of you who would not spend those last days better than all that had preceded them.

85. If you look accurately through the records of the lives that have been most useful to humanity, you will find that all that has been done best, has been done so; that to the clearest intellects and highest souls—to the true children of the father, with whom a thousand years are as one day, their poor seventy years are but as seven days. The removal of the shadow of death from them to an uncertain, but always narrow, distance, never takes away from them their intuition of its approach; the extending to them of a few hours more or less of light abates not their acknowledgement of the infinitude that must remain to be known beyond their knowledge—done beyond their deeds; the unprofitableness of their momentary service is wrought in a magnificent despair, and their very honor is bequeathed by them for the joy of others, as they lie down to their rest, regarding for themselves the voice of men no more

86. The best things, I repeat to you, have been done thus, and therefore, sorrowfully. But the greatest part of the good work of the world is done either in pure and unvexed instinct of duty, "I have stubbed Thornaby waste," or else, and better, it is cheerful and helpful doing of what the hand finds to do, in surety that at evening time, whatsoever is right, the Master will give. And that it be worthily done, depends wholly on that ultimate quantity of worth which you can measure, each in himself, by the test I have just given you. For that test, observe, will mark to you the precise force, first of your absolute courage, and then of the energy in you for the right ordering of things, and the kindly dealing with persons. You have cut away from these two instincts every selfish or common motive, and left nothing but the energies of Order and of Love.

87. Now, where those two roots are set, all the other powers and desires find right nourishment, and become to their own utmost, helpful to others and pleasurable to ourselves. And so far as those two springs of action are not in us, all other powers become corrupt or dead; even the love of truth, apart from these, hardens into an insolent and cold avarice of knowledge, which unused, is more vain than unused gold.

88. These, then, are the two essential instincts of humanity: The love of Order and the love of Kindness. By the love of order the moral energy is to deal

with the earth, and to dress it, and keep it; and with all rebellious and dissolute forces in lower creatures, or in ourselves. By the love of doing kindness it is to deal rightly with all surrounding life. And then, grafted on these, we are to make every other passion perfect; so that they may every one have full strength and yet be absolutely under control.

89. Every one must be strong, every one perfect, every one obedient as a war horse. And it is among the most beautiful pieces of mysticism to which eternal truth is attached, that the chariot race, which Plato uses as an image of moral government, and which is indeed the most perfect type of it in any visible skill of men, should have been made by the Greeks the continual subject of their best poetry and best art. Nevertheless, Plato's use of it is not altogether true. There is no black horse in the chariot of the soul. One of the driver's worst faults is in starving his horses; another, in not breaking them early enough; but they are all good. Take, for example, one usually thought of as wholly evil—that of anger, leading to vengeance. I believe it to be quite one of the crowning wickednesses of this age that we have starved and chilled our faculty of indignation, and neither desire nor dare to punish crimes justly. We have taken up the benevolent idea, forsooth, that justice is to be preventive instead of vindictive; and we imagine that we are to punish, not in anger, but in ex-

pediency; not that we may give deserved pain to the person in fault, but that we may frighten other people from committing the same fault. The beautiful theory of this non-vindictive justice is, that having convicted a man of a crime worthy of death, we entirely pardon the criminal, restore him to his place in our affection and esteem, and then hang him, not as a malefactor, but as a scarecrow. That is the theory. And the practice is, that we send a child to prison for a month for stealing a handful of walnuts, for fear that other children should come to steal more of our walnuts. And we do not punish a swindler for ruining a thousand families, because we think swindling is a wholesome excitement to trade.

90. But all true justice is vindictive to vice as it is rewarding to virtue. Only—and herein it is distinguished from personal revenge—it is vindictive of the wrong done, not of the wrong done to *us*. It is the national expression of deliberate anger, as of deliberate gratitude; it is not exemplary, or even corrective, but essentially retributive; it is the absolute art of measured recompense, giving honor where honor is due, and shame where shame is due, and joy where joy is due, and pain where pain is due. It is neither educational, for men are to be educated by wholesome habit, not by rewards and punishments; nor is it preventive, for it is to be executed without regard to any consequences; but only for righteousness' sake, a righteous nation

does judgment and justice. But in this, as in all other instances, the rightness of the secondary passion depends on its being grafted on those two primary instincts, the love of order and of kindness, so that indignation itself is against the wounding of love. Do you think the μῆνις Ἀχιλῆος came of a hard heart in Achilles, or the "*Pallas te hoc vulnere, Pallas,*" of a hard heart in Anchises' son?

91. And now, if with this clue through the labyrinth of them, you remember the course of the arts of great nations, you will perceive that whatever has prospered, and become lovely, had its beginning—for no other was possible—in the love of order in material things associated with true δικαιοσύνη, and the desire of beauty in material things, which is associated with true affection, *charitas*; and with the innumerable conditions of true gentleness expressed by the different uses of the words χάρις and *gratia*. You will find that this love of beauty is an essential part of all healthy human nature, and though it can long co-exist with states of life in many other respects unvirtuous, it is itself wholly good—the direct adversary of envy, avarice, mean worldly care, and especially of cruelty. It entirely perishes when these are willfully indulged ; and the men in whom it has been most strong have always been compassionate, and lovers of justice, and the earliest discerners and declarers of things conducive to the happiness of mankind.

92. Nearly every important truth respecting the love of beauty in its familiar relations to human life was mythically expressed by the Greeks in their various accounts of the parentage and offices of the Graces. But one fact, the most vital of all, they could not in its fullness perceive, namely, that the intensity of other perceptions of beauty is exactly commensurate with the imaginative purity of the passion of love, and with the singleness of its devotion. They were not fully conscious of, and could not therefore either mythically or philosophically express, the deep relation within themselves between their power of perceiving beauty, and the honor of domestic affection which found their sternest themes of tragedy in the infringement of its laws—which made the rape of Helen the chief subject of their epic poetry, and which fastened their clearest symbolism of resurrection on the story of Alcestis. Unhappily, the subordinate position of their most revered women, and the partial corruption of feeling toward them by the presence of certain other singular states of inferior passion which it is as difficult as grievous to analyze, arrested the ethical as well as the formative progress of the Greek mind; and it was not until after an interval of nearly two thousand years of various error and pain, that, partly as the true reward of Christian warfare nobly sustained through centuries of trial, and partly as the visionary culmination of the faith which saw in a maiden's purity the link between

God and her race, the highest and holiest strength of mortal love was reached; and, together with it, in the song of Dante, and the painting of Bernard of Luino and his fellows, the perception, and embodiment forever of whatsoever things are pure, whatsoever things are lovely, whatsoever things are of good report; that, if there be any virtue, and if there be any praise, men might think on those things.

93. You probably observed the expression I used a moment ago, the *imaginative* purity of the passion of love. I have not yet spoken, nor is it possible for me to-day to speak adequately, of the moral power of the imagination; but you may for yourselves enough discern its nature merely by comparing the dignity of the relations between the sexes, from their lowest level in moths or mollusca, through the higher creatures in whom they become a domestic influence and law, up to the love of pure men and women; and, finally, to the ideal love which animated chivalry. Throughout this vast ascent it is the gradual increase of the imaginative faculty which exalts and enlarges the authority of the passion until, at its height, it is the bulwark of patience, the tutor of honor, and the perfectness of praise.

94. You will find farther, that as of love, so of all the other passions, the right government and exaltation begins in that of the imagination, which is lord over them. For to *subdue* the passions, which is thought

so often to be the sum of duty respecting them, is possible enough to a proud dullness; but to *excite* them rightly, and make them strong for good, is the work of the unselfish imagination. It is constantly said that human nature is heartless. Do not believe it. Human nature is kind and generous; but it is narrow and blind; and can only with difficulty conceive anything but what it immediately sees and feels. People would instantly care for others as well as themselves if only they could *imagine* others as well as themselves. Let a child fall into the river before the roughest man's eyes; he will usually do what he can to get it out, even at some risk to himself; and all the town will triumph in the saving of one little life. Let the same man be shown that hundreds of children are dying of fever for want of some sanitary measure which it will cost him trouble to urge, and he will make no effort; and probably all the town would resist him if he did. So, also, the lives of many deserving women are passed in a succession of petty anxieties about themselves, and gleaning of minute interests and mean pleasures in their immediate circle, because they are never taught to make any effort to look beyond it; or to know anything about the mighty world in which their lives are fading, like blades of bitter grass in fruitless fields.

95. I had intended to enlarge on this—and yet more on the kingdom which every man holds in his

conceptive faculty, to be peopled with active thoughts and lovely presences, or left waste for the springing up of those dark desires and dreams of which it is written that "every imagination of the thoughts of man's heart is evil continually." True, and a thousand times true it is, that here at least, "greater is he that ruleth his spirit, than he that taketh a city." But this you can partly follow out for yourselves without help, partly we must leave it for future inquiry. I press to the conclusion which I wish to leave with you, that all you can rightly do, or honorably become depends on the government of these two instincts of order and kindness, by this great imaginative faculty, which gives you inheritance of the past, grasp of the present, authority over the future. Map out the spaces of your possible lives by its help; measure the range of their possible agency! On the walls and towers of this your fair city, there is not an ornament of which the first origin may not be traced back to the thoughts of men who died two thousand years ago. Whom will *you* be governing by your thoughts, two thousand years hence? Think of it, and you will find that so far from art being immoral, little else except art is moral; that life without industry is guilt, and industry without art is brutality; and for the words "good" and "wicked" used of men, you may almost substitute the words "makers" or "destroyers." Far the greater part of the seeming prosperity of the world is, so far as our present knowledge extends, vain : wholly useless for any kind of good, but having assigned to it a certain inevitable sequence of destruction and of sorrow. Its stress is only the stress of wandering storm; its beauty the hectic of plague: and what is called the history of mankind is too often the record of the whirlwind, and the map of the spreading of the leprosy. But underneath all that, or in narrow spaces of dominion in the midst of it, the work of every man, "*qui non accepit in vanitatem animam suam*" endures and prospers; a small remnant or green bud of it prevailing at last over evil. And though faint with sickness, and encumbered in ruin, the true workers redeem inch by inch the wilderness into garden ground; by the help of their joined hands the order of all things is surely sustained and vitally expanded, and although with strange vacillation, in the eyes of the watcher, the morning cometh, and also the night, there is no hour of human existence that does not draw on toward the perfect day.

96. And perfect the day shall be, when it is of all men understood that the beauty of holiness must be in labor as well as in rest. Nay, *more*, if it may be, in labor; in our strength, rather than in our weakness; and in the choice of what we shall work for through the six days, and may know to be good at their evening time, than in the choice of what we pray for on the seventh, of reward or repose. With the multitude

that keep holiday, we may perhaps sometimes vainly have gone up to the house of the Lord, and vainly there asked for what we fancied would be mercy; but for the few who labor as their Lord would have them the mercy needs no seeking, and their wide home no hallowing. Surely goodness and mercy shall *follow* them *all* the days of their life; and they shall dwell in the house of the Lord—FOREVER.

LECTURE IV.

THE RELATION OF ART TO USE.

97. Our subject of inquiry to-day, you will remember, is the mode in which fine art is founded upon, or may contribute to the practical requirements of human life.

Its offices in this respect are mainly two-fold; it gives form to knowledge, and grace to utility; that is to say, it makes permanently visible to us things which otherwise could neither be described by our science, nor retained by our memory; and it gives delightfulness and worth to the implements of daily use, and materials of dress, furniture and lodging. In the first of these offices it gives precision and charm to truth; in the second it gives precision and charm to service. For, the moment we make anything useful thoroughly, it is a law of nature that we shall be pleased with ourselves, and with the thing we have made; and become desirous therefore to adorn or complete it, in some dainty way, with finer art expressive of our pleasure.

And the point I wish chiefly to bring before you to-day, is this close and healthy connection of the fine arts with material use; but I must first try briefly to put in clear light the function of art in giving form to truth.

98. Much that I have hitherto tried to teach has been disputed on the ground that I have attached too much importance to art as representing natural facts, and too little to it as a source of pleasure. And I wish, in the close of these four prefatory lectures, strongly to assert to you, and, so far as I can in the time, convince you, that the entire vitality of art depends upon its being either full of truth, or full of use; and that, however pleasant, wonderful, or impressive it may be in itself, it must yet be of inferior kind, and tend to deeper inferiority, unless it has clearly one of these main objects—either *to state a true thing*, or to *adorn a serviceable one*. It must never exist alone—never for itself; it exists rightly only when it is the means of knowledge, or the grace of agency for life.

99. Now, I pray you to observe—for though I have said this often before, I have never yet said it clearly enough—every good piece of art, to whichever of these ends it may be directed, involves first essentially the evidence of human skill, and the formation of an actually beautiful thing by it.

Skill and beauty, always, then; and, beyond these, the formative arts have always one or other of the two objects which I have just defined to you—truth, or serviceableness; and without these aims neither the skill nor their beauty will avail; only by these can either legitimately reign. All the graphic arts begin in keeping the outline of shadow that we have loved, and they end in giving to it the aspect of life; and all the architectural arts begin in the shaping of the cup and the platter, and they end in a glorified roof.

Therefore, you see, in the graphic arts you have skill, beauty and likeness; and in the architectural arts skill, beauty and use: and you *must* have the three in each group, balanced and co-ordinate; and all the chief errors of art consist in losing or exaggerating one of these elements.

100. For instance, almost the whole system and hope of modern life are founded on the notion that you may substitute mechanism for skill, photograph for picture, cast-iron for sculpture. That is your main nineteenth-century faith, or infidelity. You think you can get everything by grinding—music, literature and painting. You will find it grievously not so; you can get nothing but dust by mere grinding. Even to have the barley-meal out of it, you must have the barley first; and that comes by growth, not grinding. But essentially, we have lost our delight in skill; in that majesty of it which I was trying to make clear to you in my last address, and which long ago I tried to express, under the head of ideas of power. The entire sense of that, we have lost, because we ourselves do

not take pains enough to do right, and have no conception of what the right costs; so that all the joy and reverence we ought to feel in looking at a strong man's work, have ceased in us. We keep them yet a little in looking at a honeycomb or a bird's nest; we understand that these differ, by divinity of skill, from a lump of wax or a cluster of sticks. But a picture, which is a much more wonderful thing than a honeycomb or a bird's nest—have we not known people, and sensible people, too, who expected to be taught to produce that, in six lessons?

101. Well, you must have the skill, you must have the beauty, which is the highest moral element; and then, lastly, you must have the verity or utility, which is not the moral, but the vital element; and this desire for verity and use is the one aim of the three that always leads in great schools, and in the minds of great masters, without any exception. They will permit themselves in awkwardness, they will permit themselves in ugliness—but they will never permit themselves in uselessness or in unveracity.

102. And farther, as their skill increases, and as their grace, so much more their desire for truth. It is impossible to find the three motives in fairer balance and harmony than in our own Reynolds. He rejoices in showing you his skill; and those of you who succeed in learning what painters' work really is, will one day rejoice also, even to laughter

—that highest laughter which springs of pure delight, in watching the fortitude and the fire of a hand which strikes forth its will upon the canvas as easily as the wind strikes it on the sea. He rejoices in all abstract beauty and rhythm and melody of design; he will never give you a color that is not lovely, nor a shade that is unnecessary, nor a line that is ungraceful. But all his power and all his invention are held by him subordinate—and the more obediently because of their nobleness—to his true leading purpose of setting before you such likeness of the living presence of an English gentleman or an English lady, as shall be worthy of being looked upon forever.

103. But farther, you remember, I hope—for I said it in a way that I thought would shock you a little, that you might remember it—my statement, that art had never done more than this, never more than given the likeness of a noble human being. Not only so, but it very seldom does so much as this, and the best pictures that exist of the great schools are all portraits, or groups of portraits, often of very simple and nowise noble persons. You may have much more brilliant and impressive qualities in imaginative pictures; you may have figures scattered like clouds, or garlanded like flowers; you may have light and shade as of a tempest, and color, as of the rainbow; but all that is child's play to the great men, though it is astonishment to us. Their real strength is tried to the

utmost, and as far as I know, it is never elsewhere brought out so thoroughly, as in painting one man or woman, and the soul that was in them; nor that always the highest soul, but often only a thwarted one that was capable of height; or, perhaps, not even that, but faultful and poor, yet seen through, to the poor best of it, by the masterful sight. So that in order to put before you in your standard series the best art possible, I am obliged, even from the very strongest men, to take the portraits, before I take the idealism. Nay, whatever is best in the great compositions themselves has depended on portraiture; and the study necessary to enable you to understand invention will also convince you that the mind of man never invented a greater thing than the form of man, animated by faithful life. Every attempt to refine or exalt such healthy humanity has weakened or caricatured it; or else consists only in giving it, to please our fancy, the wings of birds, or the eyes of antelopes. Whatever is truly great in either Greek or Christian art, is also restrictedly human; and even the raptures of the redeemed souls who enter "*celestemente ballando,*" the gate of Angelico's Paradise, were seen first in the terrestrial, yet most pure, mirth of Florentine maidens.

104. I am aware that this cannot but at present appear gravely questionable to those of my audience who are strictly cognizant of the phases of Greek art; for they know that the moment of its decline is accu-

rately marked, by its turning from abstract form to portraiture. But the reason of this is simple. The progressive course of Greek art was in subduing monstrous conceptions to natural ones; it did this by general laws; it reached absolute truth of generic human form, and if its ethical force had remained, would have advanced into healthy portraiture. But at the moment of change the national life ended in Greece; and portraiture, there, meant insult to her religion, and flattery to her tyrants. And her skill perished, not because she became true in sight, but because she became vile in heart.

105. And now let us think of our own work, and ask how that may become, in its own poor measure, active in some verity of representation. We certainly cannot begin by drawing kings or queens; but we must try, even in our earliest work, if it is to prosper, to draw something that will convey true knowledge both to ourselves and others. And I think you will find greatest advantage in the endeavor to give more life and educational power to the simpler branches of natural science; for the great scientific men are all so eager in advance that they have no time to popularize their discoveries, and if we can glean after them a little and make pictures of the things which science describes, we shall find the service a worthy one. Not only so, but we may even be helpful to science herself; for she has suffered by her proud severance from

the arts; and having made too little effort to realize her discoveries to vulgar eyes, has herself lost true measure of what was chiefly precious in them.

106. Take botany, for instance. Our scientific botanists are, I think, chiefly at present occupied in distinguishing species, which perfect methods of distinction will probably in the future show to be indistinct; in inventing descriptive names of which a more advanced science and more fastidious scholarship will show some to be unnecessary, and others inadmissible; and in microscopic investigations of structure, which through many alternate links of triumphant discovery that tissue is composed of vessels and that vessels are composed of tissue, have not hitherto completely explained to us either the origin, the energy, or the course of the sap; and which, however subtle or successful, bear to the real natural history of plants only the relation that anatomy and organic chemistry bear to the history of men. In the meantime, our artists are so generally convinced of the truth of the Darwinian theory, that they do not always think it necessary to show any difference between the foliage of an elm and an oak; and the gift-books of Christmas have every page surrounded with laboriously engraved garlands of rose, shamrock, thistle, and forget-me-not, without its being thought proper by the draughtsmen, or desirable by the public, even in the

case of those uncommon flowers, to observe the real shape of the petals of any one of them.

107. Now what we especially need at present for educational purposes is to know, not the anatomy of plants, but their biography—how and where they live and die, their tempers, benevolences, malignities, distresses, and virtues. We want them drawn from their youth to their age, from bud to fruit. We ought to see the various forms of their diminished but hardy growth in cold climates, or poor soils; and their rank or wild luxuriance, when full-fed and warmly nursed. And all this we ought to have drawn so accurately, that we might at once compare any given part of a plant with the same part of any other, drawn on the like conditions. Now, is not this a work which we may set about here in Oxford, with good hope and much pleasure? I think it so important, that the first exercise in drawing I shall put before you will be an outline of a laurel leaf. You will find in the opening sentence of Lionardo's treatise, our present text-book, that you must not at first draw from nature, but from a good master's work, *"per assuefarsi a buone membra,"* to accustom yourselves, that is, to entirely good representative organic forms. So your first exercise shall be the top of the laurel sceptre of Apollo, drawn by an Italian engraver of Lionardo's own time; then we will draw a laurel leaf itself; and little by little, I think we may both

learn ourselves, and teach to many besides, somewhat more than we know yet, of the wild olives of Greece, and the wild roses of England.

108. Next, in geology, which I will take leave to consider as an entirely separate science from the zoölogy of the past, which has lately usurped its name and interest. In geology itself we find the strength of many able men occupied in debating questions of which there are yet no data even for the clear statement; and in seizing advanced theoretical positions on the mere contingency of their being afterward tenable; while, in the meantime, no simple person, taking a holiday in Cumberland, can get an intelligible section of Skiddaw, or a clear account of the origin of the Skiddaw slates; and while, though half the educated society of London travel every summer over the great plain of Switzerland, none know, or care to know, why that is a plain, and the Alps to the south of it are Alps: and whether or not the gravel of the one has anything to do with the rocks of the other. And though every palace in Europe owes part of its decoration to variegated marbles, and nearly every woman in Europe part of her decoration to pieces of jasper or chalcedony, I do not think any geologist could at this moment with authority, tell us either how a piece of marble is stained, or what causes the streaks in a Scotch pebble.

109. Now, as soon as you have obtained the

power of drawing, I do not say a mountain, but even a stone accurately, every question of this kind will become to you at once attractive and definite; you will find that in the grain, the luster, and the cleavage-lines of the smallest fragment of rock, there are recorded forces of every order and magnitude, from those which raise a continent by one volcanic effort, to those which at every instant are polishing the apparently complete crystal in its nest, and conducting the apparently motionless metal in its vein; and that only by the art of your own hand, and fidelity of sight which it develops, you can obtain true perception of these invincible and inimitable arts of the earth herself: while the comparatively slight effort necessary to obtain so much skill as may serviceably draw mountains in distant effect will be instantly rewarded by what is almost equivalent to a new sense of the conditions of their structure.

110. And, because it is well at once to know some direction in which our work may be definite, let me suggest to those of you who may intend passing their vacation in Switzerland, and who care about mountains, that if they will first qualify themselves to take angles of position and elevation with correctness, and to draw outlines with approximate fidelity, there are a series of problems of the highest interest to be worked out on the southern edge of the Swiss plain, in the study of the relations of its molasse beds to the rocks

which are characteristically developed in the chain of the Stockhorn, Beatenberg, Pilate, Mythen above Schwytz, and High Sentis of Appenzell; the pursuit of which may lead them into many pleasant, as well as creditably dangerous walks, and curious discoveries; and will be good for the discipline of their fingers in the penciling of crag form.

111. I wish I could ask you to draw, instead of the Alps, the crests of Parnassus and Olympus, and the ravines of Delphi and of Tempe. I have not loved the arts of Greece as others have; yet I love them, and her, so much, that it is to me simply a standing marvel how scholars can endure for all these centuries during which their chief education has been in the language and policy of Greece, to have only the names of her hills and rivers upon their lips, and never one line of conception of them in their minds' sight. Which of us knows what the valley of Sparta is like, or the great mountain vase of Arcadia? which of us, except in mere airy syllabling of names, knows aught of "sandy Ladon's lilied banks, or old Lycæus, or Cyllene hoar?" "You cannot travel in Greece?" I know it; nor in Magna Græcia. But, gentlemen of England, you had better find out why you cannot, and put an end to that horror of European shame, before you hope to learn Greek art.

112. I scarcely know whether to place among the things useful to art, or to science, the systematic

record, by drawing, of phenomena of the sky. But I am quite sure that your work cannot in any direction be more useful to yourselves, than in enabling you to perceive the quite unparalleled subtilties of color and inorganic form, which occur on any ordinarily fine morning or evening horizon; and I will even confess to you another of my perhaps too sanguine expectations, that in some far distant time it may come to pass, that young Englishmen and Englishwomen may think the breath of the morning sky pleasanter than that of midnight, and its light prettier than that of candles.

113. Lastly, in zoölogy. What the Greeks did for the horse, and what, as far as regards domestic and expressional character, Landseer has done for the dog and the deer, remains to be done by art for nearly all other animals of high organization. There are few birds or beasts that have not a range of character which, if not equal to that of the horse or dog, is yet as interesting within narrower limits, and often in grotesqueness, intensity, or wild and timid pathos, more singular and mysterious. Whatever love of humor you have—whatever sympathy with imperfect, but most subtle feeling—whatever perception of sublimity in conditions of fatal power, may here find fullest occupation; all these being joined, in the strong animal races, to a variable and fantastic beauty far beyond anything that merely formative art has yet

conceived. I have placed in your educational series a wing by Albert Dürer, which goes as far as art yet has reached in delineation of plumage; while for the simple action of the pinion, it is impossible to go beyond what has been done already by Titian and Tintoret; but you cannot so much as once look at the rufflings of the plumes of a pelican pluming itself after it has been in the water, or carefully draw the contours of the wing either of a vulture or a common swift, or paint the rose and vermillion on that of a flamingo, without receiving almost a new conception of the meaning of form and color in creation.

114. Lastly. Your work, in all directions I have hitherto indicated, may be as deliberate as you choose; there is no immediate fear of the extinction of many species of flowers or animals; and the Alps, and valley of Sparta will wait your leisure, I fear, too long. But the fuedal and monastic buildings of Europe, and still more the streets of her ancient cities, are vanishing like dreams: and it is difficult to imagine the mingled envy and contempt with which future generations will look back to us, who still possessed such things, yet made no effort to preserve, and scarcely any to delineate them; for, when used as material of landscape by the modern artist, they are nearly always superficially or flatteringly represented, without zeal enough to penetrate their character, or patience enough to render it in modest harmony. As for places

of traditional interest, I do not know an entirely faithful drawing of any historical site, except one or two studies made by enthusiastic young painters in Palestine and Egypt: for which, thanks to them always; but we want work nearer home.

115. Now, it is quite probable that some of you, who will not care to go through the labor necessary to draw flowers or animals, may yet have pleasure in attaining some moderately accurate skill of sketching architecture, and greater pleasure still in directing it usefully. Suppose, for instance, we were to take up the historical scenery in Carlyle's "Frederick." Too justly the historian accuses the genius of past art, in that, types of too many such elsewhere, the galleries of Berlin, "are made up, like other galleries, of goat-footed Pan, Europa's Bull, Romulus' She-Wolf, and the Correggiosity of Correggio, and contain, for instance, no portrait of Friedrich the Great, no likeness at all, or next to none at all, of the noble series of Human Realities, or of any part of them, who have sprung, not from the idle brains of dreaming *dilettanti*, but from the head of God Almighty, to make this poor authentic earth a little memorable for us, and to do a little work that may be eternal there." So Carlyle tells us—too truly! We cannot now draw Friedrich for him, but we can draw some of the old castles and cities that were the cradles of German life—Hohenzollern, Hapsburg, Marburg, and such others; we may keep

some authentic likeness of these for the future. Suppose we were to take up that first volume of "Friedrich," and put outlines to it? shall we begin by looking for Henry the Fowler's tomb—Carlyle himself asks if he has any—at Quedlinburg, and so downward, rescuing what we can? That would certainly be making our work of some true use.

116. But I have told you enough, it seems to me, at least to-day, of this function of art in recording fact; let me now finally, and with all distinctness possible to me, state to you its main business of all; its service in the actual uses of daily life.

You are surprised, perhaps, to hear me call this its main business. That is indeed so, however. The giving brightness to picture is much, but the giving brightness to life more. And remember, were it as patterns only, you cannot, without the realities, have the pictures. You cannot have a landscape by Turner without a country for him to paint; you cannot have a portrait by Titian, without a man to be portrayed. I need not prove that to you, I suppose, in these short terms; but in the outcome I can get no soul to believe that the beginning of art is in getting our country clean and our people beautiful. I have been ten years trying to get this very plain certainty—I do not say believed—but even thought of, as anything but a monstrous proposition. To get your country clean, and your people lovely; I assure you, that is a necessary work of art to begin with! There has indeed been art in countries where people lived in dirt to serve God, but never in countries where they lived in dirt to serve the devil. There has indeed been art where the people were not all lovely—where even their lips were thick—and their skins black, because the sun had looked upon them; but never in a country where the people were pale with miserable toil and deadly shade, and where the lips of youth, instead of being full with blood, were pinched by famine, or warped with poison. And now, therefore, note this well, the gist of all these long prefatory talks. I said that the two great moral instincts were those of Order and Kindness. Now, all the arts are founded on agriculture by the hand, and on the graces, and kindness of feeding and dressing, and lodging your people. Greek art begins the gardens of Alcinous—perfect order, leeks in beds, and fountains in pipes. And Christian art, as it arose out of chivalry, was only possible so far as chivalry compelled both kings and knights to care for the right personal training of their people; it perished utterly when those kings and knights became δημοβόροι, devourers of the people. And it will become possible again only, when literally, the sword is beaten into the plowshare, when your St. George of England shall justify his name, and Christian art shall be known as its Master was, in breaking of bread.

117. Now look at the working out of this broad principle in minor detail; observe how, from highest to lowest, health of art has first depended on reference to industrial use. There is first the need of cup and platter, especially of cup; for you can put your meat on the Harpies', or any other tables; but you must have your cup to drink from. And to hold it conveniently, you must put a handle to it; and to fill it when it is empty you must have a large pitcher of some sort; and to carry the pitcher you may most advisably have two handles. Modify the forms of these needful possessions according to the various requirements of drinking largely and drinking delicately; of pouring easily out, or of keeping for years the perfume in; of storing in cellars, or bearing from fountains; of sacrificial libation of Pan, athenaic treasure of oil, and sepulchral treasure of ashes—and you have a resultant series of beautiful form and decoration, from the rude amphora of red earth up to Cellini's vases of gems and crystal, in which series, but especially in the more simple conditions of it, are developed the most beautiful lines and most perfect types of severe composition which have yet been attained by art.

118. But again, that you may fill your cup with pure water, you must go to the well or spring; you need a fence round the well; you need some tube or trough, or other means of confining the stream at the spring. For the conveyance of the current to any dis-

tance you must build either inclosed or open aqueduct; and in the hot square of the city where you set it free you find it good for health and pleasantness to let it leap into a fountain. On these several needs you have a school of sculpture founded; in the decoration of the walls of wells in level countries and of the sources of springs in mountainous ones, and chiefly of all, where the women of household or market meet at the city fountain. There is, however, a farther reason for the use of art here than in any other material service, so far as we may, by art, express our reverence or thankfulness. Whenever a nation is in its right mind, it always has a deep sense of divinity in the gift of rain from heaven, filling its heart with food and gladness; and all the more when that gift becomes gentle and perennial in the flowing of springs. It literally is not possible that any fruitful power of the muses should be put forth upon a people which disdains their Helicon; still less is it possible that any Christian nation should grow up "*tanquam lignum quod plantatum est secus decersus aquarum*," which cannot recognize the lesson meant in their being told of the places where Rebekah was met—where Rachel—where Zipporah—and she who was asked for water under Mount Gerizim by a stranger, weary, who had nothing to draw with.

119. And truly, when our mountain springs are set apart in vale or craggy glen, or glade of wood green through the drought of summer, far from cities, then

it is best let them stay in their own happy peace; but if near towns, and liable therefore to be defiled by common usage, we could not use the loveliest art more worthily than by sheltering the spring and its first pools with precious marbles; nor ought anything to be esteemed more important, as a means of healthy education, than the care to keep the streams of it afterward, to as great a distance as possible, pure, full of fish, and easily accessible to children. There used to be, thirty years ago, a little rivulet of the Wandel, about an inch deep, which ran over the carriage-road and under a foot-bridge just under the last chalk hill near Croydon. Alas! men came and went; and it— did *not* go on forever. It has long since been bricked over by the parish authorities; but there was more education in that stream with its minnows than you could get out of a hundred pounds spent yearly in the parish schools, even though you were to spend every farthing of it in teaching the nature of oxygen and hydrogen, and the names, and rate per minute of all the rivers in Asia and America.

120. Well, the gist of this matter lies here then. Suppose we want a school of pottery again in England, all we poor artists are ready to do the best we can, to show you how pretty a line may be that is twisted first to one side and then to the other; and how a plain household blue will make a pattern on white; and how ideal art may be got out of the spaniel's col-

ors, of black and tan. But I tell you beforehand, all that we can do will be utterly useless, unless you teach your peasant to say grace, not only before meat, but before drink; and having provided him with Greek cups and platters, provide him also with something that is not poisoned to put into them.

121. There cannot be any need that I should trace for you the conditions of art that are directly founded on serviceableness of dress, and of armor; but it is my duty to affirm to you, in the most positive manner, that after recovering, for the poor, wholesomeness of food, your next step toward founding schools of art in England must be in recovering, for the poor, decency and wholesomeness of dress; thoroughly good in substance, fitted for their daily work, becoming to their rank in life, and worn with order and dignity. And this order and dignity must be taught them by the women of the upper and middle classes, whose minds can be in nothing right, as long as they are so wrong in this matter as to endure the squalor of the poor, while they themselves dress gaily. And on the proper pride and comfort of both poor and rich in dress, must be founded the true arts of dress; carried on by masters of manufacture no less careful of the perfectness and beauty of their tissues, and of all that in substance and in design can be bestowed upon them, than ever the armorers of Milan and Damascus were careful of their steel.

122. Then, in the third place, having recovered some wholesome habits of life as to food and dress, we must recover them as to lodging. I said just now that the best architecture was but a glorified roof. Think of it. The dome of the Vatican, the porches of Rheims or Chartres, the vaults and arches of their aisles, the canopy of the tomb, and the spire of the belfry, are all forms resulting from the mere requirement that a certain space shall be strongly covered from heat and rain. More than that—as I have tried all through "The Stones of Venice" to show—the lovely forms of these were every one of them developed in civil and domestic building, and only after their invention employed ecclesiastically on the grandest scale. I do not know whether you have noticed, but I think you cannot but have noticed here in Oxford, as elsewhere, that our modern architects never seem to know what to do with their roofs. Be assured, until the roofs are right, nothing else will be; and there are just two ways of keeping them right. Never build them of iron, but only of wood or stone; and secondly, take care that in every town the little roofs are built before the large ones, and that everybody who wants one has got one. And we must try also to make everybody want one. That is to say, at some not very advanced period of life, men should desire to have a home, which they do not wish to quit any more, suited to their habits of life, and likely to be more

and more suitable to them until their death. And men must desire to have these, their dwelling-places, built as strongly as possible, and furnished and decorated daintily, and set in pleasant places, in bright light and good air, being able to choose for themselves that at least as well as swallows. And when the houses are grouped together in cities, men must have so much civic fellowship as to subject their architecture to a common law, and so much civic pride as to desire that the whole gathered group of human dwellings should be a lovely thing, not a frightful one, on the face of the earth. Not many weeks ago an English clergyman, a master of this university, a man not given to sentiment, but of middle age, and great practical sense, told me, by accident, and wholly without reference to the subject now before us, that he never could enter London from his country parsonage but with closed eyes, lest the sight of the blocks of houses which the railroad intersected in the suburbs should unfit him, by the horror of it, for his day's work.

123. Now, it is not possible—and I repeat to you, only in more deliberate assertion, what I wrote just twenty-two years ago in the last chapter of the "Seven Lamps of Architecture"—it is not possible to have any right morality, happiness, or art in any country where the cities are thus built, or thus, let me rather say, clotted and coagulated; spots of a dreadful mildew spreading by patches and blotches over the

country they consume. You must have lovely cities, crystallized, not coagulated, into form; limited in size, and not casting out the scum and scurf of them into an encircling eruption of shame, but girded each with its sacred pomœrium, and with garlands of gardens full of blossoming trees, and softly guided streams.

That is impossible, you say! It may be so. I have nothing to do with its possibility, but only with its indispensability. More than that must be possible, however, before you can have a school of art; namely, that you find places elsewhere than in England, or at least in otherwise unserviceable parts of England, for the establishment of manufactories needing the help of fire, that is to say, of all the τέχναι βαναυσικαί and ἐπίρρητοι of which it was long ago known to be the constant nature that 'ἀσχολίας μάλιστα ἔχουσι καὶ φίλων καὶ πόλεως συνεπιμελεῖσθαι,' and to reduce such manufactures to their lowest limit, so that nothing may ever be made of iron that can as effectually be made of wood or stone; and nothing moved by steam that can be as effectually moved by natural forces. And observe, that for all mechanical effort required in social life and in cities, water power is infinitely more than enough; for anchored mills on the large rivers, and mills moved by sluices from reservoirs filled by the tide, will give you command of any quantity of constant motive power you need.

Agriculture by the hand, then, and absolute refusal

or banishment of unnecessary igneous force are the first conditions of a school of art in any country. And until you do this, be it soon or late, things will continue in that triumphant state to which, for want of finer art, your mechanism has brought them; that, though England is deafened with spinning wheels, her people have not clothes—though she is black with digging of fuel, they die of cold—and though she has sold her soul for gain, they die of hunger. Stay in that triumph, if you choose; but be assured of this, it is not one which the fine arts will ever share with you.

124. Now, I have given you my message, containing, as I know, offense enough, and itself, it may seem to many, unnecessary enough. But just in proportion to its apparent non-necessity, and to its certain offense, was its real need, and my real duty to speak it. The study of the fine arts could not be rightly associated with the grave work of English universities, without due and clear protest against the misdirection of national energy, which for the present renders all good results of such study on a great scale, impossible. I can easily teach you, as any other moderately good draughtsman could, how to hold your pencils, and how to lay your colors; but it is little use my doing that, while the nation is spending millions of money in the destruction of all that pencil or color have to represent, and in the promotion of false forms of art, which are only the costliest and the least enjoyable of follies.

And therefore these are the things that I have first and last to tell you in this place—that the fine arts are not to be learned by locomotion, but by making the homes we live in lovely, and by staying in them—that the fine arts are not to be learned by competition, but by doing our quiet best in our own way; that the fine arts not to be learned by exhibition, but by doing what is right, and making what is honest, whether it be exhibited or not; and, for the sum of all, that men must paint and build neither for pride nor money, but for love; for love of their art, for the love of their neighbor, and whatever better love may be than these, founded on these. I know that I gave some pain, which I was most unwilling to give, in speaking of the possible abuses of religious art; but there can be no danger of any, so long as we remember that God inhabits cottages as well as churches, and ought to be well lodged there also. Begin with wooden floors; the tesselated ones will take care of themselves; begin with thatching roofs, and you shall end by splendidly vaulting them; begin by taking care that no old eyes fail over their Bibles, nor young ones over their needles, for want of rushlight, and then you may have whatever true good is to be got out of colored glass or wax candles. And in thus putting the arts to universal use, you will find also their universal inspiration, their universal benediction. I told you there was no evidence of a *special* divineness in any application of them; that they were always equally human and equally divine; and in closing these inaugural series of lectures, into which I have endeavored to compress the principles that are to be the foundations of your future work, it is my last duty to say some positive words as to the divinity of all art, when it is truly fair, or truly serviceable.

125. Every seventh day, if not oftener, the greater number of well-meaning persons in England thankfully receive from their teachers a benediction, couched in these terms: "The grace of our Lord Christ, and the love of God, and the fellowship of the Holy Ghost be with you." Now I do not know precisely what sense is attached in the English public mind to those expressions. But what I have to tell you positively is, that the three things do actually exist, and can be known if you care to know them, and possessed if you care to possess them; and that another thing exists, beside these, of which we already know too much.

First, by simply obeying the orders of the founder of your religion, all grace, graciousness, or beauty and favor of gentle life, will be given to you in mind and body, in work and in rest. The grace of Christ exists, and can be had if you will. Secondly, as you know more and more of the created world, you will find that the true will of its Maker is that its creatures should be happy—that He has made everything beautiful in its time and its place, and that it is chiefly by the fault of men, when they are allowed the liberty of thwarting His laws, that creation groans or travails in pain. The love of God exists, and you may see it, and live in it if you will. Lastly, a Spirit does actually exist which teaches the ant her path, the bird her building, and men, in an instinctive and marvelous way, whatever lovely arts and noble deeds are possible to them. Without it you can do no good thing. To the grief of it you can do many bad ones. In the possession of it is your peace and your power.

And there is a fourth thing, of which we already know too much. There is an evil spirit whose dominion is in blindness and in cowardice, as the dominion of the spirit of wisdom is in clear sight and in courage.

And this blind and cowardly spirit is forever telling you that evil things are pardonable, and you shall not die for them, and that good things are impossible, and you need not live for them: and that gospel of his is now the loudest that is preached in your Saxon tongue. You will find some day, to your cost, if you believe the first part of it, that it is not true; but you may never, if you believe the second part of it, find, to your gain, that also, untrue; and, therefore, I pray you with all earnestness to prove, and know within your hearts, that all things lovely and righteous are possible for those who believe in their possibility, and who determine that, for their part, they will make every day's work contribute to them. Let every dawn of morning be to you as the beginning of life, and every setting sun be to you as its close—then let every one of these short lives leave its sure record of some kindly thing done for others—some goodly strength or knowledge gained for yourselves; so, from day to day, and strength to strength, you shall build up indeed, by art, by thought, and by just will, an ecclesia of England, of which it shall not be said, "see what manner of stones are here," but "see wnat manner of men."

LECTURE V.

LINE.

126. You will, I doubt not, willingly permit me to begin your lessons in real practice of art in words of higher authority than mine (I ought rather to say, or *all* authority, while mine are of none), the words of the greatest of English painters: one also, than whom there is indeed no greater, among those of any nation, or any time—our own gentle Reynolds.

He says in his first discourse: "The Directors" (of the Academy) "ought more particularly to watch over the genius of those students, who being more advanced, are arrived at that critical period of study, on the nice management of which their future turn of taste depends. At that age it is natural for them to be more captivated with what is brilliant, than with what is solid, and to prefer splendid negligence to painful and humiliating exactness.

"A facility in composing—a lively and what is called a masterly handling of the chalk or pencil, are, it must be confessed, captivating qualities to young minds, and become of course the objects of their ambition. They endeavor to imitate these dazzling excellences, which they will find no great labor in attaining. After much time spent in these frivolous pursuits, the difficulty will be to retreat; but it will then be too late; and there is scarce an instance of return to scrupulous labor, after the mind has been debauched and deceived by this fallacious mastery."

127. I read you these words, chiefly that Sir Joshua, who founded, as first president, the academical schools of English painting, in these well-known discourses, may also begin, as he has truest right to do, our system of instruction in this university. But secondly, I read them that I may press on your attention these singular words, " painful and humiliating exactness." Singular, as expressing the first conditions of the study required from his pupils by the master, who, of all men except Velasquez, seems to have painted with the greatest ease. It is true that he asks this pain, this humiliation, only from youths who intend to follow the profession of artists. But if you wish yourselves to know anything of the practice of art, you must not suppose that because your study will be more desultory than that of academy students, it may therefore be less accurate. The shorter the time you have to give, the more careful you should be to spend it profitably; and I would not wish you to devote one hour to the practice of drawing, unless you

are resolved to be informed in it of all that in an hour can be taught.

128. I speak of the practice of *drawing* only; though elementary study of modeling may perhaps some day be advisably connected with it; but I do not wish to disturb or amuse you with a formal statement of the manifold expectations I have formed respecting your future work. You will not, I am sure, imagine that I have begun without a plan, nor blame my reticence as to the parts of it which cannot yet be put into execution, and which there may occur reason afterward to modify. My first task must unquestionably be to lay before you right and simple methods of drawing and coloring.

I use the word "coloring" without reference to any particular vehicle of color, for the laws of good painting are the same, whatever liquid is employed to dissolve the pigments. But the technical management of oil is more difficult than that of water-color, and the impossibility of using it with safety among books or prints, and its unavailableness for note-book sketches and memoranda, are sufficient reasons for not introducing it in a course of practice intended chiefly for students of literature. On the contrary, in the exercises of artists, oil should be the vehicle of color employed from the first. The extended practice of water-color painting, as a separate skill, is in every way harmful to the arts: its pleasant slightness and plausible dexterity divert the genius of the painter from its proper aims, and withdraw the attention of the public from excellence of higher claim; nor ought any man, who has the consciousness of ability for good work, to be ignorant of, or indolent in employing, the methods of making its results permanent as long as the laws of nature allow. It is surely a severe lesson to us in this matter, that the best works of Turner could not be shown to the public for six months without being destroyed—and that his most ambitious ones for the most part perished, even before they could be shown. I will break through my law of reticence, however, so far as to tell you that I have hope of one day interesting you greatly (with the help of the Florentine masters) in the study of the arts of molding and painting porcelain; and to induce some of you to use your future power of patronage in encouraging the various branches of this art, and turning the attention of the workmen of Italy from the vulgar tricks of minute and perishable mosaic to the exquisite subtilties of form and color possible in the perfectly ductile, afterward unalterable clay. And one of the ultimate results of such craftsmanship might be the production of pictures as brilliant as painted glass—as delicate as the most subtle water-colors, and more permanent than the Pyramids.

129. And now to begin our own work. In order that we may know how rightly to learn to draw, and

to paint, it will be necessary, will it not, that we know first what we are to aim at doing—what kind of representation of nature is best?

I will tell you in the words of Lionardo. "That is the most praiseworthy painting which has most conformity with the thing represented," "*quella pittura e piu laudabile, la quale ha piu conformita con la cosa imitata*" (chap. 276). In plain terms, "the painting which is likest nature is the best." And you will find by referring to the preceeding chapter, "*come lo specchio e maestro de' pittori,*" how absolutely Lionardo means what he says. Let the living thing (he tells us) be reflected in a mirror, then put your picture beside the reflection, and match the one with the other. And indeed the very best painting is unquestionably so like the mirrored truth, that all the world admit its excellence. Entirely first-rate work is so quiet and natural that there can be no dispute over it; you may not particularly admire it, but you will find no fault with it. Second-rate painting pleases one person much, and displeases another; but first-rate painting pleases all a little, and intensely pleases those who can recognize its unostentatious skill.

130. This, then, is what we have first got to do—to make our drawing look as like the thing we have to draw as we can.

Now, all objects are seen by the eye as patches of color of a certain shape, with gradations of color within them. And, unless their colors be actually luminous, as those of the sun, or of fire, these patches of different hues are sufficiently inimitable, except so far as they are seen stereoscopically. You will find Lionardo again and again insisting on the stereoscopic power of the double sight; but do not let that trouble you; you can only paint what you can see from one point of sight, but that is quite enough. So seen, then, all objects appear to the human eye simply as masses of color of variable depth, texture, and outline. The outline of any object is the limit of its mass, as relieved against another mass. Take a crocus, and put it on a green cloth. You will see it detach itself as a mere space of yellow from the green behind it, as it does from the grass. Hold it up against the window—you will see it detach itself as a dark space against the white or blue behind it. In either case its outline is the limit of the space of color by which it expresses itself to your sight. That outline is therefore infinitely subtle—not even a line, but the place of a line, and that, also, made soft by texture. In the finest painting, it is therefore slightly softened; but it is necessary to be able to draw it with absolute sharpness and precision. The art of doing this is to be obtained by drawing it as an actual line, which art is to be the subject of our present inquiry; but I must first lay the divisions of the entire subject completely before you.

131. I have said that all objects detach themselves

as masses of color. Usually, light and shade are thought of as separate from color; but the fact is that all nature is seen as a mosaic composed of graduated portions of different colors, dark or light. There is no difference in the quality of these colors, except as affected by texture. You will constantly hear lights and shades spoken of as if these were different in nature, and to be painted in different ways. But every light is a shadow compared to higher lights, till we reach the brightness of the sun; and every shadow is a light compared to lower shadows, till we reach the darkness of night.

Every color used in painting, except pure white and black, is therefore a light and shade at the same time. It is a light with reference to all below it, and a shade with reference to all above it.

132. The solid forms of an object, that is to say, the projections or recessions of its surface within the outline, are, for the most part, rendered visible by variations in the intensity or quantity of light falling on them. The study of the relations between the quantities of this light, irrespectively of its color, is the second division of the regulated science of painting.

133 Finally, the qualities and relations of natural colors. the means of imitating them, and the laws by which they become separately beautiful, and in association harmonious, are the subjects of the third and final division of the painter's study. I shall endeavor

at once to state to you what is most immediately desirable for you to know on each of these subjects, in this and the two following lectures.

134. What we have to do, then, from beginning to end, is, I repeat once more, simply to draw spaces of their true shape, and to fill them with colors which shall match their colors; quite a simple thing in the definition of it, not quite so easy in the doing of it.

But it is something to get this simple definition; and I wish you to notice that the terms of it are complete, though I do not introduce the terms "light" or "shadow." Painters who have no eye for color have greatly confused and falsified the practice of art by the theory that shadow is an absence of color. Shadow is, on the contrary, necessary to the full presence of color; for every color is a diminished quantity or energy of light; and, practically, it follows, from what I have just told you (that every light in painting is a shadow to higher lights, and every shadow a light to lower shadows) that also every color in painting must be a shadow to some brighter color, and a light to some darker one—all the while being a positive color itself. And the great splendor of the Venetian school arises from their having seen and held from the beginning this great fact—that shadow is as much color as light, often much more. In Titian's fullest red the lights are pale rose-color, passing into white—the shadows warm deep crimson. In Veronese's most splendid orange, the lights are pale, the shadows crocus color; and so on. In nature, dark sides, if seen by reflected lights, are almost always fuller or warmer in color than the lights; and the practice of the Bolognese and Roman schools, in drawing their shadows always dark and cold, is false from the beginning, and renders perfect painting forever impossible in those schools, and all that follow them.

135. Every visible space, then, be it dark or light is a space of color of some kind, or of black or white. And you have to inclose it with a true outline, and to paint it with its true color.

But before considering how we are to draw this enclosing line, I must state to you something about lines in general, and their use by different schools. I said just now that there was no difference between the masses of color of which all visible nature is composed except in *texture*.

1. Textures are principally of three kinds:
   (I.) Lustrous, as of water and glass.
   (II.) Bloomy, or velvety, as of a rose-leaf or peach.
   (III.) Linear, produced by filaments or threads, as in feathers, fur, hair, and woven or reticulated tissues.

All the three sources of pleasure to the eye in texture are united in the best ornamental work. A fine picture by Fra Angelico, or a fine illuminated page of missal, has large spaces of gold, partly burnished and lustrous, partly dead; some of it chased and enriched with linear texture, and mingled with imposed or inlaid colors, soft in bloom like that of the rose-leaf. But many schools of art depend for the most part on one kind of texture only, and a vast quantity of the art of all ages rests for great part of its power especially on texture produced by multitudinous lines. Thus, wood engraving, line engraving properly so called, and countless varieties of sculpture, metal work and textile fabric, depend for great part of the effect of their colors, or shades, for their mystery, softness, and clearness, on modification of the surfaces by lines or threads; and even in advanced oil painting, the work often depends for some part of its effect on the texture of the canvas.

136. Again, the arts of etching and mezzotint engraving depend principally for their effect on the velvety, or bloomy texture of their darkness, and the best of all painting is the fresco work of great colorists, in which the colors are what is usually called dead; but they are anything but dead, they glow with the luminous bloom of life. The frescoes of Correggio, when not repainted, are supreme in this quality; and you have a lovely example in the university galleries, in the untouched portion of the female head by Raphael, partly restored by Lawrence.

137. While, however, in all periods of art these different textures are thus used in various styles, and for various purposes, you will find that there is a broad historical division of schools, which will materially assist you in understanding them. The earliest art in most countries is linear, consisting of interwoven or richly spiral and otherwise involved arrangements of sculptured or painted lines, on stone, wood, metal, or clay. It is generally characteristic of savage life, and of feverish energy of imagination. I shall examine these schools with you hereafter, under the general head of the "Schools of line."

Secondly, even in the earliest periods, among powerful nations, this linear decoration is more or less filled with checkered or barred shade, and begins at once to represent animal or floral form, first in mere outline, and then by outlines filled with flat shadow, or with flat color. And here we instantly find two great divisions of temper and thought. The Greeks look upon all color first as light; they are, as compared with other races, insensitive to hue, exquisitely sensitive to phenomena of light. And their linear school passes into one of flat masses of light and darkness, represented in the main by four tints—white, black, and two reds, one brick color, more or less vivid, the other dark purple; these two representing their favorite πορφύρεος color, in its light and dark powers. On the other hand, many of the northern nations are at first entirely insensible to light and shade, but exquisitely sensitive to color, and their linear decoration is filled with flat tints, infinitely varied, having no expression of light and shade. Both these schools have a limited but absolute perfection of their own, and their peculiar successes can in no wise be imitated, except by the strictest observance of the same limitations.

138. You have then, line for the earliest art, branching into:

(1.) Greek, Line with Light.
(2.) Gothic, Line with Color.

Now, as art completes itself, each of these schools retain their separate characters, but they cease to depend on lines, and learn to represent masses instead, becoming more refined at the same time in all modes of perception and execution.

And thus there arise the two vast mediæval schools; one of flat and infinitely varied color, with exquisite character and sentiment added, in the forms represented; but little perception of shadow. The other, of light and shade, with exquisite drawing of solid form, and little perception of color; sometimes as little of sentiment. Of these, the school of flat color is the more vital one; it is always natural and simple, if not great—and when it is great, it is very great.

The school of light and shade associates itself with that of engraving; it is essentially an academical school; broadly dividing light from darkness, and begins by assuming that the light side of all objects shall be represented by white, and the extreme shadow by black. On this conventional principle it reaches a limited excellence of its own, in which the best existing types of engraving are executed, and ultimately, the most regular expressions of organic form in painting.

Then, lastly—the schools of color advance steadily till they adopt from those of light and shade, whatever is compatible with their own power—and then you have perfect art, represented centrally by that of the great Venetians.

The schools of light and shade, on the other hand, are partly, in their academical formulas, too haughty, and partly in their narrowness of imagination, too weak, to learn much from the schools of color; and they pass into a decadence, consisting partly in proud endeavors to give painting the qualities of sculpture, and partly in the pursuit of effects of light and shade, carried at last to extreme sensational subtlety by the Dutch school. In their fall, they drag the schools of color down with them; and the recent history of art is one of confused effort to find lost roads, and resume allegiance to violated principles.

139. That, briefly, is the map of the great schools, easily remembered by this form:

Line.
Early schools.

Line and Light.	**Line and Color.**
Greek clay.	Gothic glass.
Mass and Light.	**Mass and Color.**
(Represented by Lionardo, and his schools.)	(Represented by Giorgione, and his schools.)

Mass, Light, and Color.
(Represented by Titian, and his schools.)

I will endeavor hereafter to show you the various relations of all these branches; at present, I am only concerned with your own practice. My wish is that you should with your own eyes and fingers trace, and in your own progress follow, the method of advance traced for you by these great schools. I wish you to begin by getting command of line, that is to say, by learning to draw a steady line, limiting with absolute correctness the form or space you intend it to limit; to proceed by getting command over flat tints, so that you may be able to fill the spaces you have enclosed, evenly, either with shade or color; according to the school you adopt; and finally to obtain the power of adding such fineness of drawing within the masses, as shall express their undulation, and their characters of form and texture.

140. Those who are familiar with the methods of existing schools must be aware that I thus nearly invert their practice of teaching. Students at present learn to draw details first, and to color and mass them afterward. I shall endeavor to teach you to arrange broad masses and colors first; and you shall put the details into them afterward. I have several reasons for this audacity, of which you may justly require me to state the principal ones. The first is that, as I have shown you, this method I wish you to follow, is the natural one. All great artist-nations *have* actually learned to work in this way, and I believe it therefore the right, as the hitherto successful one. Secondly, you will find it less irksome than the reverse method, and more definite. When a beginner is set at once to draw details, and make finished studies in light and shade, no master can correct his innumerable errors, or rescue him out of his endless difficulties. But in the natural method, he can correct, if he will, his own errors. You will have positive lines to draw, presenting no more difficulty, except in requiring greater steadiness of hand than the outlines of a map. They will be generally sweeping and simple, instead of being jagged into promontories and bays; but assuredly, they may be drawn rightly (with patience), and their rightness tested with mathematical accuracy. You

have only to follow your own line with tracing paper, and apply it to your copy. If they do not correspond, you are wrong, and you need no master to show you where. Again; in washing in a flat tone of color or shade, you can always see yourself if it is flat, and kept well within the edges; and you can set a piece of your color side by side with that of the copy; if it does not match, you are wrong; and, again, you need no one to tell you so, if your eye for color is true. It happens, indeed, more frequently than would be supposed, that there is real want of power in the eye to distinguish colors; and this I even suspect to be a condition which has been sometimes attendant on high degrees of cerebral sensitiveness in other directions: but such want of faculty would be detected in your first two or three exercises by this simple method, while otherwise you might go on for years endeavoring to color from nature in vain. Lastly, and this is a very weighty collateral reason, such a method enables me to show you many things, besides the art of drawing. Every exercise that I prepare for you will be either a portion of some important example of ancient art, or of some natural object. However rudely or unsuccessfully you may draw it (though I anticipate from you neither want of care nor success), you will nevertheless have learned what no words could have as forcibly or completely taught you, either respecting early art or organic structure; and I am thus certain that not a moment you spend attentively will be altogether wasted, and that, generally, you will be twice gainers by every effort. There is, however, yet another point in which I think a change of existing methods will be advisable.

141. You have here in Oxford one of the finest collections in Europe of drawings in pen, and chalk, by Michael Angelo and Raphael. Of the whole number, you cannot but have noticed that not one is weak or student-like—all are evidently master's work.

You may look the galleries of Europe through, and so far as I know, or as it is possible to make with safety any so wide generalization, you will not find in them a childish or feeble drawing, by these, or by any other great master.

And farther—by the greatest men—by Titian, Velasquez, or Veronese—you will hardly find an authentic drawing at all. For, the fact is, that while we moderns have always learned, or tried to learn, to paint by drawing, the ancients learned to draw by painting—or by engraving, more difficult still. The brush was put into their hands when they were children, and they were forced to draw with that, until, if they used the pen or crayon, they used it either with the lightness of a brush or the decision of a graver. Michael Angelo uses his pen like a chisel; but all of them seem to use it only when they are in the height of their power, and then for rapid notation of thought or for study of models; but never as a practice helping them to paint. Probably exercises of the severest kind were gone through in minute drawing by the apprentices of the goldsmiths, of which we hear and know little, and which were entirely a matter of course. To these, and to the exquisiteness of care and touch developed in working precious metals, may probably be attributed the final triumph of Italian sculpture. Michael Angelo, when a boy, is said to have copied engravings by Schöngauer and others with his pen, in fac-simile so true that he could pass his drawings as the originals. But I should only discourage you from all farther attempts in art, if I asked you to imitate any of these accomplished drawings of the gem-artificers. You have, fortunately, a most interesting collection of them already in your galleries, and may try your hands on them if you will. But I desire rather that you should attempt nothing except what can by determination be absolutely accomplished, and be known and felt by you to be accomplished when it is so. Now, therefore, I am going at once to comply with that popular instinct which, I hope, so far as you care for drawing at all, you are still boys enough to feel, the desire to paint. Paint you shall; but remember, I understand by painting what you will not find easy. Paint you shall; but daub or blot you shall not: and there will be even more care required, though care of a pleasanter kind, to follow the lines traced for you with the point of the brush than if they had been drawn with that of a crayon. But from the very beginning (though carrying on at the same time an incidental practice with crayon and lead pencil), you shall try to draw a line of absolute correctness with the point, not of pen or crayon, but of the brush, as Apelles did, and as all colored lines are drawn on Greek vases. A line of absolute correctness, observe. I do not care how slowly you do it, or with how many alterations, junctions, or retouchings; the one thing I ask of you is, that the line shall be right, and right by measurement, to the same minuteness which you would have to give in a government chart to the map of a dangerous shoal.

142. This question of measurement is, as you are probably aware, one much vexed in art schools; but it is determined indisputably by the very first words written by Lionardo: "*Il giovane deve prima imparare prospettiva, per le misure d' ogni cosa.*"

Without absolute precision of measurement, it is certainly impossible for you to learn perspective rightly; and, as far as I can judge, impossible to learn anything else rightly. And in my past experience of teaching, I have found that such precision is of all things the most difficult to inforce on the pupils. It is easy to persuade to diligence, or provoke to enthusiasm; but I have found it hitherto impossible to humiliate one student into perfect accuracy.

It is, therefore, necessary, in beginning a system of drawing for the university, that no opening should be left for failure in this essential matter. I hope you will trust the words of the most accomplished draughtsman of Italy, and the painter of the great sacred picture which, perhaps beyond all others, has influenced the mind of Europe, when he tells you that your first duty is " to learn perspective by the *measures* of everything." For perspective, I will undertake that it shall be made, practically, quite easy to you; but I wish first to make application to the trustees of the National Gallery for the loan to Oxford of Turner's perspective diagrams, which are at present lying useless in a folio in the National Gallery; and therefore we will not trouble ourselves about perspective till the autumn; unless, in the meanwhile, you care to master the mathematical theory of it, which I have carried as far as is necessary for you in my treatise written in 1859, of which copies shall be placed at your disposal in your working room. But the habit and dexterity of measurement you must acquire at once, and that with engineer's accuracy. I hope that in our now gradually developing system of education, elemetary architectural or military drawing will be required at all public schools; so that when youths come to the university, it may be no more necessary for them to pass through the preliminary exercises of drawing than of grammar. For the present, I will place in your series examples simple and severe enough for all necessary practice.

143. And while you are learning to measure, and to draw, and lay flat tints, with the brush, you must also get easy command of the pen ; for that is not only the great instrument for the finest sketching, but its right use is the foundation of the art of illumination. In nothing is fine art more directly connected with service than in the close dependence of decorative illumination on good writing. Perfect illumination is only writing made lovely ; the moment it passes into picture-making it has lost its dignity and function. For pictures, small or great, if beautiful, ought not to be painted on leaves of books, to be worn with service; and pictures, small or great, not beautiful, should be painted nowhere. But to make writing *itself* beautiful—to make the sweep of the pen lovely—is the true art of illumination ; and I particularly wish you to note this, because it happens continually that young girls who are incapable of tracing a single curve with steadiness, much more of delineating any ornamental or organic form with correctness, think that the work which would be intolerable in ordinary drawing becomes tolerable when it is employed for the decoration of texts; and thus they render all healthy progress impossible, by protecting themselves in inefficiency under the shield of a good motive. Whereas the right way of setting to work is to make themselves first

mistresses of the art of writing beautifully; and then to apply that art in its proper degrees of development to whatever they desire permanently to write. And it is indeed a much more truly religious duty for girls to acquire a habit of deliberate legible, and lovely penmanship in their daily use of the pen, than to illuminate any quantity of texts. Having done so, they may next discipline their hands into the control of lines of any length, and, finally, add the beauty of color and form to the flowing of these perfect lines. But it is only after years of practice that they will be able to illuminate noble words rightly for the eyes, as it is only after years of practice that they can make them melodious rightly, with the voice.

144. I shall not attempt, in this lecture, to give you any account of the use of the pen as a drawing instrument. That use is connected in many ways with principles both of shading and of engraving, hereafter to be examined at length. But I may generally state to you that its best employment is in giving determination to the forms in drawings washed with neutral tint; and that, in this use of it, Holbein is quite without a rival. I have therefore placed many examples of his work among your copies. It is employed for rapid study by Raphael and other masters of delineation, who, in such cases, give with it also, partial indications of shadow; but it is not a proper instrument for shading, when drawings are intended to be delib-

crate and complete, nor do the great masters ever so employ it. Its virtue is the power of producing a perfectly delicate, equal, and decisive line with great rapidity; and the temptation allied with that virtue is to licentious haste, and chance-swept instead of strictly-commanded curvature. In the hands of very great painters it obtains, like the etching needle, qualities of exquisite charm in this free use; but all attempts at imitation of these confused and suggestive sketches must be absolutely denied to yourselves while students. You may fancy you have produced something like them with little trouble; but, be assured, it is in reality as unlike them as nonsense is unlike sense; and that, if you persist in such work, you will not only prevent your own executive progress, but you will never understand in all your lives what good painting means. Whenever you take a pen in your hand, if you cannot count every line you lay with it, and say why you make it so long and no longer, and why you drew it in that direction and no other, your work is bad. The only man who can put his pen to full speed, and yet retain command over every separate line of it, is Dürer. He has done this in the illustrations of a missal preserved at Munich, which have been fairly fac-similed; and of these I have placed several in your copying series, with some of Turner's landscape etchings and other examples of deliberate pen work, such as will advantage you in early study. The proper use of them you will find explained in the catalogue.

145. And, now, but one word more to-day. Do not impute to me the impertinence of setting before you what is new in this system of practice as being certainly the best method. No English artists are yet agreed entirely on early methods; and even Reynolds expresses with some hesitation his conviction of the expediency of learning to draw with the brush. But this method that I show you rests in all essential points on his authority, on Lionardo's, or on the evident as well as recorded practice of the most splendid Greek and Italian draughtsmen; and you may be assured it will lead you, however slowly, to a great and certain skill. To what degree of skill, must depend greatly on yourselves; but I know that in practice of this kind you cannot spend an hour without definitely gaining, both in true knowledge of art, and in useful power of hand; and for what may appear in it too difficult, I must shelter or support myself, as in beginning, so in closing, this first lecture on practice, by the words of Reynolds: "The impetuosity of youth is disgusted at the slow approaches of a regular siege, and desires from mere impatience of labor to take the citadel by storm. They must, therefore, be told again and again that labor is the only price of solid fame, and that, whatever their force of genius may be, there is no easy method of becoming a good painter."

LECTURE VI.

LIGHT.

146. The plan of the divisions of art schools which I gave you in the last lecture is, of course, only a first germ of classification, on which we are to found farther and more defined statement; but for this very reason it is necessary that every term of it should be very clear in your minds.

And especially I must ask you to note the sense in which I use the word "mass." Artists usually employ that word to express the spaces of light and darkness, or of color, into which a picture is divided. But this habit of theirs arises partly from their always speaking of pictures in which the lights represent solid form. If they had instead been speaking of flat tints, as, for instance, of the gold and blue in this missal page (S. 7), they would not have called them "masses," but "spaces" of color. Now both for accuracy and convenience sake, you will find it well to observe this distinction, and to call a simple flat tint a space of color; and only the representation of solid or projecting form a mass.

At all events, I mean myself always to make this distinction; which I think you will see the use of by comparing the missal page (S. 7) with a piece of finished painting (Edu. 2). The one I call space with color; the other, mass with color; I use, however, the word "line" rather than "space" in our general scheme, because you cannot limit a flat tint but by a line, or the locus of a line; whereas a gradated tint, expressive of mass, may be lost at its edges in another without any fixed limit; and practically is so, in the works of the greatest masters.

147. You have thus, in your hexagonal scheme, the expression of the universal manner of advance in painting. Line first; then line enclosing flat spaces colored or shaded; then the lines vanish, and the solid forms are seen within the spaces. That is the universal law of advance—1, line; 2, flat space; 3, massed or solid space. But, as you see, this advance may be made, and has been made, by two different roads; one advancing always through color, the other through light and shade. And these two roads are taken by two entirely different kinds of men. The way by color is taken by men of cheerful, natural and entirely sane disposition in body and mind, much resembling, even at its strongest, the temper of well brought up children—too happy to think deeply, yet with powers of imagination by which they can live other lives than their actual ones; make-believe lives, while yet they

remain conscious all the while that they *are* making believe—therefore entirely sane. They are also absolutely contented; they ask for no more light than is immediately around them, and cannot see anything like darkness, but only green and blue, in the earth and sea.

148. The way by light and shade is, on the contrary, taken by men of the highest powers of thought and most earnest desire for truth; they long for light, and for knowledge of all that light can show. But seeking for light, they perceive also darkness; seeking for truth and substance, they find vanity. They look for form in the earth—for dawn in the sky; and seeking these, they find formlessness in the earth, and night in the sky.

Now remember, in these introductory lectures I am putting before you the roots of things, which are strange, and dark, and often, it may seem, unconnected with the branches. You may not at present think these metaphysical statements necessary; but as you go on, you will find that having hold of the clue to methods of work through their springs in human character, you may perceive unerringly where they lead, and what constitutes their wrongness and rightness; and when we have the main principles laid down, all others will develop themselves in due succession, and everything will become more clearly intelligible to you in the end, for having been apparently vague in the beginning. You know when one is laying the foundation of a house, it does not show directly where the rooms are to be.

149. You have then these two great divisions of human mind: one, content with the colors of things, whether they are dark or light; the other seeking light pure, as such, and dreading darkness as such. One, also, content with the colored aspects and visionary shapes of things; the other seeking their form and substance. And, as I said, the school of knowledge, seeking light, perceives, and has to accept and deal with obscurity; and seeking form, it has to accept and deal with formlessness, or death.

Farther, the school of color in Europe, using the word Gothic in its broadest sense, is essentially Gothic-Christian; and full of comfort and peace. Again, the school of light is essentially Greek, and full of sorrow. I cannot tell you which is right, or least wrong. I tell you only what I know—this vital distinction between them; the Gothic or color school is always cheerful, the Greek always oppressed by the shadow of death; and the stronger its masters are, the closer that body of death grips them. The strongest whose work I can show you in recent periods is Holbein; next to him is Lionardo; and then Dürer: but of the three Holbein is the strongest, and with his help I will put the two schools in their full character before you in a moment

150. Here is, first, an entirely characteristic piece of the great color school. It is by Cima of Conegliano, a mountaineer, like Luini, born under the Alps of Friuli. His Christian name was John Baptist: he is here painting his name-Saint; the whole picture full of peace and intense faith and hope, and deep joy in light of sky, and fruit and flower and weed of earth. The picture was painted for the church of Our Lady of the Garden at Venice, La Madonna dell' Orto (properly Madonna of the *Kitchen* Garden), and it is full of simple flowers, and has the wild strawberry of Cima's native mountains gleaming through the grass.

Beside it I will put a piece of strongest work of the school of light and shade—strongest, because Holbein was a colorist also; but he belongs, nevertheless, essentially to the chiaroscuro school. You know that his name is connected, in ideal work, chiefly with his "Dance of Death." I will not show you any of the terror of that; only his deepest thought of death, his well-known "Dead Christ." It will at once show you how completely the Christian art of this school is oppressed by its veracity, and forced to see what is fearful, even in what it most trusts. You may think I am showing you contrasts merely to fit my theories. But there is Dürer's "Knight and Death," his greatest plate; and if I had Lionardo's "Medusa" here, which he painted when only a boy, you would have seen how he was held by the same chain. And you cannot but wonder why, this being the melancholy temper of the great Greek or naturalistic school, I should have called it the school of light. I call it so because it is through its intense love of light that the darkness becomes apparent to it, and through its intense love of truth and form that all mystery becomes attractive to it. And when, having learned these things, it is joined to the school of color, you have the perfect, though always, as I will show you, pensive, art of Titian and his followers.

151. But remember, its first development, and all its final power, depends on Greek sorrow, and Greek religion.

The school of light is founded in the Doric worship of Apollo and the Ionic worship of Athena, as the spirits of life in the light, and of life in the air, opposed each to their own contrary deity of death—Apollo to the Python, Athena to the Gorgon—Apollo as life in light, to the earth spirit of corruption in darkness, Athena as life by motion, to the Gorgon spirit of death by pause, freezing, or turning to stone: both of the great divinities taking their glory from the evil they have conquered; both of them, when angry, taking to men the form of the evil which is their opposite —Apollo slaying by poisoned arrow, by pestilence; Athena by cold, the black ægis on her breast. These are the definite and direct expressions of the Greek thoughts respecting death and life. But underlying both these, and far more mysterious, dreadful, and yet beautiful, there is the Greek conception of spiritual darkness; of the anger of fate, whether foredoomed or avenging; the root and theme of all Greek tragedy; the anger of the Erinnyes, and Demeter Erinnys, compared to which the anger of either of Apollo or Athena is temporary and partial—and also, while Apollo or Athena only slay, the power of Demeter and the Eumenides is over the whole life; so that in the stories of Bellerophon, of Hippolytus, of Orestes, of Œdipus, you have an incomparably deeper shadow than any that was possible to the thought of later ages, when the hope of the resurrection had become definite. And if you keep this in mind, you will find every name and legend of the oldest history become full of meaning to you. All the mythic accounts of Greek sculpture begin in the legends of the family of Tantalus. The main one is the making of the ivory shoulder of Pelops after Demeter has eaten the shoulder of flesh. With that you have Broteas, the brother of Pelops, carving the first statue of the mother of the gods; and you have his sister, Niobe, weeping herself to stone under the anger of the deities of light. Then Pelops himself, the dark-faced, gives name to the Peloponnesus, which you may therefore read as the "isle of darkness;" but its central city, Sparta, the "sown city," is connected with all the ideas of the earth as life-giving. And from her you have Helen, the representative of light in beauty, and the Fratres Helenæ—"*lucida sidera*;" and, on the other side of the hills, the brightness of Argos, with its correlative darkness over the Atreidæ, marked to you by Helios turning away his face from the feast of Thyestes.

152. Then join with these the northern legends connected with the air. It does not matter whether you take Dorus as the son of Apollo or the son of Hellen; he equally symbolizes the power of light: while his brother, Æolus, through all his descendants, chiefly in Sisyphus, is confused or associated with the real god of the winds, and represents to you the power of the air. And then, as this conception enters into art, you have the myths of Dædalus, the flight of Icarus, and the story of Phrixus and Helle, giving you continual associations of the physical air and light, ending in the power of Athena over Corinth as well as over Athens. Now, once having the clue, you can work out the sequels for yourselves better than I can for you; and you will soon find even the earliest or slightest grotesques of Greek art become full of interest to you. For nothing is more wonderful than the depth of meaning which nations in their first days of thought, like children, can attach to the rudest symbols; and what to us is grotesque or ugly, like a little child's doll, can speak to them the loveliest things. I have brought you to-day a few more examples of

early Greek vase painting, respecting which remember generally that its finest development is for the most part sepulchral. You have, in the first period, always energy in the figures, light in the sky or upon the figures;* in the second period, while the conception of the divine power remains the same, it is thought of as in repose, and the light is in the god, not in the sky; in the time of decline, the divine power is gradually disbelieved, and all form and light are lost together. With that period I wish you to have nothing to do. You shall not have a single example of it set before you, but shall rather learn to recognize afterward what is base by its strangeness. These, which are to come early in the third group of your standard series, will enough represent to you the elements of early and late conception in the Greek mind of the deities of light.

153. First (S. 204), you have Apollo ascending from the sea; thought of as the physical sunrise; only a circle of light for his head; his chariot horses, seen foreshortened, black against the daybreak, their feet not yet risen above the horizon. Underneath is the painting from the opposite side of the same vase; Athena as the morning breeze, and Hermes as the morning cloud, flying across the waves before the sunrise. At the distance I now hold them from you, it is scarcely possible for you to see that they are figures at

---

* See note in the catalogue on No. 201.

all, so like are they to broken fragments of flying mist; and when you look close, you will see that as Apollo's face is invisible in the circle of light, Mercury's is invisible in the broken form of cloud; but I can tell you that it is conceived as reverted, looking back to Athena; the grotesque appearance of feature in the front is the outline of his hair.

These two paintings are excessively rude, and of the archaic period; the deities being yet thought of chiefly as physical powers in violent agency.

Underneath these two are Athena and Hermes, in the types attained about the time of Phidias; but, of course, rudely drawn on the vase, and still more rudely in this print from Le Normant and De Witt. For it is impossible (as you will soon find if you try for yourself) to give on a plane surface the grace of figures drawn on one of solid curvature, and adapted to all its curves; and among other minor differences, Athena's lance is in the original nearly twice as tall as herself, and has to be cut short to come into the print at all. Still, there is enough here to show you what I want you to see—the repose, and entirely realized personality, of the deities as conceived in the Phidian period. The relation of the two deities is, I believe, the same as in the painting above, though probably there is another added of more definite kind. But the physical meaning still remains—Athena unhelmeted, as the *gentle* morning wind, commanding the cloud

Hermes to slow flight. His petasus is slung at his back, meaning that the clouds are not yet opened or expanded in the sky.

154. Next (S. 205), you have Athena, again unhelmeted and crowned with leaves, walking between two nymphs, who are crowned also with leaves; and all the three hold flowers in their hands, and there is a fawn walking at Athena's feet.

This is still Athena as the morning air, but upon the earth instead of in the sky, with the nymphs of the dew beside her; the flowers and leaves opening as they breathe upon them. Note the white gleam of light on the fawn's breast; and compare it with the next following examples (underneath this one is the contest of Athena and Poseidon, which does not bear on our present subject).

Next (S. 206), Artemis as the moon of morning, walking low on the hills, and singing to her lyre; the fawn beside her, with the gleam of light of sunrise on its ear and breast. Those of you who are often out in the dawn-time know that there is no moon so glorious as that gleaming crescent ascending before the sun, though in its wane.

Underneath, Artemis and Apollo, of Phidian time.

Next (S. 207), Apollo walking on the earth, god of the morning, singing to his lyre; the fawn beside him, again with the gleam of light on its breast. And underneath, Apollo, crossing the sea to Delphi, of the Phidian time.

155. Now you cannot but be struck in these three examples with the similarity of action in Athena, Apollo, and Artemis, drawn as deities of the morning; and with the association in every case of the fawn with them. It has been said (I will not interrupt you with authorities) that the fawn belongs to Apollo and Diana because stags are sensitive to music (are they?). But you see the fawn is here with Athena of the dew, though she has no lyre; and I have myself no doubt that in this particular relation to the gods of morning it always stands as the symbol of wavering and glancing motion on the ground, as well as of the light and shadows through the leaves, checkering the ground as the fawn is dappled. Similarly the spots on the nebris of Dionysus, thought of sometimes as stars ($\dot{a}\pi\grave{o}\ \tau\tilde{\eta}s\ \tau\tilde{\omega}\nu\ \ddot{a}\sigma\tau\rho\omega\ \pi o\iota\varkappa\iota\lambda\iota as$, Diodorus, II. 1) as well as those of his panthers, and the cloudings of the tortoise-shell of Hermes, are all significant of this light of the sky broken by cloud shadow.

156. You observe also that in all the three examples the fawn has light on its ears, and face, as well as its breast. In the earliest Greek drawings of animals, bars of white are used as one means of detaching the figures from the ground; ordinarily on the under side of them, marking the lighter color of the hair in wild animals. But the placing of this bar of white, or the

direction of the face in deities of light (the faces and flesh of women being always represented as white) may become expressive of the direction of the light, when that direction is important. Thus we are enabled at once to read the intention of this Greek symbol of the course of a day (in the center-piece of S. 208, which gives you the types of Hermes). At the top you have an archaic representation of Hermes stealing Io from Argus. Argus is here the night; his grotesque features monstrous; his hair overshadowing his shoulders; Hermes on tiptoe, stealing upon him, and taking the cord which is fastened to the horn of Io out of his hand without his feeling it. Then, underneath, you have the course of an entire day. Apollo first, on the left, dark, entering his chariot, the sun not yet risen. In front of him Artemis, as the moon, ascending before him, playing on her lyre, and looking back to the sun. In the center, behind the horses, Hermes, as the cumulus cloud at mid-day, wearing his petasus heightened to a cone, and holding a flower in his right hand; indicating the nourishment of the flowers by the rain from the heat-cloud. Finally, on the right, Latona, going down as the evening, lighted from the right by the sun, now sunk; and with her feet reverted, signifying the unwillingness of the departing day.

Finally, underneath, you have Hermes of the Phidian period, as the floating cumulus cloud, almost shapeless (as you see him at this distance); with the tortoise-shell lyre in his hand, barred with black, and a fleece of white cloud, not level, but *oblique*, under his feet. (Compare the 'διὰ τῶν κοίλων—πλάγιαι,' and the relations of the 'αἰγίδος ἡνίοχος Ἀθάνα,' with the clouds as the moon's messengers, in Aristophanes; and note of Hermes generally, that you never find him flying as a Victory flies, but always, if moving fast at all, clambering along, as it were, as a cloud gathers and heaps itself: the Gorgons stretch and stride in their flight, half kneeling, for the same reason, running or gliding shapelessly along in this stealthy way.)

157. And now take this last illustration, of a very different kind. Here is an effect of morning light by Turner (S. 301), on the rocks of Otley-hill, near Leeds, drawn long ago, when Apollo, and Artemis, and Athena, still sometimes were seen, and felt, even near Leeds. The original drawing is one of the great Farnley series, and entirely beautiful. I have shown, in the last volume of "Modern Painters," how well Turner knew the meaning of Greek legends: he was not thinking of them, however, when he made this design: but, unintentionally, has given us the very effect of morning light we want: the glittering of the sunshine on dewy grass, half dark; and the narrow gleam of it on the sides and head of the stag and hind.

158. These few instances will be enough to show

you how we may read in early art of the Greeks their strong impressions of the power of light. You will find the subject entered into at somewhat greater length in my "Queen of the Air;" and if you will look at the beginning of the 7th book of Plato's "Polity," and read carefully the passages in the context respecting the sun and intellectual sight, you will see how intimately this physical love of light was connected with their philosophy, in its search, as blind and captive, for better knowledge. I shall not attempt to define for you to-day, the more complex but much shallower forms which this love of light, and the philosophy that accompanies it, take in the mediæval mind; only remember that in future, when I briefly speak of the Greek school of art with reference to questions of delineation, I mean the entire range of the schools, from Homer's days to our own, which concern themselves with the representation of light, and the effects it produces on material form—beginning practically for us with these Greek vase paintings, and closing practically for us with Turner's sunset on the Temeraire; being throughout a school of captivity and sadness, but of intense power; and which in its technical method of shadow on material form, as well as in its essential temper, is centrally represented to you by Dürer's two great engravings of the "Melencolia" and the "Knight and Death." On the other hand, when I briefly speak to you of the Gothic school, with reference to delineation, I mean the entire and much more extensive range of schools extending from the earliest art in Central Asia and Egypt down to our own day in India and China—schools which have been content to obtain beautiful harmonies of color without any representation of light; and which have, many of them, rested in such imperfect expressions of form as could be so obtained; schools usually in some measure childish, or restricted in intellect, and similarly childish or restricted in their philosophies or faiths; but contented in the restriction; and in the more powerful races, capable of advance to nobler development than the Greek schools, though the consummate art of Europe has only been accomplished by the union of both. How that union was affected, I will endeavor to show you in my next lecture; to-day I shall take note only of the points bearing on our immediate practice.

159. A certain number of you, by faculty and natural disposition—and all, so far as you are interested in modern art—will necessarily have to put yourselves under the discipline of the Greek or chiaroscuro school, which is directed primarily to the attainment of the power of representing form by pure contrast of light and shade. I say, the "discipline" of the Greek school, both because, followed faithfully, it is indeed a severe one, and because to follow it at all is, for persons fond of color, often a course of painful self-denial,

from which young students are eager to escape. And yet, when the laws of both schools are rightly obeyed the most perfect discipline is that of the colorists; for they see and draw everything, while the chiaroscurists must leave much indeterminate in mystery, or invisible in gloom; and there are therefore many licentious and vulgar forms of art connected with the chiaroscuro school, both in painting and etching, which have no parallel among the colorists. But both schools, rightly followed, require, first of all, absolute accuracy of delineation. This you need not hope to escape. Whether you fill your spaces with colors, or with shadows, they must equally be of the true outline and in true gradations. I have been thirty years telling modern students of art this in vain. I mean to say it to you only once, for the statement is too important to be weakened by repetition.

Without perfect delineation of form and perfect gradation of space, neither noble color is possible, nor noble light.

160. It may make this more believable to you if I put beside each other a piece of detail from each school. I gave you the St. John of Cima da Conegliano for a type of the color school. Here is one of the sprays of oak which rise against the sky of it in the distance, enlarged to about its real size (Edu. 12). I hope to draw it better for you at Venice; but this will show you with what perfect care the colorist has followed

the outline of every leaf in the sky. Beside it, I put a chiaroscurist drawing (at least, a photograph of one), Dürer's, from nature, of the common wild wall-cabbage (Edu. 32). It is the most perfect piece of delineation by flat tint I have even seen, in its mastery of the perspective of every leaf, and its attainment almost of the bloom of texture, merely by its exquisitely tender and decisive laying of the color. These two examples ought, I think, to satisfy you as to the precision of outline of both schools, and the power of expression which may be obtained by flat tints laid within such outline.

161. Next, here are two examples of the gradated shading expressive of the forms within the outline, by two masters of the chiaroscuro school. The first (S. 12) shows you Lionardo's method of work, both with chalk and the silver point. The second (S. 302), Turner's work in mezzotint; both masters doing their best. Observe that this plate of Turner's, which he worked on so long that it was never published, is of a subject peculiarly depending on effects of mystery and concealment, the fall of the Reuss under the Devil's Bridge on the St. Gothard (the *old* bridge; you may still see it under the existing one, which was built since Turner's drawing was made). If ever outline could be dispensed with, you would think it might be so in this confusion of cloud, foam, and darkness. But here is Turner's own etching on the plate, (Edu. 35 F),

made under the mezzotint; and of all the studies of rock outline made by his hand, it is the most decisive and quietly complete.

162. Again; in the Lionardo sketches, many parts are lost in obscurity, or are left intentionally uncertain and mysterious, even in the light; and you might at first imagine some permission of escape had been here given you from the terrible law of delineation. But the slightest attempts to copy them will show you that the terminal lines are inimitably subtle, unaccusably true and filled by gradations of shade so determined and measured, that the addition of a grain of the lead or chalk as large as the filament of a moth's wing, would make an appreciable difference in them.

This is grievous, you think, and hopeless. No, it is delightful and full of hope: delightful, to see what marvelous things can be done by men; and full of hope, if your hope is the right one, of being one day able to rejoice more in what others are, than in what you are yourself, and more in the strength that is forever above you, than in that you can ever attain.

163. But you can attain much, if you will work reverently and patiently, and hope for no success through ill-regulated effort. It is, however, most assuredly at this point of your study that the full strain on your patience will begin. The exercises in line-drawing and flat laying of color are irksome; but they are definite, and within certain limits, sure to be suc-

cessful if practiced with moderate care. But the expression of form by shadow requires more subtle patience, and involves the necessity of frequent and mortifying failure, not to speak of the self-denial which I said was needful in persons fond of color, to draw in mere light and shade. If, indeed, you were going to be artists, or could give any great length of time to study, it might be possible for you to learn wholly in the Venetian school, and to reach form through color. But without the most intense application this is not possible; and practically, it will be necessary for you, as soon as you have gained the power of outlining accurately, and of laying flat color, to learn to express solid form as shown by light and shade only. And there is this great advantage in doing so, that many forms are more or less disguised by color, and that we can only represent them completely to others, or rapidly and easily record them for ourselves, by the use of shade alone. A single instance will show you what I mean. Perhaps there are few flowers of which the impression on the eye is more definitely of flat color than the scarlet geranium. But you will find, if you were to try to paint it—first, that no pigment could approach the beauty of its scarlet; and secondly, that the brightness of the hue dazzled the eye, and prevented its following the real arrangement of the cluster of flowers. I have drawn for you here (at least this is a mezzotint from my drawing), a single cluster of the scarlet geranium, in mere light and shade (Edu. 32 B.), and I think you will feel that its domed form, and the flat lying of the petals one over the other, in the vaulted roof of it, can be seen better thus than if they had been painted scarlet.

164. Also this study will be useful to you, in showing how entirely effects of light depend on delineation and gradation of spaces, and not on methods of shading. And this is the second great practical matter I want you to remember to-day. All effects of light and shade depend, not on the method or execution of shadows, but on their rightness of place, form and depth. There is indeed a loveliness of execution *added* to the rightness, by the great masters, but you cannot obtain that till you become one. Shadow cannot be laid thoroughly well, any more than lines can be drawn steadily, but by a long practiced hand, and the attempts to imitate the shading of fine draughtsmen, by dotting and hatching, are just as ridiculous as it would be to endeavor to imitate their instantaneous lines by a series of re-touchings. You will often indeed see in Lionardo's work and in Michael Angelo's, shadow wrought laboriously to an extreme of fineness; but when you look into it, you will find that they have always been drawing more and more form within the space, and never finishing for the sake of added texture, but of added fact. And all those effects of transparency and reflected light, aimed at in com-

mon chalk drawings, are wholly spurious. For since, as I told you, all lights are shades compared to higher lights, and lights only as compared to lower ones, it follows that there can be no difference in their quality as such; but that light is opaque when it expresses substance, and transparent when it expresses space; and shade is also opaque when it expresses substance, and transparent when it expresses space. But it is not, even then, transparent in the common sense of that word; nor is its appearance to be obtained by dotting or cross hatching, but by touches so tender as to look like mist. And now we find the use of having Lionardo for our guide. He is supreme in all questions of execution, and in his twenty-eighth chapter, you will find that shadows are to be "*dolce e sfumose,*" to be tender, and look as if they were exhaled, or breathed on the paper. Then, look at any of Michael Angelo's finished drawings, or of Correggio's sketches and you will see that the true nurse of light is in art, as in nature, the cloud; a misty and tender darkness, made lovely by gradation.

165. And how absolutely independent it is of material or method of production, how absolutely dependent on rightness of place and depth—there are now before you instances enough to prove. Here is Dürer's work in flat color, represented by the photograph in its smoky brown; Turner's in washed sepia, and in mezzotint; Lionardo's, in pencil and in chalk; on the

screen in front of you a large study in charcoal. In every one of these drawings, the material of shadow is absolutely opaque. But photograph-stain, chalk, lead, ink, or charcoal—every one of them, laid by the master's hand, becomes full of light by gradation only. Here is a moonlight (Edu. 31 B.), in which you would think the moon shone through every cloud; yet the clouds are mere single dashes of sepia, imitated by the brown stain of a photograph; similarly, in these plates from the Liber Studiorum the white paper becomes transparent or opaque, exactly as the master chooses. Here, on the granite rock of the St. Gothard (S. 302), is white paper made opaque, every light represents solid bosses of rock, or balls of foam. But in this study of twilight (S. 303), the same white paper (coarse old stuff it is, too!) is made as transparent as crystal, and every fragment of it represents clear and far away light in the sky of evening in Italy. From which the practical conclusion for you is, that you are never to trouble yourselves with any questions as to the means of shade or light, but only with the right government of the means at your disposal. And it is a most grave error in the system of many of our public drawing-schools that the students are permitted to spend weeks of labor in giving attractive appearance, by delicacy of texture, to chiaroscuro drawings in which every form is false, and every relation of depth untrue. A most unhappy form of error; for it not only delays, and often wholly arrests, their advance in their own art; but it prevents what ought to take place co-relatively with their executive practice, the formation of their taste by the accurate study of the models from which they draw. I do not doubt but that you have more pleasure in looking at the large drawing of the arch of Bourges, behind me (Ref. 1), than at common sketches of sculpture. The reason you like it is, that the whole effort of the workman has been to show you, not his own skill in shading, but the play of the light on the surfaces of the leaves, which is lovely, because the sculpture itself is first-rate. And I must so far anticipate what we shall discover when we come to the subject of sculpture, as to tell you the two main principles of good sculpture: first, that its masters think before all other matters of the right placing of masses; secondly, that they give life by flexure of surface, not by quantity of detail; for sculpture is indeed only light and shade drawing in stone.

166. Much that I have endeavored to teach on this subject has been gravely misunderstood, by both young painters and sculptors, especially by the latter. Because I am always urging them to imitate organic forms, they think if they carve quantities of flowers and leaves, and copy them from the life, they have done all that is needed. But the difficulty is not to carve quantities of leaves. Anybody can do that. The difficulty is, never anywhere to have an unneces-

sary leaf. Over the arch on the right, you see there is a cluster of seven, with their short stalks springing from a thick stem. Now, you could not turn one of those leaves a hair's-breath out of its place, nor thicken one of their stems, nor alter the angle at which each slips over the next one, without spoiling the whole, as much as you would a piece of melody by missing a note. That is disposition of masses. Again, in the group on the left, while the placing of every leaf is just as skillful, they are made more interesting yet by the lovely undulation of their surfaces, so that not one of them is in equal light with another. And that is so in all good sculpture, without exception. From the Elgin marbles down to the lightest tendril that curls round a capital in the thirteenth century, every piece of stone that has been touched by the hand of a master, becomes soft with under-life, not resembling nature merely in skin-texture, nor in fibres of leaf, or veins of flesh; but in the broad, tender unspeakably subtle undulation of its organic form.

167. Returning then to the question of our own practice, I believe that all difficulties in method will vanish, if only you cultivate with care enough the habit of accurate observation, and if you think only of making your light and shade true, whether it be delicate or not. But there are three divisions or degrees of truth to be sought for, in light and shade, by three several modes of study, which I must ask you to distinguish carefully.

I. When objects are lighted by the direct rays of the sun, or by direct light entering from a window one side of them is of course in light, the other in shade, and the forms in the mass are exhibited systematically by the force of the rays falling on it; (those having most power of illumination which strike most vertically); and note that there is, therefore, to every solid curvature of surface, a necessarily proportioned gradation of light, the gradation on a parabolic solid being different from the gradation on an elliptical or spherical one. Now, when your purpose is to represent and learn the anatomy, or otherwise characteristic forms, of any object, it is best to place it in this kind of direct light, and to draw it as it is seen when we look at it in a direction at right angles to that of the ray. This is the ordinary academical way of studying form. Lionardo seldom practises any other in his real work, though he directs many others in his treatise.

168. The great importance of anatomical knowledge to the painters of the sixteenth century rendered this method of study very frequent with them; it almost wholly regulated their schools of engraving, and has been the most frequent system of drawing in art-schools since (to the very inexpedient exclusion of others). When you study objects in this way, and it will indeed be well to do so often, though not exclusively, observe always one main principle. Divide the light from the

darkness frankly at first: all over the subject let there be no doubt which is which. Separate them one from the other as they are separated in the moon, or on the world itself, in day and night. Then gradate your lights with the utmost subtilty possible to you; but let your shadows alone, until near the termination of the drawing: then put quickly into them what farther energy they need, thus gaining the reflected lights out of their original flat gloom; but generally not looking much for reflected lights. Nearly all young students (and too many advanced masters) exaggerate them. It is good to see a drawing come out of its ground like a vision of light only; the shadows lost, or disregarded in the vague of space. In vulgar chiaroscuro the shades are so full of reflection that they look as if some one had been walking round the object with a candle, and the student, by that help, peering into its crannies.

169. II. But in the reality of nature, very few objects are seen in this accurately lateral manner, or lighted by unconfused direct rays. Some are all in shadow, some all in light, some near, and vigorously defined; others dim and faint in aerial distance. The study of these various effects and forces of light, which we may call aerial chiaroscuro, is a far more subtle one than that of the rays exhibiting organic form (which for distinction's sake we may call "formal" chiaroscuro), since the degrees of light from the sun

itself to the blackness of night, are far beyond any literal imitation. In order to produce a mental impression of the facts, two distinct methods may be followed: the first, to shade downward from the lights making everything darker in due proportion, until the scale of our power being ended, the mass of the picture is lost in shade. The second, to assume the points of extreme darkness for a basis, and to light everything above these in due proportion, till the mass of the picture is lost in light.

170. Thus, in Turner's sepia drawing "Isis" (Edu. 31), he begins with the extreme light in the sky, and shades down from that till he is forced to represent the near trees and pool as one mass of blackness. In his drawing of the Greta (S. 2) he begins with the dark brown shadow of the bank on the left, and illuminates up from that, till, in his distance, trees, hills, sky, and clouds, are all lost in broad light, so that you can hardly see the distinction between hills and sky. The second of these methods is in general the best for color, though great painters unite both in their practice, according to the character of their subject. The first method is never pursued in color but by inferior painters. It is, nevertheless, of great importance to make studies of chiaroscuro in this first manner for some time, as a preparation for coloring; and this for many reasons, which it would take too long to state now. I shall expect you to have confidence in

me when I assure you of the necessity of this study, and ask you to make good use of the examples from the Liber Studiorum which I have placed in your educational series.

171. III. Whether in formal or aerial chiaroscuro it is optional with the student to make the local color of objects a part of his shadow, or to consider the high lights of every color as white. For instance, a chiaroscurist of Lionardo's school, drawing a leopard, would take no notice whatever of the spots, but only give the shadows which expressed the anatomy. And it is indeed necessary to be able to do this, and to make drawings of the forms of things as if they were sculptured, and had no color. But in general and more especially in the practice which is to guide you to color, it is better to regard the local color as part of the general dark and light to be imitated; and, as I told you at first, to consider all nature merely as a mosaic of different colors, to be imitated one by one in simplicity. But good artists vary their methods according to their subject and material. In general, Dürer takes little account of local color; but in woodcuts of armorial bearings (one with peacock's feathers I shall get for you some day) takes great delight in it; while one of the chief merits of Bewick is the ease and vigor with which he uses his black and white for the colors of plumes. Also, every great artist looks for and expresses, that character of his subject which is

best to be rendered by the instrument in his hand, and the material he works on. Give Valasquez or Veronese a leopard to paint, the first thing they think of will be its spots; give it to Dürer to engrave, and he will set himself at the fur and whiskers; give it a Greek to carve, and he will only think of its jaws and limbs; each doing what is absolutely best with the means at his disposal.

172. The details of practice in these various methods I will endeavor to explain to you by distinct examples in your educational series, as we proceed in our work; for the present, let me, in closing, recommend to you once more with great earnestness the patient endeavor to render the chiaroscuro of landscape in the manner of the Liber Studiorum; and this the rather, because you might easily suppose that the facility of obtaining photographs which render such effects, as it seems, with absolute truth and with unapproachable subtlety, superceded the necessity of study, and the use of sketching. Let me assure you, once for all, that photographs supercede no single quality nor use of fine art, and have so much in common with nature, that they even share her temper of parsimony, and will themselves give you nothing valuable that you do not work for. They supercede no good art, for the definition of art is "human labor regulated by human design," and this design or evidence of active intellect in choice and arrangement, is the essential part of the work; which, so long as you cannot

perceive, you perceive no art whatsoever; which, when once you do perceive, you will perceive also to be replaceable by no mechanism. But, farther, photographs will give you nothing you do not work for. They are invaluable for record of some kinds of facts, and for giving transcripts of drawings by great masters; but neither in the photographed scene, nor photographed drawing will you see any true good, more than in the things themselves, until you have given the appointed price in your own attention and toil. And when once you have paid this price, you will not care for photographs of landscape. They are not true, though they seem so. They are merely spoiled nature. If it is not human design you are looking for, there is more beauty in the next wayside bank than in all the sun-blackened paper you could collect in a lifetime. Go and look at the real landscape, and take care of it; do not think you can get the good of it in a black stain portable in a folio. But if you care for human thought and passion, then learn yourselves to watch the course and fall of the light by whose influence you live, and to share in the joy of human spirits in the heavenly gifts of sunbeam and shade. For I tell you truly, that to a quiet heart, and healthy brain, and industrious hand there is more delight, and use, in the dappling of one wood-glade with flowers and sunshine, than to the restless, heartless, and idle could be brought by a panorama of a belt of the world, photographed round the equator.

LECTURE VII.

COLOR.

173. To-day I must try to complete our elementary sketch of schools of art, by tracing the course of those which were distinguished by faculty of color, and afterward to deduce from the entire scheme advisable methods of immediate practice.

You remember that, for the type of the early schools of color, I chose their work in glass; as for that of the early schools of chiaroscuro, I chose their work in clay.

I had two reasons for this. First, that the peculiar skill of colorists is seen most intelligibly in their work in glass or in enamel; secondly, that nature herself produces all her loveliest colors in some kind of solid or liquid glass or crystal. The rainbow is painted on a shower of melted glass, and the colors of the opal are produced in vitreous flint mixed with water; the green and blue, and golden or amber brown of flowing water is in surface glossy, and in motion, "*splendidor vitro.*" And the loveliest colors ever granted to human sight—those of morning and evening clouds before or after rain—are produced on minute particles of finely-divided water, or perhaps sometimes, ice. But more than this. If you examine with a lens some of the richest colors of flowers, as, for instance, those of the gentian and dianthus, you will find their texture is produced by a crystalline or sugary frost-work upon them. In the lychnis of the high Alps, the red and white have a kind of sugary bloom, as rich as it is delicate. It is indescribable; but if you can fancy very powdery and crystalline snow mixed with the softest cream, and then dashed with carmine, it may give you some idea of the look of it. There are no colors, either in the nacre of shells, or the plumes of birds and insects, which are so pure as those of clouds-opal or flowers; but the *force* of purple and blue in some butterflies, and the methods of clouding, and strength of burnished luster, in plumage like the peacock's, give them more universal interest; in some birds, also, as in our own kingfisher, the color nearly reaches a floral preciousness. The luster in most, however, is metallic rather than vitreous; and the vitreous always gives the purest hue. Entirely common and vulgar compared with these, yet to be noticed as completing the crystalline or vitreous system, we have the colors of gems. The green of the emerald is the best of these; but at its best is as vulgar as house-painting beside the green of bird's plumage or of clear water. No diamond shows color so pure as a dewdrop; the ruby is like the pink of an ill-dyed and half-washed-out print, compared to the dianthus; and the carbuncle is usually quite dead unless set with a foil, and even then is not prettier than the seed of a pomegranate. The opal is, however, an exception. When pure and uncut in its native rock, it presents the most lovely colors that can be seen in the world, except those of clouds.

We have thus in nature, chiefly obtained by crystalline conditions, a series of groups of entirely delicious hues; and it is one of the best signs that the bodily system is in a healthy state when we can see these clearly in their most delicate tints, and enjoy them fully and simply, with the kind of enjoyment that children have in eating sweet things. I shall place a piece of rock opal on the table in your working-room; if on fine days you will sometimes dip it in water, take it into sunshine, and examine it with a lens of moderate power, you may always test your progress in sensibility to color by the degree of pleasure it gives you.

174. Now, the course of our main color schools is briefly this: First, we have, returning to our hexagonal scheme, line; then *spaces* filled with pure color; and then *masses* expressed or rounded with pure color. And during these two stages the masters of color delight in the purest tints, and endeavor as far as possible to rival those of opals and flowers. In saying

"the purest tints," I do not mean the simplest types of red, blue and yellow, but the most pure tints obtainable by their combinations.

175. You remember I told you, when the colorists painted masses or projecting spaces, they, aiming always at color, perceived from the first and held to the last the fact that shadows, though of course darker than the lights with reference to which they *are* shadows are not therefore necessarily less vigorous colors, but perhaps more vigorous. Some of the most beautiful blues and purples in nature, for instance, are those of mountains in shadow against amber sky; and the darkness of the hollow in the center of a wild rose is one glow of orange fire, owing to the quantity of its yellow stamens.

Well, the Venetians always saw this, and all great colorists see it, and are thus separated from the non-colorists or schools of mere chiaroscuro, not by difference in style merely but by being right while the others are wrong. It is an absolute fact that shadows are as much colors as lights are; and whoever represents them by merely the subdued or darkened tint of the light, represents them falsely. I particularly want you to observe that this is no matter of taste, but fact. If you are especially sober-minded, you may indeed choose sober colors where Venetians would have chosen gay ones; that is a matter of taste: you may think it proper for a hero to wear a dress without patterns on it, rather than an embroidered one ; that is similary a matter of taste : but, though you may also think it would be dignified for a hero's limbs to be all black, or brown, on the shaded side of them, yet, if you are using color at all you cannot so have him to your mind, except by falsehood ; he never, under any circumstances, could be entirely black or brown on one side of him.

176. In this, then, the Venetians are separate from other schools by rightness, and they are so to their last days. Venetian painting is in this matter always right. But also in their early days, the colorists are separated from other schools by their contentment with tranquil cheerfulness of light; by their never wanting to be dazzled. None of their lights are flashing or blinding; they are soft, winning, precious ; lights of pearl, not of lime : only, you know, on this condition they cannot have sunshine : their day is the day of Paradise ; they need no candle, neither light of the sun, in their cities ; and everything is seen clear, as through crystal, far or near.

This holds to the end of the fifteenth century. Then they begin to see that this, beautiful as it may be, is still a make-believe light ; that we do not live in the inside of a pearl ; but in an atmosphere through which a burning sun shines thwartedly, and over which a sorrowful night must far prevail. And then the chiaroscurists succeed in persuading them of the fact that there is mystery in the day as in the night, and show them how constantly to see truly, is to see dimly. And also they teach them the brilliancy of light, and the degree in which it is raised from the darkness; and, instead of their sweet and pearly peace, tempt them to look for the strength of flame and coruscation of lightning, and flash of sunshine on armor and on points of spears.

177. The noble painters take the lesson nobly, alike for gloom or flame. Titian with deliberate strength, Tintoret with stormy passion, read it, side by side. Titian deepens the hues of his Assumption, as of his Entombment, into a solemn twilight; Tintoret involves his earth in coils of volcanic cloud, and withdraws, through circle flaming above circle, the distant light of Paradise. Both of them, becoming naturalist and human, add the veracity of Holbein's intense portraiture to the glow and the dignity they had themselves inherited from the Masters of Peace: at the same moment another, as strong as they, and in pure felicity of art-faculty, even greater than they, but trained in a lower school—Velasquez—produced the miracles of color and shadow-painting, which made Reynolds say of him, "What we all do with labor, he does with ease;" and one more, Correggio, uniting the sensual element of the Greek schools with their gloom, and their light with their beauty, and all these with the Lombardic color, became, as since I think it

has been admitted without question, the captain of the painter's art as such. Other men have nobler or more numerous gifts, but as a painter, master of the art of laying color so as to be lovely, Correggio is alone.

178. I said the noble men learned their lesson nobly. The base men also, and necessarily, learn it basely. The great men rise from color to sunlight. The base ones fall from color to candlelight. To-day, "*non ragiouiam di lor,*" but let us see what this great change which perfects the art of painting mainly consists in, and means. For though we are only at present speaking of technical matters, every one of them, I can scarcely too often repeat, is the outcome and sign of a mental character, and you can only understand the folds of the veil, by those of the form it veils.

179. The complete painters, we find, have brought dimness and mystery into their method of coloring. That means that the world all round them has resolved to dream, or to believe, no more; but to know, and to see. And instantly all knowledge and sight are given, no more as in the Gothic times, through a window of glass brightly, but as through a telescope-glass, darkly. Your cathedral window shut you from the true sky, and illumined you with a vision; your telescope leads you to the sky, but darkens its light, and reveals nebula beyond nebula, far and farther, and to no conceiveable farthest—unresolvable. That is what the mystery means.

180. Next, what does that Greek opposition of black and white mean?

In the sweet crystalline time of color, the painters, whether on glass or canvas, employed intricate patterns, in order to mingle hues beautifully with each other, and make one perfect melody of them all. But in the great naturalist school, they like their patterns to come in the Greek way, dashed dark on light—gleaming light out of dark. That means also that the world round them has again returned to the Greek conviction, that all nature, especially human nature, is not entirely melodious nor luminous; but a barred and broken thing; that saints have their foibles, sinners their forces; that the most luminous virtue is often only a flash, and the blackest-looking fault is sometimes only a stain: and, without confusing in the least black with white, they can forgive, or even take delight in things that are like the $νεβρίς$, dappled.

181. You have then—first, mystery. Secondly, opposition of dark and light. Then, lastly, whatever truth of form the dark and light can show.

That is to say, truth altogether, and resignation to it, and quiet, and quiet resolve to make the best of it. And therefore, portraiture of living men, women, and children, no more of saints, cherubs, or demons. So here I have brought for your standards of perfect art, a little maiden of the Strozzi family, with her dog, by Titian; and a little princess of the house of Savoy, by

Vandyke; and Charles the Fifth, by Titian; and a queen by Velasquez; and an English girl in a brocaded gown, by Reynolds; and an English physician in his plain coat and wig, by Reynolds: and if you do not like them, I cannot help myself, for I can find nothing better for you.

182. Better? I must pause at the word. Nothing stronger, certainly, nor so strong. Nothing so wonderful, so inimitable, so keen in unprejudiced and unbiased sight.

Yet better, perhaps, the sight that was guided by a sacred will; the power that could be taught to weaker hands; the work that was faultless, though not inimitable, bright with felicity of heart, and consummate in a disciplined and companionable skill. You will find, when I can place in your hands the notes on Verona, which I read at the Royal Institution, that I have ventured to call the æra of painting represented by John Bellini, the time " of the masters." Truly, they deserved the name, who did nothing but what was lovely, and taught only what was right. These mightier, who succeeded them, crowned, but closed, the dynasties of art, and since their day painting has never flourished more.

183. There were many reasons for this, without fault of theirs. They were exponents, in the first place, of the change in all men's minds from civil and religious to merely domestic passion; the love of their

gods and their country had contracted itself now into that of their domestic circle, which was little more than the halo of themselves. You will see the reflection of this change in painting at once by comparing the two Madonnas (S. 37, John Bellini's, and Raphael's, called "*della Seggiola*"). Bellini's Madonna cares for all creatures through her child; Raphael's, for her child only.

Again, the world round these painters had become sad and proud, instead of happy and humble—its domestic peace was darkened by irreligion, and made restless by pride. And the Hymen, whose statue this fair English girl of Reynold's thought must decorate (S. 43), is blind and holds a coronet.

Again, in the splendid power of realization, which these greatest of artists had reached, there was the latent possibility of amusement by deception, and of excitement by sensualism. And Dutch trickeries of base resemblance, and French and English fancies of insidious beauty, soon occupied the eyes of the populace of Europe, too restless and wretched now to care for the sweet earth-berries and Madonna's ivy of Cima, and too ignoble to perceive Titian's color, or Correggio's shade.

184. Enough sources of evil were here, in the temper and power of the consummate art. In its practical methods there was another, the fatallest of all. These great artists brought with them mystery, de-

spondency, domesticity, sensuality; of all these, good came, as well as evil. One thing more they brought, of which nothing but evil ever comes, or can come— liberty.

By the discipline of five hundred years they had learned and inherited such power, that whereas all former painters could be right only by effort, they could be right with ease; and whereas all former painters could be right only under restraint, they could be right free. Tintoret's touch, Luini's, Correggio's, Reynold's, and Velasquez's, are all as free as the air, and yet right. "How very fine," said everybody. Unquestionably, very fine. Next, said everybody, "What a grand discovery! Here is the finest work ever done, and it is quite free. Let us all be free then, and what fine things shall we not do also!" With what results we too well know.

Nevertheless, remember you are to delight in the freedom won by these mighty men through obedience though you are not to covet it. Obey, and you also shall be free in time; but in these minor things, as well as in great, it is only right service which is perfect freedom.

185. This, broadly, is the history of the early and late color-schools. The first of these I shall call generally, henceforward, the school of crystal; the other that of clay: potter's clay, or human, are too sorrowfully the same, as far as art is concerned. Now re-

member, in practice, you cannot follow both these schools; you must distinctly adopt the principles of one or the other. I will put the means of following either within your reach; and according to your dispositions you will choose one or the other: all I have to guard you against is the mistake of thinking you can unite the two. If you want to paint (even in the most distant and feeble way) in the Greek school, the school of Lionardo, Correggio, and Turner, you cannot design colored windows, nor Angelican paradises. If on the other hand, you choose to live in the peace of paradise, you cannot share in the gloomy triumphs of the earth.

186. And, incidentally note, as a practical matter of immediate importance, that painted windows have nothing to do with chiaroscuro. The virtue of glass is to be transparent everywhere. If you care to build a palace of jewels, painted glass is richer than all the treasures of Aladdin's lamp; but if you like pictures better than jewels, you must come into broad daylight to paint them. A picture in colored glass is one of the most vulgar of barbarisms, and only fit to be ranked with the gauze transparencies and chemical illuminations of the sensational stage. Also, put out of your minds at once all question about difficulty of getting color; in glass we have all the colors that are wanted, only we do not know either how to choose, or how to connect them; and we are always trying to get them

bright, when their real virtue is to be deep, and tender and subdued. We will have a thorough study of painted glass soon : meanwhile I merely give you a type of its perfect style, in two windows from Chalons sur Marne (S. 141).

187. You will have then to choose between these two modes of thought: for my own part, with what poor gift and skill is in me, I belong wholly to the chiaroscurist school; and shall teach you therefore chiefly that which I am best able to teach : and the rather, that it is only in this school that you can follow out the study either of natural history or landscape. The form of a wild animal, or the wrath of a mountain torrent, would both be revolting (or in a certain sense invisible) to the calm fantasy of a painter in the schools of crystal. He must lay his lion asleep in St. Jerome's study beside his tame partridge and spare slippers; lead the appeased river by alternate azure promontories, and restrain its courtly little streamlets with margins of marble. But, on the other hand, your studies of mythology and literature may best be connected with these schools of purest and calmest imagination ; and their discipline will be useful to you in yet another direction, and that a very important one. It will teach you to take delight in little things, and develop in you the joy which all men should feel in purity and order, not only in pictures but in reality. For, indeed, the best art of this school of fantasy may at last be

in reality, and the chiarosurists, true in ideal, may be less helpful in act. We cannot arrest sunsets nor carve mountains, but we may turn every English homestead, if we choose, into a picture by Cima or John Bellini, which shall be "no counterfeit, but the true and perfect image of life indeed."

188. For the present, however, and yet for some little time during your progress, you will not have to choose your school. For both, as we have seen, begin in delineation, and both proceed by filling flat spaces with an even tint. And therefore this will be the course of work for you, founded on all that we have seen.

Having learned to measure, and draw a pen line with some steadiness (the geometrical exercises for this purpose being properly school, not university work), you shall have a series of studies from the plants which are of chief importance in the history of art; first from their real forms, and then from the conventional and heraldic expressions of them; then we will take examples of the filling of ornamental forms with flat color in Egyptian, Greek, and Gothic design ; and then we will advance to animal forms treated in the same severe way, and so to the patterns and color designs on animals themselves. And when we are sure of our firmness of hand and accuracy of eye, we will go on into light and shade.

189. In process of time, these series of exercises

will, I hope, be sufficiently complete and systematic to show its purpose at a glance. But during the present year, I shall content myself with placing a few examples of these different kinds of practice in your rooms for work, explaining in the catalogue the position they will ultimately occupy, and the technical points of process into which it is of no use to enter in a general lecture. After a little time spent in copying these, your own predilections must determine your future course of study; only remember, whatever school you follow, it must be only to learn method, not to imitate result, and to acquaint yourselves with the minds of other men, but not to adopt them as your own. Be assured that no good can come of your work but as it arises simply out of your own true natures and the necessities of the time around you, though in many respects an evil one. You live in an age of base conceit and baser servility—an age whose intellect is chiefly formed by pillage and occupied in desecration; one day mimicking, the next destroying, the works of all the noble persons who made its intellectual or art life possible to it: an age without honest confidence enough in itself to carve a cherry-stone with an original fancy, but with insolence enough to abolish the solar system, if it were allowed to meddle with it. In the midst of all this, you have to become lowly and strong; to recognize the powers of others and to fulfill your own. I shall try to bring before you every form of ancient art, that you may read and profit by it, not imitate it. You shall draw Egyptian kings dressed in colors like the rainbow, and Doric gods, and Runic monsters, and Gothic monks—not that you may draw like Egyptians or Norsemen, nor yield yourselves passively to be bound by the devotion or infected with the delirium of the past, but that you may know truly what other men have felt during their poor span of life ; and open your own hearts to what the heavens and earth may have to tell you in yours.

Do not be surprised, therefore, nor provoked, if I give you at first strange things, and rude, to draw. As soon as you try them, you will find they are difficult enough, yet, with care, entirely possible. As you go on drawing them they will become interesting, and, as soon as you understand them, you will be on the way to understand yourselves also.

190. In closing this first course of lectures, I have one word more to say respecting the possible consequence of the introduction of art among the studies of the university. What art may do for scholarship, I have no right to conjecture ; but what scholarship may do for art, I may in all modesty tell you. Hitherto, great artists, though always gentlemen, have yet been too exclusively craftsmen. Art has been less thoughtful than we suppose ; it has taught much, but much, also, falsely. Many of the greatest pictures are enigmas ; others, beautiful toys ; others, harmful

and corrupting toys. In the loveliest there is something weak; in the greatest there is something guilty. And this, gentlemen, if you will, is the new thing that may come to pass—that the scholars of England may resolve to teach also with the silent power of the arts; and that some among you may so learn and use them, that pictures may be painted which shall not be enigmas any more, but open teachings of what can no otherwise be so well shown; which shall not be fevered or broken visions any more, but shall be filled with the indwelling light of self-possessed imagination; which shall not be stained or enfeebled any more by evil passion, but glorious with the strength and chastity of noble human love; and which shall no more degrade or disguise the work of God in heaven, but testify of Him as here dwelling with men, and walking with them, not angry, in the garden of the earth.

THE END.

www.ingramcontent.com/pod-product-compliance
Lightning Source LLC
Chambersburg PA
CBHW031853220426
43663CB00006B/605